PROTECTING CONSTITUTIONAL FREEDOMS

Recent Titles in
Contributions in Legal Studies

The Law School Papers of Benjamin F. Butler: New York University
Law School in the 1830s
Ronald L. Brown, editor and compiler

The Civil Rights Revolution: The Old Court and Individual Rights
John Braemen

Whom Does the Constitution Command? A Conceptual Analysis with
Practical Implications
Larry Alexander and Paul Horton

Constitutionalism: The Philosophical Dimension
Alan S. Rosenbaum, editor

Human Rights in the States: New Directions in Constitutional
Policymaking
Stanley H. Friedelbaum, editor

Death by Installments: The Ordeal of Willie Francis
Arthur S. Miller and Jeffrey H. Bowman

Truman's Court: A Study in Judicial Restraint
Frances Howell Rudko

The Gladsome Light of Jurisprudence: Learning the Law in England
and the United States in the 18th and 19th Centuries
Michael H. Hoeflich, editor and compiler

James Madison on the Constitution and the Bill of Rights
Robert J. Morgan

Lawyers, Courts, and Professionalism: The Agenda for Reform
Rudolph J. Gerber

John Marshall's Achievement: Law, Politics, and Constitutional
Interpretations
Thomas C. Shevory, editor

Affirmative Action and Principles of Justice
Kathanne W. Greene

Unfounded Fears: Myths and Realities of a Constitutional
Convention
Paul J. Weber and Barbara Perry

PROTECTING CONSTITUTIONAL FREEDOMS

A Role for Federal Courts

Daan Braveman

Contributions in Legal Studies, Number 56
Paul L. Murphy, Series Editor

GREENWOOD PRESS
NEW YORK • WESTPORT, CONNECTICUT • LONDON

347.73
B826p

Library of Congress Cataloging-in-Publication Data

Braveman, Daan.
   Protecting constitutional freedoms : a role for federal courts /
Daan Braveman.
      p.   cm.—(Contributions in legal studies, ISSN 0147-1074 ;
no. 56)
      Bibliography: p.
      Includes index.
      ISBN 0-313-26833-9 (lib. bdg. : alk. paper)
      1. Constitutional torts—United States.   2. Civil rights—United
States.   3. Judicial review—United States.   4. Jurisdiction—United
States.   5. United States.   Supreme Court.   I. Title.   II. Series.
KF1306.C64B73   1989
347.73'12—dc20
[347.30712]   89-7531

British Library Cataloguing in Publication Data is available.

Library of Congress Catalog Card Number: 89-7531
ISBN: 0-313-26833-9
ISSN: 0147-1074

First published in 1989

Greenwood Press, Inc.
88 Post Road West, Westport, Connecticut   06881

Printed in the United States of America

The paper used in this book complies with the
Permanent Paper Standard issued by the National
Information Standards Organization (Z39.48-1984).

10 9 8 7 6 5 4 3 2 1

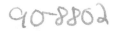

Copyright Acknowledgments

The author gratefully acknowledges permission to quote from the following sources:

Brennan, "State Constitutions and the Protection of Individual Rights," 90 *Harvard Law Review*, 489, 502–3 (1976). Copyright © 1977 by the Harvard Law Review Association.

Chayes, "The Role of the Judge in Public Law Litigation," 89 *Harvard Law Review*, 1281, 1282–83 (1976). Copyright © 1976 by the Harvard Law Review Association.

Braveman & Goldsmith, *Rules of Preclusion and Challenges to Official Action: An Essay on Finality, Fairness and Federalism, All Gone Awry*, 39 Syracuse L. Rev. 599 (1988). Copyright © 1988 by the Syracuse University College of Law. Reprinted with permission of the Syracuse Law Review.

To Lorraine and Adam

Contents

Preface   xi

Chapter 1 Introduction   1

Chapter 2 Opening the Federal Courthouse
             Doors   11

Chapter 3 Crossing the Threshold   57

Chapter 4 Our Federalism and Injunctions   79

Chapter 5 Damages   101

Chapter 6 Rules of Preclusion   135

Chapter 7 Institutional Character   165

Bibliography   193

Index   201

Preface

This book examines the closing of the federal courts to individuals challenging the constitutionality of conduct by state and local officials. In recent years the Supreme Court has used various legal doctrines to restrict federal courts, and resurrect state courts as the primary guardians of constitutional rights. The Court has frequently invoked vague notions of federalism to support these doctrines and the door-closing developments.

I criticize the Court's departure from the plan for protection of constitutional rights that was established in principle after the Civil War and finally became a reality after the 1954 school desegregation case. I argue that, notwithstanding the potential for friction in state-federal relations, the protection of constitutional rights is a national issue that transcends local interests and local control. It is an issue that should be part of the business of the federal courts, including not only the Supreme Court but the lower courts as well.

I should stress that the book does not focus primarily on the role of the Supreme Court or on the legitimacy of judicial review. These topics have been covered extensively elsewhere. My principal concern is the role of the entire federal judiciary in protecting constitutional rights. To be sure, the book examines doctrines developed by the Supreme Court; my interest is the impact of those doctrines on the ability of lower federal courts to hear cases involving unconstitutional conduct by public officials.

Many of the developments examined in the book have been the subject of scholarly articles in law review journals. For the most part, however, these articles treat the doctrines separately and are addressed to an expert audience. In writing this book, I have attempted to present the material in a nontechnical, readable fashion in the hopes of expanding the discussion to include nonexperts in the field. As we celebrate the 200th anniversary of the establishment of our federal judicial system, it is appropriate to reassess our commitment to protection of constitutional freedoms. And in my view the general public has a right to participate in the debate about the proper role of the federal judiciary in securing those freedoms.

I have many to thank for their help on this project. My colleagues, Bill Wiecek and Bill Banks, made especially helpful comments on drafts of portions of the book. The Syracuse University Center for Interdisciplinary Legal Studies granted research support for aspects of the project. Lisa DiPoala (class of 1989) and Margaret Babb (class of 1990) provided valuable assistance in the preparation of footnotes and the bibliography. Randy Krupa, Lynn Oatman, Mary Ann McClanahan, Cathie Soccocio, and Joyce Robertson took turns deciphering my scribbled notes. My sincere thanks to all of you.

PROTECTING CONSTITUTIONAL FREEDOMS

Chapter 1

Introduction

The conditions were shocking, although certainly not uncommon. Pennhurst State School and Hospital, owned and operated by the Commonwealth of Pennsylvania, was a typical state residential institution for the retarded. It housed 1,200 residents, most of whom were profoundly retarded with an IQ less than thirty-five. Many were also physically handicapped. These patients were deposited in Pennhurst either as a result of a court order or upon request of a parent or guardian, and once in the institution stayed on average for twenty-one years. While at Pennhurst patients were forced to endure conditions that even the staff conceded fell distressingly far below minimally accepted professional standards. The residents had no privacy, slept in overcrowded wards, spent their waking hours in large dayrooms, and ate in group settings. They conformed to a schedule that allowed no individual flexibility. Overcrowding and inadequate staffing made the physical environment hazardous to the residents. There was often excrement and urine on ward floors. Most toilet areas did not have soap, towels, or toilet paper, and were filthy as well as broken. Obnoxious odors and loud noises filled the atmosphere. Indeed, the noise in the dayrooms was so loud that many residents simply stopped speaking.

The institution utterly failed in providing any education, training, or care for the patients. A resident had one psychological evaluation every three years and one vocational adjustment service report every ten years. Physical restraints, confinement in seclusion rooms, and drugs were used as substitutes for treatment and programs. Conditions were so inhumane and dangerous that many of the residents suffered physical deterioration as well as intellectual and behavioral regression during their stay.[1]

The residents at Pennhurst were among society's throwaways and, as such, they were voiceless. The patients obviously lacked the ability and power to appeal directly to the politicians who control the purse and could allocate money to improve the conditions. Moreover, locked away in an isolated setting, they were literally out of sight of a public that might react with justifiable horror.

Fortunately, a few groups and individuals did attempt to speak on behalf of the Pennhurst residents. In May 1974, a class action lawsuit was filed on their behalf in federal court in Philadelphia seeking to challenge the conditions at the institution. The case was assigned to District Judge Raymond Broderick who eventually held a thirty-two-day trial to consider the patients' allegations. On December 23, 1977, he issued a decision, finding that the state and its officials had subjected patients to intolerable conditions and thereby had denied the patients' rights protected by the U.S. Constitution, by federal statute, and by the state's own laws, which were designed to guarantee minimum adequate care and treatment to residents of Pennhurst. Three months later, in March 1978, he ordered that immediate steps be taken to remove patients from Pennhurst. Judge Broderick directed the officials to provide suitable community living arrangements and community services for the Pennhurst residents and those on its waiting list. Additionally, he prohibited the county officials from recommending or in any way counseling that an individual be committed to Pennhurst. Judge Broderick also directed that officials stop the excessive use of physical restraints and drugs either as a means of punishing residents or as substitutes for programs. Finally, he appointed a special master to monitor and supervise the implementation of his order.[2]

The state and its officials appealed to the U.S. Court of Appeals for the Third Circuit seeking to overturn Judge Broderick's order. Instead, in December 1979, that court substantially affirmed the district judge's directive. Unlike Judge Broderick, however, the third circuit did not rely on the federal constitution as a basis for providing relief. Rather, it ruled that the defendants had deprived the patients of rights given by a federal law, known as the Developmentally Disabled Assistance and Bill of Rights Act, and by state law. The appellate court affirmed Judge Broderick's order except insofar as it ordered Pennhurst to be closed.[3] It remanded the case to the district court for individual determinations as to the appropriateness of an improved Pennhurst for each patient. The appellate court directed that in making the individual determination, the district judge should begin with a presumption in favor of placing individuals outside the institution in community living arrangements.[4]

Five years had passed since the start of the lawsuit and the state had lost twice. But the officials were not to be deterred and sought review by the Supreme Court. There they found a receptive ear. On April 20, 1981, the Court issued an opinion in which it held that the federal Developmentally Disabled Assistance and Bill of Rights Act—the principal basis for the third circuit's decision—did nothing more than announce a national policy in favor of better care and treatment for the retarded. It did not, the Court concluded, require the state to provide any kind of treatment or care.[5] The Supreme Court, therefore, sent the case back to the third circuit to consider whether the broad relief was required by the Constitution, by state law, or by other sections of the federal law not previously considered.

When the case returned to the third circuit, that court again held that the state officials must provide relief to the Pennhurst residents.[6] This time the court relied on a state law that recently had been held by Pennsylvania's highest court to require use of the "least restrictive environment" in caring for the mentally retarded. The third circuit found that this state law fully supported its prior judgment, and consequently it did not reach the remaining issues of whether the Constitution or some other federal law required the state to make the previously ordered changes.

Unfortunately, this decision by the court of appeals did not put an end to the lengthy litigation. Defendants again appealed to the Supreme Court and again found a sympathetic audience.

On January 23, 1984, ten years after the lawsuit commenced, the Supreme Court ruled in a closely divided decision that a federal court lacked the power to direct state officials to comply with state law.[7] Although in certain limited circumstances a federal court could order state officials to comply with federal law, it could not direct compliance with state law. Its conclusion, said the Court, was compelled by the Eleventh Amendment to the Constitution, which states: "The Judicial Power of the United States shall not be construed to extend to any suit in law or equity, commenced or prosecuted against one of the United States by citizens of another State, or by Citizens or Subjects of any Foreign State." The majority observed that the amendment embodies not only principles of sovereign immunity, but also notions of federalism, and plays a vital role in relieving the tensions created by making one sovereign appear in the courts of the other. The Court again reversed the judgment of the court of appeals.

The immediate impact of the decision was clear: additional delays would result before the patients could obtain a final judicial statement about their legal right to humane treatment. The case would have to be returned to the lower court for further litigation. Eighteen months later the parties agreed to end the litigation battle and settle the case. Under the settlement the institution would remain open, but the state and local officials would provide community living arrangements to those for whom placement outside the institution is appropriate.[8] The officials agreed to develop and provide individualized habilitation plans for patients both in and outside the institution, and to monitor and annually review their plans. They also agreed that all patients covered by the agreement would be (1) protected from harm; (2) provided with safe conditions and adequate shelter, clothing, and medical care; and (3) protected from physical and psychological abuse, from unreasonable restraint, and from the administration of unnecessary medication. To pay for the cost of implementing the settlement, the state agreed to make sufficient funds available. After eleven years, twenty-eight published court opinions, 500 court orders, and three arguments before the Supreme Court, the Pennhurst patients saw a promise of some relief.

The long-term impact of the *Pennhurst* decision on future litigants was even more troubling than its effect on the patients. To obtain relief in a lawsuit, litigants must establish that they have been injured by their opponent's conduct and that some principle of law authorizes recovery for the injury. Often litigants assert many different legal theories as grounds for recovery. The patients at Pennhurst, for example, claimed that they had been severely injured by the deplorable conditions at the hospital and that they were entitled to a judicial remedy by virtue of the U.S. Constitution, certain federal statutes, and specified state laws.

The *Pennhurst* decision creates a significant problem for individuals injured by state officials who may be acting in violation of both state and federal law. As a result of that decision, the federal court generally lacks power to award any relief based on state law. Thus, potential litigants have three choices. First, they can sue in federal court basing the case solely on federal law and omitting any reference to state law. In so doing, however, individuals may be giving up a winning legal theory derived from state law. Second, victims of official misconduct can bring two lawsuits, one in federal court raising the federal law theories and one in state court asserting state law as a basis for recovery. Such an option is especially, sometimes prohibitively, costly because it requires two separate lawsuits focusing on the identical, alleged misconduct. Third, litigants can elect to bypass the federal court completely and bring the lawsuit in a state court. With regard to the third option, it should be stressed that the *Pennhurst* decision spoke only of the federal court's power to grant relief against state officials on the basis of state laws. After the decision, state courts continue to be available to individuals who claim that their rights under both state and federal law have been denied by state officials.

The justices who joined the majority opinion in the *Pennhurst* case, I submit, were pushing litigants toward the third option. Indeed, that decision was part of a much larger effort to rid the federal courts of lawsuits challenging the conduct of state officials and to force such lawsuits into the state court system. The larger plan had become clear well before *Pennhurst*, and was intended to dismantle the federal courts as guardians of rights secured by the Constitution and U.S. laws.

Justice Stevens wrote a powerful dissenting opinion in *Pennhurst*, which began with the observation that "this case has illuminated the character of an institution."[9] The institution to which he referred was not Pennhurst Hospital but the Supreme Court itself. The character he portrayed was not a particularly appealing one. He accused the majority of repudiating years of well-settled doctrine and voyaging into the "sea of undisciplined law-making" in its rush to reach a "perverse result."[10]

The *Pennhurst* decision does, indeed, illuminate the character of the present Supreme Court as well as the lower federal courts that must follow the higher court's direction. It is a character that emerged quite clearly in the past two decades during the so-called Burger Court.[11] Its distinguishing trait is an unwillingness to hear claims that state officials are depriving individuals of their federal constitutional rights.

Recently it has become fashionable to argue that the Burger Court did not cause a feared counter-revolution in individual rights.[12] As one commentator observed, "When Warren E. Burger succeeded Earl Warren as Chief Justice of the United States in 1969, many expected to see the more striking constitutional doctrines of the Warren years rolled back or even abandoned."[13] The work of the Burger Court, however, may not be so easily characterized. Retrenchment did take place in certain areas, whereas in other areas the scope of individual freedoms may have been expanded.[14] The Burger Court appeared to have been "drifting" in its attempts to define the precise contours of individual rights.[15] But at the same time, a clear and rather disturbing picture emerged regarding the Burger Court's view of the role of federal courts in protecting those freedoms. In short, it sought to eliminate federal courts and resurrect state courts as the principal guardians of individual rights.

Such a restrictive role for the federal courts is truly counter-revolutionary, representing a significant departure from the vision that existed in the late 1960s. By that time, "the Supreme Court had implanted in American jurisprudence the precept that the Federal Courthouse doors were to be generally left open to all individuals seeking constitutional relief."[16] In 1972 the Supreme Court itself proclaimed that federal courts were placed "between the States and the people, as guardians of the people's federal rights—to protect the people from unconstitutional actions under color of state law 'whether that action be executive, legislative or judicial.' "[17]

This book examines the radical change in character that took place over the course of the past twenty years. Chapter 2 traces the emergence of the federal courts as the primary protectors of federal constitutional rights. Under the original scheme established by the Judiciary Act of 1789, the state rather than the federal courts were assigned the task of guarding such rights. The Civil War, however, began a transformation in the role of the federal government, including the federal judiciary, in protecting individuals from state interference with the exercise of constitutional rights. Completion of the transformation process was slow. Nevertheless, after the decision in the school desegregation case (*Brown v. Board of Education*),[18] and certainly by the time the Burger Court was in high gear, the federal courts were firmly entrenched as the primary guardians of constitutional rights.

After tracing the historical background, the book discusses the various doctrines that have operated to close the federal courts to individuals seeking to assert constitutional claims. Chapter 3 focuses on the "standing to sue" doctrine, which requires a litigant attempting to gain access to a federal forum to show "injury" directly caused by the state officials' conduct. Although the doctrine may have a legitimate basis, it has been applied by the Burger Court with an illegitimate vengeance. It has been used to close the federal courthouse doors to individuals most in need of judicial protection.

Even assuming litigants can meet the threshold standing requirement and at least walk through the federal courthouse doors, they will then be confronted with additional obstacles to the award of any relief. Chapter 4 describes one of those hurdles—the difficulty in obtaining an injunction that restrains public officials from violating constitutional rights. Quite often, civil rights litigants request the court to grant injunctive relief directing state officials to refrain from unconstitutional conduct or compelling them to make changes necessary to conform their conduct to constitutional standards. In the years after the *Brown* case, the civil rights injunction emerged as a powerful weapon combating official misconduct. It was the only weapon in the arsenal of the patients at Pennhurst. However, in recent years the Court has exhibited a distinct distaste for such relief and an unwillingness to allow federal courts to use the injunction to remedy constitutional violations. Indeed, it has held in various circumstances that federal courts must refrain from awarding such relief.

Similarly, the Court has placed hurdles in the path of federal court litigants attempting to recover damage awards against officials who violate constitutionally protected rights. This development is traced in chapter 5, which explores the Burger Court's excessive reliance on the Eleventh Amendment and judge-made doctrines to protect public officials from paying damages to those injured by their unconstitutional conduct.

The various doctrines discussed in these chapters force those seeking to litigate constitutional violations to bring their lawsuits in state courts to obtain complete relief. As revealed in chapter 6, the Court has put the final nail in the federal courthouse door by holding that, in most circumstances, those who litigate in state court are precluded from later attempting to relitigate their constitutional claims in federal court. Through reliance on judicially created doctrines, as well as the full, faith and credit statute, the Court completed its dismantling of the lower federal courts as guardians of constitutional rights.[19]

Finally, chapter 7 addresses the question, "So What?" Why should it matter whether an individual is forced to litigate a constitutional case in state, rather than federal, court? I argue that it does indeed matter and examine the reasons for that conclusion. The developments discussed in the earlier chapters are based on the underlying assumption that state courts are as competent as their federal counterparts to protect constitutional rights. Although individual state and federal judges may be equally competent, institutional differences between the two court systems render the federal courts generally more capable of guarding individual liberties. At the very least, litigants like those in *Pennhurst* should have the right to make their own decision on whether the state or federal court is a more favorable forum. Moreover, the Constitution assigns Congress, not the Supreme Court, the task of determining the jurisdiction of the lower federal courts. The Court thus usurps legislative power when it develops doctrines that operate as a limit on the business of the federal judiciary. In addition, regardless of the quality of state courts, protection of constitutional rights is a national issue that transcends local interests and local protection, and the business of the federal courts should include that task. Finally, closing the federal courts to litigants asserting constitutional rights, but leaving the doors open to other classes of litigants, reinforces perceptions of unfairness and discriminatory treatment.

The issues examined in this book have been the subject of numerous articles in scholarly journals. Unfortunately, the general public has not been included in the debate about the role of the federal judiciary in guarding constitutional rights. It has been observed that although the founders of our country "differed over many important matters, they shared a belief that the constitutional system created between 1787 and 1791 (when the Bill of Rights received approval) should be fully comprehensible to the American people."[20] This book is written with that spirit in mind. The patients in Pennhurst Hospital fell victim to the federal judiciary's change in character. As revealed in the following pages, there have been other victims as well. The general public, I believe, is entitled to hear their stories and participate in the debate about the proper character of federal courts in our constitutional system.

Notes

1. For a detailed discussion of the conditions, see Judge Raymond Broderick's opinion in Halderman v. Pennhurst State School and Hospital, 446 F. Supp. 1295 (E. D. Pa. 1977).
2. *Id.* at 1326.
3. 612 F.2d 84 (3d Cir. 1979) (en banc).
4. On remand, the district court established detailed procedures for individual determinations.
5. 451 U.S. 1, 32–33 (1981).
6. 673 F.2d 647 (3d Cir. 1982) (en banc).
7. 465 U.S. 89 (1984).
8. 610 F. Supp. 1221, 1222 (E. D. Pa. 1985). For further discussion of Pennhurst, see Althouse, *How to Build a Separate Sphere: Federal Courts and State Power*, 100 HARV. L. REV. 1485 (1987); Chemerinsky, *State*

Sovereignty and Federal Court Power: The Eleventh Amendment After Pennhurst v. Halderman, 12 HASTINGS CONST. L. Q. 643 (1985); Dwyer, *Pendent Jurisdiction and the Eleventh Amendment,* 75 CALIF. L. REV. 129 (1987); Rudenstine, *Pennhurst and the Scope of Judicial Power to Reform Social Institution,* 6 CARDOZO L. REV. 71 (1984); Shapiro, *Wrong Turns: The Eleventh Amendment and the Pennhurst Case,* 98 HARV. L. REV. 61 (1985).

9. 454 U.S. 89, 165–66 (1984).

10. *Id.*

11. Warren Burger became chief justice of the United States in 1969. Although the chief justice may not dominate the Court over which he presides, it is a "common expedient to use changes in identity of the chief justice as dividing lines for demarcating segments of Supreme Court history" THE BURGER COURT: THE COUNTER REVOLUTION THAT WASN'T xix (V. BLASI ed. [1983]).

12. *Id.*

13. *Id.* at vii.

14. *See* the essays in THE BURGER YEARS: RIGHTS AND WRONGS IN THE SUPREME COURT, 1969–1986 (H. SCHWARTZ ed. 1987) and V. BLASI (ed.), *supra* note 11.

15. V. BLASI (ed.) *supra* at xxi.

16. S. 35, 95th Cong., 1st Sess., 123 Cong. Rec. 555 (1977) (remarks of Sen. Mathias, R-Md).

17. Mitchum v. Foster, 407 U.S. 225, 242 (1972) (quoting *Ex parte Virginia,* 100 U.S. 339, 346 (1879)).

18. 347 U.S. 483 (1954).

19. 28 U.S.C. § 1738.

20. M. KAMMEN, A MACHINE THAT WOULD GO OF ITSELF 3 (1986).

Chapter 2
Opening the Federal Courthouse Doors

Over 100 years ago Salmon P. Chase, the chief justice of the United States, observed that "the Constitution, in all its provisions, looks to an indestructible Union, composed of indestructible states."[1] This observation captures the essential characteristic of the continuing American experiment with federalism. We have a dual system of government, and one of the fundamental issues in our development has been, and continues to be, the relationship between the two indestructible components of that system. Indeed, much of our constitutional history has involved a struggle to find a proper distribution of power between the states and the central government.

Today it is taken for granted that a feature of our federalism is the existence of a dual judicial system. Each state has a court system, usually composed of trial courts, intermediate appellate courts, and a supreme court. So too, the federal government has a similarly structured judicial system: trial courts (called district courts), intermediate appellate courts (known as courts of appeal), and, of course, a highest court, the Supreme Court. The story told in the following chapters concerns the allocation of power between the state and federal courts in cases involving constitutional challenges to conduct by states and local officials. Should federal courts be open to hear such cases? Or, should such cases be confined to the state courts? This story involves an ongoing potential for friction not only between the two court systems but also between the federal courts and the other branches of state government.

To fully develop that story it is important to cast a historical light on the existing dual court system. It has been said that "the Federal judiciary seems so natural and inevitable now that it may be difficult to imagine a time when its establishment and existence were controversial."[2] The present structure of the federal judiciary, however, was not inevitable, and its power to protect individual freedoms did not fully emerge until decades after adoption of the Constitution.

For nearly two centuries before the Revolution, the American people lived under colonial charters that provided the method of establishing governments in the colonies. The settlers attached great importance to these charters that were viewed as "the bulwark of people against repression, the stepping stones to a larger freedom."[3] The charters were looked upon not as "revocable grants but as agreements inviolable except by mutual consent."[4] For our purposes, they are significant because colonial experience under them helped shape later concepts of individual freedom. For example, in 1641, Massachusetts adopted the "Body of Liberties," which guaranteed many rights later appearing in the Bill of Rights, such as ancestors of the right to equal protection of the laws, and prohibitions against double jeopardy and cruel or unusual punishment. Similarly, the Rhode Island Charter provided a right of religious liberty as a fundamental aspect of the framework of the government.[5] In protecting these liberties, the colonists relied primarily on the assembly rather than the courts. Nevertheless, colonial courts did exist and "formed an important if subordinate part of the structure of local government" in the colonial period.[6]

After the Declaration of Independence and during the period under the Articles of Confederation (1776–89), the states were the source of individual rights.[7] Colonial leaders spent much of the revolutionary period writing state constitutions, and these documents often included explicit guarantees of individual liberties.[8] The 1776 Virginia Constitution, for example, provided that "all men are by nature equally free and independent, and have certain inherent rights...; namely, the enjoyment of life and liberty, with the means of acquiring and possessing property, and pursuing and obtaining happiness and safety."[9] During the Confederation period, as in the colonial era, protection of such rights was left to the states, but the state courts played an uncertain role. "Beyond the settlement of private disputes, the role of the [state] judiciary under the separation of powers was as yet unclear."[10] One issue was clear: The Articles of Confederation did not create a national judicial system except to handle certain specialized matters such as admiralty and boundary disputes.

By the time the framers met in Philadelphia in 1787 there was widespread dissatisfaction with the state courts and strong demand for a national judiciary.[11] As one commentator recently observed, during the Constitutional Convention "there were dozens of imaginative phrases to describe the ghastly consequences of a legislative branch run wild or an executive branch turned despotic. But a search of the debates for comparable words about the third branch of government will be in vain, for the notion that judges could become dangerous seems not to have occurred to the delegates."[12] That observation may be a bit overstated; certainly, the states-rightists feared that a system of lower federal courts would dilute the power of the states.[13] Those at the convention, however, were much more concerned about the other two branches of the federal government.

In his famous *Federalist No. 78*, Alexander Hamilton explained the basis for the view that the judiciary will always be the least dangerous of the three branches:

The Executive not only dispenses the honors, but holds the sword of the community. The legislature not only commands the purse but prescribes the rules by which the duties and rights of every citizen are to be neglected. The judiciary, on the contrary, has no influence over either the sword or the purse; no directions either of the strength or of the wealth of the society; and can take no active resolutions whatever. It may truly be said to have neither FORCE NOR WILL, but merely judgment; and must ultimately depend upon the aid of the executive arm even for the efficacy of its judgments.[14]

It is not surprising, therefore, that the total time debating the creation of a national judiciary would fit into a single afternoon.[15] The proponents of a national judiciary argued that an independent national judicial system was necessary to ensure the supremacy of federal law as well as its uniform application throughout the states.[16] State courts, it was urged, could not be trusted with the administration of federal laws.[17] A local or sectional spirit might well prevent state judges from impartially applying national laws. Such a possibility was not fanciful because many state judges held their office at the pleasure of other state officials or for short periods.[18] Additionally, the proponents stressed that judicial authority and legislative authority must be co-extensive to ensure an effective national government. James Madison, a leading supporter of a strong national judiciary, observed that "an effective Judiciary establishment commensurate to the legislative authority was essential. A government without a proper Executive and Judiciary would be the mere trunk of a body without arms or legs to act or move."[19]

The opponents of a federal judiciary, like Roger Sherman of Connecticut, focused on the expense of a new set of courts when existing state courts could serve the same purpose.[20] Moreover, they asserted the states' rights theme that was so prevalent during the entire convention. Quite simply, a national court system would diminish the authority of the states.[21] The states-rightists particularly feared creation of lower federal courts with judges dispersed throughout the country.[22] "The states," said Pierce Butler of South Carolina, "will revolt at such an encroachment."[23]

Madison proposed in his Virginia Plan that the Constitution create a Supreme Court and mandate the establishment of lower federal courts.[24] In a related matter, he also proposed that Congress be given power to veto state laws violating the Constitution.[25] Both proposals were defeated and, in the spirit that seemed to dominate the convention, compromises were reached with respect to the national judiciary. The delegates agreed to Madison's fallback position—the Constitution would establish a supreme court and not direct creation of lower federal courts but instead authorize Congress to create such courts if it so desired.[26] The real fight over lower federal courts was thus avoided at least for the time.

Madison's plan for a congressional veto was also rejected because it was seen as a real threat to state power. The veto would, in effect, have made Congress a part of the state legislatures. Additionally, to review all state legislation, Congress would have to be in session continuously.[27] The compromise offered by Luther Martin of Maryland[28] eventually resulted in the Supremacy Clause that made the Constitution and federal law the supreme law of the land and directed that judges in every state "shall be bound thereby."[29] Although the clause did not authorize appeals from state to federal courts, it implied such judicial review and many delegates assumed the existence of federal judicial power to rule on the constitutionality of state laws as the way to preserve the supremacy and uniform application of federal law.[30]

The final judiciary article that emerged from the convention not only provided for a Supreme Court and for the discretionary power of Congress to create lower federal courts, but also designated the kinds of cases that the federal judiciary could hear.[31] Article III provides that the judicial power of the United States extends to nine kinds of cases or controversies: (1) those arising under the Constitution, laws, and treaties of the United States; (2) those affecting ambassadors, other public ministers, and consuls; (3) admirality and maritime cases; (4) those to which the United States is a party; (5) those between two or more states; (6) those between a state and citizens of another state; (7) those between citizens of different states; (8) those between citizens of the same state claiming lands under grants of different states; and finally (9) those between a state, or its citizens, and foreign states or citizens.

Article III does not attempt to delineate the precise way the "judicial power" over these nine kinds of cases would be distributed between the Supreme Court and any inferior federal courts that might be created. That task is left to Congress. It does state, however, that the Supreme Court has original jurisdiction in two of the nine categories—cases affecting ambassadors or other public ministers and consuls, and cases in which the state shall be a party. Those two kinds of cases, thus, would begin in the Supreme Court. In the other seven categories of cases, the Supreme Court would have appellate jurisdiction (i.e., would review another court's judgment) "with such Exceptions, and under such Regulations as the Congress shall make."

One final aspect of article III plays an important role in the story that unfolds in the following chapters. The framers provided that federal judges would have lifetime tenure, holding office during good behavior subject to impeachment for high crimes and misdemeanors.[32] Moreover, they further protected the judiciary by providing that the judges' compensation could not be diminished during their time in office.[33] These two provisions were designed to guarantee an independent federal judiciary, free from pressure by the other branches of government and immune from political accountability to the people. The need for such protection was readily apparent. One commentator recently reported that "eighteenth-century judges had been whipped for their rulings by the Regulators in Georgia and beaten and terrorized by the Shaysites in Massachusetts."[34] Other states used more gentle methods: In Pennsylvania legislators displeased with judges cut their salaries and in Rhode Island and elsewhere judges were fired.

Hamilton argued that an independent federal judiciary was necessary to "guard the Constitution and the rights of individuals." He wrote in *Federalist No. 78*:

That inflexible and uniform adherence to the rights of the Constitution, and of individuals, which we perceive to be indispensable in the courts of justice, can certainly not be expected from judges who hold their offices by a temporary commission. Periodical appointments, however regulated, or by whomsoever made, would, in some way or other, be fatal to their necessary independence. If the power of making them was committed either to the Executive or legislature, there would be danger of an improper complaisance to the branch which possessed it; if to both, there would be an unwillingness to hazard the displeasure of either; if to the people or to persons chosen by them for the special purpose, there would be too great a disposition to consult popularity, to justify a reliance that nothing would be consulted but the Constitution and the laws.[35]

Our story about the respective roles of the state and the federal judiciary in protecting constitutional rights thus begins with many uncertainties. The constitutional convention produced a compromise that left completion of the details to future congresses. Those who gathered in Philadelphia avoided any decision on the precise allocation of power between state and federal courts, particularly the lower federal courts. The framers, however, plainly recognized that a supreme court was necessary to ensure the supremacy of federal law as well as its uniform application. Moreover, they recognized the need for an independent federal judiciary that could adhere to constitutional principles without fear of retaliation by the other branches of government, or by the people themselves.

During the debates over ratification of the Constitution, the antifederalists took aim at the national judiciary envisioned by article III. At the Virginia ratifying convention, George Mason urged that state courts would be annihilated and that the federal courts would not be fair and impartial.[36] He warned, for example, that the federal sheriff might go into a poor man's home, beat him, and then receive protection from the federal court.[37] John Marshall (later, chief justice of the United States) responded to such attacks by reminding those at the Virginia convention that state courts would not lose their power over cases they presently decided and, as to those cases listed in article III, state courts would have concurrent jurisdiction with the federal courts.[38]

Hamilton also tried to dispel the fears of the antifederalists by arguing in *Federalist No. 82* that the state and federal governments are "kindred systems" and parts of "*one whole*."[39] When viewed in this light "the inference seems to be conclusive, that the State courts would have a concurrent jurisdiction in all cases arising under the laws of the Union, where it was not expressly prohibited."[40] Moreover, because the state and federal governments are kindred systems, the former should not fear the prospects of Supreme Court review of state court judgments. The state courts, he wrote, will be "natural auxiliaries to the execution of the laws of the Union, and an appeal from them will as naturally lie to that tribunal which is destined to unite and assimilate the principles of national justice and the rules of national decisions."[41]

The Constitution was ratified despite the antifederalist concerns about article III. But, ratification did not end the disagreement over the role of the federal courts. Article III authorized the legislature to work out the details of the federal judicial system, and the First Congress undertook that task. The legislation that was introduced rekindled the debate, the federalists arguing that federal judicial power should be coextensive with national legislative authority and the antifederalists urging that a national court system with lower federal courts would destroy the independence of the states.[42] The product of this debate was the great Judiciary Act of 1789,[43] a compromise between the states'-rightists and the centralists.[44]

The latter succeeded in creating a system of lower federal courts. Besides providing that the Supreme Court would have six justices, the act established (1) thirteen district courts each having one judge, and (2) three circuit courts each consisting of two Supreme Court justices and one district judge. The centralists also prevailed in another important respect. Section 25 of the act authorized Supreme Court review of decisions by the highest state courts in three instances: (1) where the state court held against the validity of a federal law or treaty; (2) where it upheld a state law that had been challenged as contrary to the Constitution, treaties, or U.S. laws; and finally, (3) where a state court decided against a title, right privilege, or exemption claimed under the Constitution, treaties, or federal law.

Section 25, thus, resolved an issue that was left open during the Convention—namely, whether appeals could be taken from the state courts to the federal system. In providing that such appeals could be taken to the Supreme Court when a state court ruled against a federal claim, the judiciary act allowed the Court to play its intended role of guarding the supremacy of federal law and ensuring its uniform application.

However, the victory of the centralists was tempered by the antifederalists' success in limiting the jurisdiction of the lower federal courts. Some federalists argued that the lower national courts should be granted the full extent of the "judicial power" described in article III. They would have given the lower federal courts power to hear all the cases or controversies listed in section 2 (except, of course, the two that are within the Supreme Court's original jurisdiction). The federalists, however, were unsuccessful and the resulting judiciary act vested only part of the federal judicial power in the inferior federal courts. These courts were given exclusive power to hear admiralty cases and those cases involving crimes under federal law. The circuit courts were given power to hear civil cases falling within article III where the amount in controversy exceeded $500. The state courts, however, retained their authority to hear civil cases as well and thus had concurrent jurisdiction with the lower federal courts. Most notably, the lower federal courts were not given jurisdiction over cases arising under the Constitution or U.S. laws. These cases instead would be commenced in state courts and, if the highest state court ruled against the federal claim, could be appealed to the Supreme Court pursuant to section 25.[45]

Although years later the judiciary act was described as "probably the most important and the most satisfactory Act ever passed by Congress," opinion in 1789 was much more critical, notwithstanding the successes of the antifederalists.[46] Senator William Maclay of Pennsylvania described the act as a "vile law system, calculated for expense, and with a design to draw by degrees all law business into the Federal Courts. The Constitution is meant to swallow all the State Constitutions, by degrees, and to swallow, by degrees, all the State Judiciaries."[47] Senator William Grayson of Virginia wrote more bluntly that the act was "monstrous."[48]

With respect to the concern here—the power of federal courts to hear constitutional challenges to state conduct—the judiciary act was hardly monstrous, at least from the antifederalists' viewpoint. Their struggle to keep these cases out of the lower federal courts had succeeded. Under the act such challenges would be brought to state courts in the first instance and reach the Supreme Court only after appeals in the state system were exhausted. State courts would be the primary guardians of federal constitutional rights and, despite minor changes, would retain that position until well after the Civil War.

Even the ratification of the Bill of Rights did not alter the scheme established by the judiciary act. The Constitution, as originally ratified, had no detailed declaration of individual rights. The document, of course, was not silent on the protection of individual freedom. It guaranteed the right of representative government,[49] prohibited ex post facto laws or bills of attainder,[50] preserved the writ of habeas corpus[51] and the right to jury trials,[52] and prohibited states from impairing the obligation of contracts,[53] or from denying out of state citizens the privileges and immunities extended to their own citizens.[54]

It did not contain a bill of rights, however, and various explanations have been offered for the omission.[55] First, the framers focused much of their attention on establishing a structure of government and it was believed that the structure itself would protect against the invasion of individual rights. Second, because the powers of the central government were limited to those enumerated, Madison, Hamilton, and others argued that it was unnecessary to include a bill of rights that set forth in further detail what the government could not do. Third, state constitutions already contained relatively noncontroversial protections for individual freedoms. Finally, some suggested that a bill of rights would be dangerous because, as James Wilson urged, it might be assumed that rights not expressly mentioned were purposely omitted.

Despite these arguments, it soon became clear that a bill of rights was necessary, at the very least for political reasons. During the ratification period, the federalists won some support by promising amendments that included a bill of rights. Also, opponents of the Constitution indicated they would seek a second constitutional convention for the stated purpose of adopting a bill of rights but for the real purpose of destroying the plan that had emerged from the first convention.[56] In his inaugural address, President Washington asked the First Congress to consider amendments. Madison, then a member of the House of Representatives, introduced twelve proposed amendments, ten of which were ratified by the requisite number of states and added to the Constitution in 1791.[57]

The newly ratified amendments, however, had no immediate impact on the balance of federal and state power. Indeed, the amendments simply recognized rights that would have been assumed to exist even without their formal inclusion. Moreover, the Bill of Rights served as a limitation on the federal government only and placed no restrictions on the states. This principle was firmly established by the Supreme Court in *Barron v. Mayor and City Council of Baltimore*.[58] That case involved a challenge to Baltimore's decision to construct streets in a manner that caused masses of earth and sand to be deposited in front of Barron's large wharf. As a result, the waters became so shallow that the wharf could no longer be used for most vessels. Barron sued the city claiming that it had violated the Fifth Amendment by taking his property without just compensation. The state trial court awarded Barron $4,500, but the state appellate court reversed its finding for the city. Barron then sought review by the U.S. Supreme Court. Under section 25 of the judiciary act the Court could review the state court judgment only if that court had found against a federal right. The Supreme Court's jurisdiction, therefore, would turn on whether the Fifth Amendment protects an individual from the state or its local government. That question, Chief Justice John Marshall observed, is "of great importance, but not of much difficulty."[59] He went on to conclude on behalf of the Court that the Bill of Rights was intended solely as a limit on the exercise of power by the central government.

It is a part of the history of the day, that the great revolution which established the constitution of the United States, was not effected without immense opposition. Serious fears were extensively entertained that those powers which the patriot statesmen, who then watched over the interest of our country, deemed essential to union, and to the attainment of those invaluable objects for which union was sought, might be exercised in a manner dangerous to liberty. In almost every convention, by which the constitution was adopted, amendments demanded security against the apprehended encroachments of the general—not against those of the local government. In compliance with a sentiment thus generally expressed, to quiet fears thus extensively entertained, amendments were proposed by the required majority in congress, and adopted by the states. These amendments contain no expression indicating an intention to apply them to the state governments. This court cannot so apply them.[60]

The Court therefore held that because Barron was challenging state—not federal—conduct, no federal right was involved and it lacked power to review the state court judgment.

Consequently, the Bill of Rights had no immediate effect on the relations between the state and the federal government generally and plainly did not affect the balance between state and federal courts. The amendments did not alter the 1789 Judiciary

Act's scheme, one that gave the state courts the first opportunity to decide federal constitutional questions and denied the lower federal courts any role. *Barron* itself illustrates the act's plan; the party claiming that officials were violating the federal constitution started his lawsuit in state court and entered the federal judicial system only by appeal to the Supreme Court. Under this scheme there was no opportunity for conflict between the lower federal courts and the states because the former had virtually no role in the protection of constitutional rights.

Although not directly related to the enforcement of constitutional rights, one early confrontation provided a spark that could have ignited a real clash in all aspects of the relationship between federal courts and the states. In 1793, two South Carolina citizens brought a lawsuit against the state of Georgia to collect a debt. Article III provides that the Supreme Court shall have original jurisdiction in all cases in which a state shall be a party, and so the South Carolinians started their case in that court. At that time it was well established that a state was immune from a lawsuit and could not be sued in its own court unless it consented.[61] Despite the absence of any such consent, the Supreme Court concluded in *Chisholm v. Georgia* that by virtue of article III it had power to hear the case against Georgia.[62] In effect, article III was construed to have waived the state's sovereign immunity from lawsuit in the federal courts.

The response to *Chisholm* was extreme. One newspaper asserted that *Chisholm* could lead to "the overthrow of the State Governments, to the consolidation of the Union for the purpose of arbitrary power, to the downfall of liberty and the subversion of the rights of the people."[63] The Georgia House of Representatives was so outraged it passed a bill providing that anyone attempting to execute process in the *Chisholm* case would be guilty of a felony and sentenced to death by hanging. Moreover, the legislature added that the unfortunate person would suffer that fate even if it was a first offense.[64]

Georgia's reaction was shared by the other states as well and the Eleventh Amendment was proposed less than a month after final judgment was entered in *Chisholm*. Within a year the requisite number of states ratified the amendment.[65] This provision, which eventually figures prominently in our story, was designed to overrule that case.

A potential for ongoing battles between the federal judiciary and the states was averted for a time. On a different front, the Supreme Court was beginning to strengthen its hand, first with respect to the other branches of the federal government and then with respect to the states themselves. The Court asserted its power to review the constitutionality of the actions of the co-equal branches of the federal government in the famous case, *Marbury v. Madison*.[66] The case arose out of the appointment of "midnight judges" in the final moments of President John Adams' administration. The judges were confirmed by the Senate and their commissions were signed and sealed by the secretary of state (who, at the time, was John Marshall). Some of the commissions, including that of William Marbury, were not delivered, however. When Jefferson assumed office he instructed his secretary of state (James Madison) to disregard the appointments and withhold the undelivered commissions. Marbury then sued to compel Madison to deliver the commission and, relying on section 13 of the Judiciary Act of 1789, started the proceedings in the Supreme Court itself rather than in a lower federal court.

Chief Justice Marshall began his opinion for the Court by concluding that Marbury plainly had a right to the commission and that the laws gave him a remedy in the nature of a writ that directs an officer of government to take particular action. The important issue, however, was whether the Supreme Court had power to issue the writ as part of its original jurisdiction. Section 13 appeared to confer such original jurisdiction but, in so doing, ran into a head-on collision with article III.[67] It will be recalled that article III granted the Supreme Court original jurisdiction in only two categories of cases, neither of which applied to Marbury. In all other cases, article III provided that the Court would have "appellate Jurisdiction, with such Exceptions, and under such Regulations as the Congress shall make."

For Marshall, the issue was whether "an act, repugnant to the constitution, can become law of the land."[68] Having thus framed the issue, it is not surprising that he concluded with a resounding "no." He wrote: "Certainly all those who have framed written constitutions contemplate them as forming the fundamental and paramount law of the nation, and, consequently, the theory of every such government must be, that an act of the legislature, repugnant to the constitution, is void."[69]

Marshall then considered whether the courts are nevertheless bound to apply a law that is void as repugnant to the Constitution. Again, he concluded with an answer that may seem obvious. Courts, as well as the other branches of government, are bound by the Constitution and cannot apply a law that is inconsistent with that document. To hold otherwise, said Marshall, would "subvert the foundation of all written constitutions," give the legislature a "practical and real omnipotence," and reduce "to nothing what we have deemed the greatest improvement on political institutions, a written constitution."[70] A court, therefore, must refuse to enforce an unconstitutional law. Accordingly, on behalf of the Court, Marshall held that because section 13 was unconstitutional it could not be enforced and the Court lacked power to grant Marbury's request for a writ.

Marshall's seductive reasoning, as Professor Alexander Bickel argued, "begged the question-in-chief."[71] If a statute and the Constitution conflict, a court must obey the latter, the superior law. But whether a statute does in fact conflict with the Constitution is in many instances not self-evident. In *Marbury* itself it was not clear that section 13 was repugnant to article III.[72] The real questions, then, are: Who decides whether a law is repugnant to the Constitution? And, who serves as the umpire and determines whether a branch of government has played by the rules set forth in the Constitution? In *Marbury*, Marshall assumed that power for the Supreme Court. And, it is a remarkable power indeed because it allows federal judges, appointed for life and not directly accountable to the people, to declare invalid the acts of their elected representatives. Professor Bickel argued:

The root difficulty is that judicial review is a countermajoritarian force in our system. . . . When the Supreme Court declares unconstitutional a legislative act or the action of an elected executive, it thwarts the will of representatives of the actual people of the here and now; it exercises control, not in behalf of the prevailing majority, but against it.[73]

Marshall's decision in *Marbury* and his conclusion that a court can review the constitutionality of actions taken by the other branches of government have provoked a massive outpouring of scholarly discussions over the past two centuries.[74] For purposes here, *Marbury* helps set the stage for the eventual emergence of the federal judiciary as guardians of constitutional rights. The decision placed the Supreme Court in the umpire position, authorizing it to have the "final say" on the meaning of the Constitution. *Marbury* did not directly involve the states, but it had the potential for placing the Supreme Court in a similar role with respect to state conduct. Under the Judiciary Act of 1789 the Court was given power to review state court judgments finding against a federal right. That provision, together with *Marbury*, threatened to thrust the Supreme Court into the business of the state governments, and it did not take long for that potential to ripen into a full-scale clash.

The battle lines were drawn in a dispute over title to Virginia land previously held by Lord Fairfax, a British national who had been a citizen of Virginia. The state claimed that it had properly taken the land from the British loyalist and then conveyed the property to David Hunter and his heirs. The Fairfax heirs, however, asserted that their right to the property was protected by federal treaties. In 1791, Hunter brought an action in state court seeking to evict Denny Martin, one of the Fairfax heirs. Hunter asserted his right to this property based on state law, whereas Martin claimed the land belonged to him under the federal treaties. After almost twenty years of complicated negotiations (involving John Marshall, the future chief justice, and his brother[75]) the Virginia Court of Appeals upheld the legality of the state's seizure of the Fairfax land and ruled for Hunter.[76]

Relying on section 25 of the judiciary act, Martin appealed to the Supreme Court, which reversed the determination of Virginia's highest court. In 1813, the Supreme Court held that the federal treaties gave title to Martin. Because the Supremacy Clause requires that inconsistent state law yield to federal treaties, the Supreme Court returned the case to the Virginia court with instructions to enter judgment for Martin.[77]

The Virginia Court of Appeals, however, refused to follow this command, holding instead that the Supreme Court could not review state court judgments and that section 25, which authorized such review, was itself unconstitutional. The state judges reasoned that such review by a branch of the federal government is an intrusion into the state's sovereignty. Judge Cabell said:

Before one Court can dictate to another, the judgment it shall pronounce, it must bear, to that other, the relation of an appellate Court. The term appellate, however, necessarily includes the idea of superiority. But one Court cannot be correctly said to be superior to another, unless both of them belong to the same sovereignty. It would be a misapplication of terms to say that a Court of Virginia is superior to a Court of Maryland, or vice versa. The Courts of the United States, therefore, belonging to one sovereignty, cannot be appellate Courts in relation to the State Courts, which belong to a different sovereignty—and of course, their commands or instructions impose no obligation.[78]

In the view of the Virginia judges, article III authorized Congress to provide only for Supreme Court review of lower federal courts, not state courts. Section 25 exceeded this authority and, therefore, was void.

It should be stressed that the Virginia Court of Appeals did not deny that under the Supremacy Clause federal law prevails over inconsistent state provisions. The court, however, concluded that the Fairfax interests had been validly seized and that there was no conflict between state and federal law. The state judges vigorously disputed the power of the Supreme Court to tell them that they had misinterpreted the applicable law. Such power was an impermissible—indeed, unconstitutional—intrusion into the state's sovereignty.

The impact of this decision, if allowed to stand, was far-reaching. It would have severely restricted the ability of the Supreme Court to perform the functions envisioned by the framers—to guarantee the supremacy of federal law as well as its uniform application. State courts would have the final say on the meaning of federal rights in their respective jurisdictions and the interpretation of those rights might vary from state to state. The Supreme Court, of course, would be able to review lower federal court judgments, but, under the 1789 Judiciary Act, the lower federal courts were not given permission to hear cases arising under federal law. The antifederalists in the First Congress had succeeded in requiring that such cases start in the state courts, subject to appeal to the Supreme Court under section 25. The Virginia Court of Appeals' decision in the Fairfax case effectively cut off the only avenue for federal court review. Congress could have tried to amend the judiciary act to authorize lower federal courts to hear cases arising under federal law. But, such an attempt would have met with the strong opposition of those in Congress who distrusted a federal judiciary lurking in their states.

It is not surprising that the Supreme Court did not allow the Virginia Court of Appeals' decision to stand. In *Martin v. Hunter's Lessee*, Justice Story, writing for the Court, reversed the judgment of the Virginia Court of Appeals and held that Congress did not violate the Constitution when it provided in section 25 for Supreme Court review of a state court decision.[79] The *Martin* case allowed Justice Story to address a subject that was "particularly close to his heart."[80] Story had previously devoted considerable effort to securing enactment of legislation that would give lower federal courts the full range of jurisdiction described in article III, including power to hear cases arising under federal law. His efforts had failed but nevertheless reflected an ardent support for the federal judiciary.[81]

In *Martin* he observed that the framers plainly contemplated that "cases" within the scope of article III might also arise in state courts and that the appellate jurisdiction of the Supreme Court would extend to review of such cases. "The appellate process is not limited by the terms of the third article to any particular court... It is the case, then, and not the court, that gives the jurisdiction."[82]

After rejecting Virginia's narrow construction of article III, he attacked the state's sovereignty arguments and, in so doing, refuted the notion that the Constitution was not intended to limit the sovereignty of the states. To the contrary, he wrote, the Constitution "is crowded with provisions which restrain or annul the sovereignty of the states in some of the highest branches of their prerogatives."[83] As Justice Story noted, article I, section 10 contains a long list of limits on state power. When the states are "stripped of some of the highest attributes of sovereignty," he reasoned, it is difficult to accept the argument that appellate review of state decisions is somehow a dangerous act or contrary to the spirit of the constitution.[84] Justice Story wrote:

The courts of the United States can, without question, revise the proceedings of the executive and legislative authorities of the states, and if they are found to be contrary to the constitution, may declare them to be of no legal validity. Surely the exercise of the same right over judicial tribunals is not a higher or more dangerous act of sovereign power.[85]

Finally, he concluded by reaffirming the arguments for a single national court with power to review all cases—even those coming from state court—that fell within the confines of article III. Such power must rest in the Court to protect against the "state attachments, state prejudices, state jealousies and state interests" that might sometimes obstruct or confront the regular administration of justice.[86] In addition, a separate and distinct reason, "perfectly compatible with the most sincere respect for state tribunals," is the necessity for uniform decisions on the meaning of federal law.[87]

Judges of equal learning and integrity, in different states, might differently interpret a statute, or a treaty of the United States, or even the constitution itself. If there were no revising authority to control these jarring and discordant judgments, and harmonize them into uniformity, the laws, the treaties, and the constitution of the United States would be different in different states, and might, perhaps, never have precisely the same construction, obligation, or efficacy, in any two states. The public mischiefs that would attend such a state of things would be truly deplorable, and it cannot be believed that they could have escaped the enlightened convention which formed the constitution.[88]

Supreme Court review of state court cases arising under federal law, thus, was justified not only by the language of article III and the spirit of the constitutional scheme but also by reasons "touching the safety, peace and sovereignty of the nations."[89] Despite the potential for friction between the state and federal governments, *Martin* held that the Supreme Court could indeed review state court judgments in cases that fell within the categories listed in article III.

The decision in *Martin* did not end state resistance to section 25 and Supreme Court review of state court judgments. Five years after that decision the Court was again asked to address the issue, this time in the context of a criminal case. Two brothers had been convicted for selling District of Columbia lottery tickets in violation of Virginia law. On appeal to the Supreme Court they argued that they were immune from state prosecution for selling lottery tickets authorized by Congress. In *Cohens v. Virginia*, the Court rejected this argument but, before doing so, considered whether it had power to review a state court judgment in a criminal case.[90] Section 25 conferred such power and *Martin* had sustained the validity of that law. The state's lawyer, however, argued that *Martin* should not control because that case involved a dispute between private parties. By contrast, in *Cohens* the state itself was a party and Supreme Court review would be a more serious intrusion on state sovereignty. Chief Justice Marshall emphatically rejected Virginia's suggestion and held that the Supreme Court has power to review state criminal cases involving federal constitutional rights. In so doing he expressed a rather harsh view of the reliability of state judges to protect constitutional rights:

It would be hazarding too much to assert, that the judicatures of the States will be exempt from the prejudices by which the legislatures and people are influenced, and will constitute perfectly impartial tribunals. In many States the judges are dependent for office and for salary on the will of the legislature.... When we observe the importance which that constitution attaches to the independence of judges, we are the less inclined to suppose that it can have intended to leave these constitutional questions to tribunals where this independence may not exist, in all cases where a State shall prosecute an individual who claims the protection of an act of Congress.... No government ought to be so defective in its organization, as not to contain within itself the means of securing the execution of its own laws against other dangers than those which occur every day. Courts of justice are the means most usually employed; and it is reasonable to expect that a government should repose on its own Courts, rather than on others. There is certainly nothing in the circumstances under which our constitution was formed; nothing in the history of the times, which would justify the opinion that the confidence reposed in the States was so implicit as to leave in them and their tribunals the power of resisting or defeating, in the form of law, the legitimate measures of the Union.[91]

Martin, Cohens, and *Marbury* significantly increased the power of the Supreme Court. These decisions served over time as the vehicles for transforming the Supreme Court into "the most extraordinarily powerful court of law the world has ever known."[92] They did not, however, have a direct impact on the power of lower federal courts, which under the judiciary act were denied any role in protecting constitutional rights. While the Supreme Court's authority to guard these rights was being enhanced, similar efforts on behalf of the lower federal courts during the early 1800s were less successful.

Some, like Justice Story, firmly believed that lower federal courts should be given broad powers to protect federal rights. Indeed, he argued that federal courts should be given the full power conferred by the Constitution and be allowed to hear cases arising under the Constitution or federal law.[93] The 1789 Judiciary Act, of course, plainly rejected this approach. In 1801, however, Congress made a move, although short-lived, toward Story's position. That move was motivated by the economic and political interests of the federalists.

In the late 1790s the federal judiciary became strategically important in economic and political controversies and, as a result, attracted heightened interest.[94] The economic controversies involved land speculation by federalists in Georgia, Kentucky, Pennsylvania, and Virginia, states controlled by Republicans. Disputes arose in these states over the application of state law to the land companies and, because of the Judiciary Act of 1789, these matters fell within the jurisdiction of state court. The federalist land speculators, facing litigation in unfriendly state courts, renewed efforts to change the jurisdiction of the federal courts and thereby obtain a more favorable forum.

On a political level, the federalists were threatened by the rise of the Republican party. As part of the effort to quash the opposition, the federalists enacted the Sedition Act of 1798, which made it illegal to print or publish any "false, scandalous and malicious writing" against the federal government, the president, or the Congress with intent to defame or bring them "into contempt or disrepute, or to excite against them . . . the hatred of the good people of the United States."[95] The Adams' administration brought a number of prosecutions against Republicans, and the federal courts, staffed with federalist judges, conducted the trials in a partisan manner.[96] As tension mounted, the federalists saw the expansion of the federal judiciary as a further means for controlling the opposition.[97]

The product of these developments was the Judiciary Act of 1801, which created six new federal circuit courts as well as several new district courts.[98] In addition, the act increased the size of the federal judiciary, paving the way for Adams' appointment of the "midnight judges." The federalists' political purposes were further reflected in the provision reducing the number of Supreme Court justices from six to five, thereby depriving President Jefferson of an appointment. Finally, and most importantly, the 1801 act greatly expanded the jurisdiction of the lower federal courts, eliminating the $500 jurisdictional amount requirement for civil cases, expanding power to hear disputes between citizens of different states and giving them power to hear certain cases involving land disputes. Most relevant, the act authorized lower federal courts to hear cases arising under the Constitution and federal law. Although the immediate purpose of the act was to protect the federalist interests, this motivation "should not obscure the corollary aim of reforming the circuit court system, nor the effect the law had in promoting a more uniform administration of justice and bringing the federal judiciary closer to the people."[99]

The changes created by the 1801 act were the subject of intense criticism by the Republicans who assumed power during the Jefferson administration. Provoked in part by Marbury's attempt to compel delivery of his commission as a justice of the peace, the Republicans began efforts to repeal the 1801 law.[100] These efforts were successful and, effective March 31, 1802, the previous year's changes were repealed.[101] The effect was to reinstate the federal judicial system created by the Judiciary Act of 1789 in which lower federal courts did not have power to hear cases arising under the Constitution or U.S. laws. Once again these cases would be heard by state courts with the possibility of appellate review by the Supreme Court.

For the most part, this scheme remained intact until after the Civil War, and during the next sixty-five years Congress made only a few minor alterations that expanded federal judicial power. In 1815, for example, it provided that suits against federal officers enforcing the collection of war revenues could be removed from state to federal courts.[102] Subsequent legislation permitted removal of lawsuits against federal officers based on acts done under the revenue laws, and removal of state court cases where the defendant asserted some federal immunity.[103] As (then professor) Felix Frankfurter noted regarding these changes: "All this was *ad hoc* legislation—not abstract or systematic assertion of federal power, but measures governing restricted types of controversies, and directed towards demonstrated inadequacy of state agencies."[104]

In short, during the first half of the nineteenth century there was little opportunity for friction between the lower federal courts and the states with regard to enforcement of the Constitution or federal law. Without a bill of rights that limited states, the Constitution itself placed relatively few restraints on the states in their dealings with individuals. Moreover, the lower federal courts had virtually no power to enforce whatever restraints existed. For the most part, the first seventy-five years of our history were largely uneventful with regard to enforcement of constitutional rights by lower federal courts against state governments.

The slavery crisis and the Civil War, however, profoundly changed the character of our nation, and the constitutional structure for protecting individual freedoms was very much a part of the new order. I do not intend to review the vast literature on the slavery crisis, the Civil War, and the resulting reconstruction efforts.[105] Rather, it is sufficient to note that after the war a concept of national citizenship began emerging and that concept would have implications for the relations between the federal and state governments generally and for the role of federal courts specifically.[106] Before the war, the concept of an "American citizen" was not only ill-defined but "largely insignificant."[107] Individuals defined themselves with reference to their states. As others have commented, "the Civil War changed all that by establishing that a citizen's primary allegiance was to the federal government."[108]

The constitutional amendments adopted in the wake of the Civil War gave content to the idea of national citizenship. The Thirteenth Amendment, ratified in December 1865, was designed to achieve a "revolution in federalism," fundamentally restructuring the federal system and providing for federal authority in the area of personal liberty.[109] The amendment states that neither slavery nor involuntary servitude shall exist and, moreover, gives Congress power to enforce that prohibition. The immense significance of the language has been too often ignored. Professor Jacobus tenBroek wrote in his account of the Civil War amendments that the few words of the Thirteenth Amendment embody fundamental concepts of liberty and equality. The amendment, said tenBroek, was seen as "not merely cutting loose the fetters which bound the physical person of the slave, but restoring him to his natural inalienable, and civil rights . . . guaranteeing to him the privilege and immunities of citizens of the United States. . . . If slavery were abolished then liberty must exist."[110]

Unfortunately the Thirteenth Amendment failed to have the broad reach intended by its sponsors. Indeed, shortly after the amendment had been ratified, the southern states began to enact black codes that discriminated on the basis of race.[111] The laws extended to all aspects of the lives of the freed slaves. They imposed a system of passes that controlled the movement of blacks, prohibited blacks from congregating in groups, from residing in certain areas or pursuing jobs, and forbade racial intermarriage. They even made certain conduct criminal only if done by blacks. The codes, for example, prohibited blacks from directing insulting language at whites and provided for the death penalty when a black raped a white woman but not when a white raped a black woman. Some codes also prohibited blacks from voting, sitting on juries, or holding public office. The southern states plainly intended to ignore and defeat the national attempt to redefine citizenship and guarantee equality and liberty to all citizens.

The black codes and actions of the southern state officials

persuaded Congress that legislation was needed to ensure the guarantees of the Thirteenth Amendment. The amendment gave Congress power to "enforce this article by appropriate legislation," and Congress quickly invoked that power. In 1866 it enacted the first of a series of civil rights acts that became part of the Reconstruction effort. The Civil Rights Act of 1866 conferred citizenship on all persons born in the United States and granted all, including black citizens, the right to make and enforce contracts, the right to inherit, buy, and sell real and personal property, the right to sue, and the right to the full and equal benefit of all laws for the security of person and property.[112] The 1866 act imposed criminal sanctions on those who, acting under color of state law, deprive citizens of these rights. Finally, section 3 of the act expressly gave lower federal courts power to hear civil and criminal matters involving persons who were denied the enumerated rights or who could not enforce those rights in state court.

The sponsors of the 1866 Civil Rights Act maintained that the Thirteenth Amendment gave Congress power to enact those far-reaching provisions. Nevertheless, considerable doubt remained about whether the amendment in fact granted such broad powers to guarantee equality, particularly when such a guarantee conflicted with existing state laws. To remove any doubts and to ensure that the statutory rights would be beyond the control of future congressional majorities, members of the Thirty-ninth Congress proposed the Fourteenth Amendment. On June 13, 1866, both houses passed the amendment that became part of the Constitution two years later in July 1868, when it was ratified by the states. The Fourteenth Amendment would eventually emerge as the principal constitutional vehicle for safeguarding individual rights from intrusion by the states. It states:

All persons born or naturalized in the United States and subject to the jurisdiction thereof, are citizens of the United States and of the State wherein they reside. No State shall make or enforce any law which shall abridge the privileges or immunities of citizens of the United States; nor shall any State deprive any person of life, liberty, or property, without due process of law; nor deny to any person within its jurisdiction the equal protection of the laws.

Moreover, it gave Congress power to enact legislation enforcing these provisions. One issue was clear—the Fourteenth Amendment was intended to place the constitutionality of the civil rights bill beyond any doubt.[113]

Relying on this new source of power, Congress enacted a number of laws designed to give content to the national citizenship conferred by the Fourteenth Amendment. First, in 1870, it passed the Enforcement Act, which included the provisions of the 1866 Civil Rights Act and, in addition, gave federal courts power to hear lawsuits involving interference with the right to vote.[114] Next it enacted the Civil Rights Act of 1871, which provided a civil remedy against persons who, acting under color of state law, deprive others of rights secured by the Constitution.[115] The 1871 act, which was directed at the Ku Klux Klan, also provided civil remedies and criminal sanctions against those who conspire to deprive others of constitutional rights. Finally, in 1875 Congress passed another civil rights act prohibiting racial discrimination by places of public accommodations and authorized civil and criminal sanctions for violations.[116]

Among these many provisions was the predecessor of the law now known as "Section 1983." That statute would become the principal statutory vehicle for enforcing federal rights against state officials and deserves special mention. As originally drafted in 1871, the statute protected rights secured by the Constitution. In 1874, it was amended to provide protection for rights secured by federal law as well. Most significantly, Section 1983 authorized both damages and injunctive relief to be awarded against persons who, acting under color of state law, subject others to the deprivation of federal constitutional and statutory rights. In its amended form, Section 1983 now provides:

Every person who, under color of any statute, ordinance, regulation, custom, or usage, of any State or Territory, subjects, or causes to be subjected, any citizen of the United States or other person within the jurisdiction thereof to the deprivation of any rights, privileges, or immunities secured by the Constitution and laws, shall be liable to the party injured in an action at law, suit in equity, or other proper proceeding for redress.[117]

It should be noted that Section 1983 went well beyond protection of the recently freed slaves. As one legislator stated during the debate over Section 1983's predecessor, the law "not only
provides a civil remedy for persons whose former condition may
have been that of slaves, but also to all people where, under color
of state law, they or any of them may be deprived of rights to
which they are entitled under the Constitution by reason and
virtue of their national citizenship."[118] It is clear from the legislative debates that Section 1983 was intended to protect citizens
from state action, "whether that action be executive, legislative
or judicial."[119]

Congress, however, did not trust the states to enforce these
new rights, and rightly so. According to Representative Hoar,
"The principal danger that menaces us today is from the effort
within the states to deprive considerable numbers of persons of
the civil and equal rights which the General Government is en-
deavouring to secure to them."[120] Representative Lowe specifically attacked the state courts for their failure to provide effective
redress for deprivation of the federal rights.[121]

To fill the void and provide a meaningful forum for protecting
the rights created by the amendments and the civil rights acts,
Congress greatly expanded the power of lower federal courts.
The 1871 Civil Rights Act, for example, authorized lower federal
courts to hear proceedings brought to redress the deprivation,
under color of state law, of rights secured by the Constitution.[122]
In 1874, the jurisdiction of the federal courts was expanded to
include cases brought under those federal laws providing protection for equal and civil rights.[123] Finally, in 1875 Congress
returned to the short-lived approach tried seventy-four years
earlier in the 1801 Judiciary Act and granted lower federal courts
power to hear any civil cases arising under the Constitution or
federal law.[124] For the first time in our history, the federal courthouse doors were opened wide to citizens complaining of the
denial of federal rights by state officials. Although the 1875 act
received relatively little attention at the time, it produced significant and permanent expansion of the role of lower federal
courts. It was a "remarkable instance of quiet constitutional
change,"[125] placing the federal courts as the "primary and dom-

inant instruments for vindicating rights given by the Constitution, Laws and Treaties of the United States."[126]

As Justice Blackmun recently observed, "Taken together, the
Reconstruction Amendments, the Civil Rights Acts, and the new
jurisdictional statutes, all emerging from the caldron of the War
between the States, marked a revolutionary shift in the relationship among individuals, the States, and the Federal Government."[127] The post-Civil War period produced a radical
transformation in the legal structure for protecting federal
rights. The Constitution and civil rights acts imposed restraints
on the states. Individuals were given remedies to enforce these
restraints. And, a federal forum was provided for enforcement
proceedings. In short, this revolution created a new structure of
law in which individuals had "federal rights, federal remedies,
and federal forums" to protect themselves from the states.[128] As
a result of this new structure "the role of the Federal Government as a guarantor of basic federal rights against state power
was clearly established."[129] One must quickly add that this role
was clearly established only in theory. In fact, the transformation
process was slow and would take many decades to become a
reality. Indeed, during the last quarter of the nineteenth century
the Supreme Court did its best to destroy the newly created legal
structure.

In the *Slaughterhouse Cases* the Court struck a devastating
blow at those seeking constitutional protection from misconduct by state officials.[130] The cases arose out of efforts of the
butchers of New Orleans to challenge state legislation that
granted a monopoly to others. They maintained that the state
law prevented them from practicing their trade and violated
the civil war amendments in several respects. First, the state
law, they argued, imposed a form of involuntary servitude in
violation of the Thirteenth Amendment. Second, the grant of
a monopoly (which had been "greased through the Louisiana
legislature by bribery"[131]) abridged their privileges as citizens of
the United States, deprived them of property without due process, and denied them equal protection of the law—all in direct
violation of the Fourteenth Amendment.

The Court quickly disposed of the Thirteenth Amendment

argument holding that the ban on "involuntary servitude" did not apply to these circumstances. That amendment was intended to ban slavery and all vestiges of slavery including forms of forced apprenticeships or other such servitude. It had no application whatsoever, the Court said, to a state law allowing a specified company to operate a slaughterhouse within New Orleans.

The Court found the equal protection and due process arguments equally unpersuasive. The equal protection clause, the Court held, applied only to laws that discriminate against blacks. "The existence of laws in the states where the newly emancipated negroes resided, which discriminated with gross injustice and hardship against them as a class, was the evil to be remedied by this clause, and by it such laws are forbidden."[132] So too the due process clause provided no protection because it was limited to guaranteeing fair procedures, a matter not raised in this case.

The real blow to the Fourteenth Amendment came from the Court's discussion of national citizenship and the privileges and immunities clause. The amendment states that all persons born or naturalized in the United States are "citizens of the United States and of the state wherein they reside." It then prohibits a state from abridging the "privileges or immunities of citizens of the United States." Justice Miller wrote for the majority and concluded that individuals possess two separate groupings, or sets, of rights—one group includes rights we hold as state citizens, the other encompasses the separate and distinct rights we possess as national citizens.[133] This latter set of rights owes its existence to the federal government and includes, for example, the right to petition the federal government, the right to use the navigable waters of the United States, the privilege of habeas corpus, and rights secured by federal treaties. All other rights, those that do not owe their existence to the federal government, are possessed by virtue of state citizenship. These rights, the rights of state citizenship, in many respects were more significant because they relate to the daily activities of the people. The Fourteenth Amendment, said Justice Miller, prohibits only state abridgement of rights of national citizens and does not apply to state interference with rights held as state citizens.

The dissenters vigorously disputed Justice Miller's simplistic division of the universe of rights. They pointed out that the Constitution contains another privilege and immunities clause, article IV, section 2, that prohibits a state from discriminating against citizens of other states. Article IV, however, left open the possibility that a state might discriminate against its own citizens, and the recent history of the black codes revealed that some states were taking advantage of the opening. The Fourteenth Amendment, the dissenters argued, was designed to close that gap. Just as article IV prevented states from discriminatory treatment of citizens of other states, the Fourteenth Amendment prevented states from discriminatory treatment of their own citizens.

Under the majority's view, the butchers' claim had to be rejected. The right asserted by the butchers—the right to engage in their trade—did not owe its existence to federal law. If such a right existed at all, it was derived from state law and the Fourteenth Amendment did not prevent a state from discriminating against its own citizens with respect to such rights.

The majority's view that the Fourteenth Amendment privileges and immunities clause restricts only state abridgement of federal rights reduced that clause to a nullity. Even before ratification of the amendment, the supremacy clause made federal law the supreme law of the land and prevented state attempts to abridge federal rights.[134] Under Justice Miller's analysis, the Fourteenth Amendment added no additional protection from state legislation hostile to its own citizens. Even worse, his position stood in stark contrast to that of the Civil War amendments' sponsors who had attempted to create a concept of national citizenship in which privileges and immunities were defined and protected by the federal government. Indeed, one has the very distinct sense that Justice Miller was trying to hold onto a past in which states remained the primary source and protector of rights. He simply did not comprehend, or want to understand, that the Civil War amendments envisioned a new order in federal and state relations.[135] He certainly acknowledged the recent sentiment that the states presented the "true danger to the perpetuity of the Union." Nevertheless, he wrote, "however prevading this sentiment, and however it may have contributed to the adoption of the amendments we have been considering, we do not

see in those amendments any purpose to destroy the main features of the general system."[136]

Although the opinion in *Slaughterhouse Cases* did not directly involve the recently freed slaves, it had implications for them as well. To secure those rights affecting their daily existence, the blacks would have to depend on the state officials, precisely the officials least likely to protect them. Because it left blacks to the mercy of state officials, *Slaughterhouse* has been described as "the first great judicial setback [in the post-Civil War period] suffered by blacks in their quest for effective constitutional protection of their liberties."[137]

Slaughterhouse finally had an impact, although indirect, on the role of lower federal courts in protecting constitutional rights. The jurisdictional statutes enacted during Reconstruction had greatly expanded the power of federal courts, authorizing them to hear claims that state officials were depriving citizens of rights secured by the Constitution and U.S. laws. The Court, however, had ruled in *Slaughterhouse* that perhaps the most significant privileges and immunities—those affecting daily lives—were held as state citizens and not embraced by the Fourteenth Amendment. As a result, a case claiming state deprivation of such a right would not raise any federal constitutional issue but rather would present a state law claim that would have to be brought in state court. *Slaughterhouse*, thus, not only restricted the reach of the Fourteenth Amendment but also limited any role that might be played by the federal courts.

Slaughterhouse was a preview of things to come and served as a warning that the transformation from state to federal protection of constitutional rights would be dreadfully slow. Indeed, during the final quarter of the nineteenth century "reconciliation grew into a nationwide amnesia about the events of the Civil War and Reconstruction."[138] To win the 1876 presidential election, Rutherford B. Hayes needed the electoral votes of South Carolina, Louisiana, and Florida. In return for that support Hayes agreed to provide federal benefits to the South and, most significantly, remove all federal troops from the region.[139] "Back in the saddle, Southern Democrats moved at once to make sure they would not be unhorsed again."[140] The southern states began a process of disenfranchising the blacks, and by 1910, had reduced the black man to a "political cipher."[141] The Fifteenth Amendment, which had been ratified in 1870 and guaranteed that the right to vote shall not be abridged on the basis of race or color, was simply evaded.

The withdrawal of the federal troops symbolized the overall pattern of federal abandonment of the blacks and the enforcement effort. The former slave owners were once again in charge. Lynching of blacks became an ordinary event and it is reported that more than 3,000 people were killed during this period.[142] Not surprisingly, few if any whites were ever punished or even tried for these murders. Moreover, during this period racial segregation became an accepted fact of life, encouraged in significant part by the Supreme Court. It ruled in 1883, that the civil rights acts, which outlawed racial discrimination in hotels, inns, railroads, and other places of public accommodations, were unconstitutional. The acts had been passed pursuant to section 5 of the Fourteenth Amendment, which gave Congress power to enforce the amendment. In the *Civil Rights Cases*, however, the Supreme Court held that under the Fourteenth Amendment, Congress could only prohibit state action and had no power to prohibit segregation by privately owned places of public accommodation.[143]

Thirteen years later, the Court conferred its blessing on state-sponsored segregation activities. In *Plessy v. Ferguson* the Court upheld the constitutionality of a Louisiana law requiring railroads to provide separate but equal accommodations for whites and blacks.[144] Justice Brown wrote for the Court that such Jim Crow laws are not repugnant to the Fourteenth Amendment. "The object of the amendment was undoubtedly to enforce the absolute equality of the two races before the law, but in the nature of things it could not have been intended to abolish distinctions based upon color, or to enforce social, as distinguished from political equality, or a commingly of the two races upon terms unsatisfactory to either."[145] The segregation law was a reasonable attempt to promote the "preservation of the public peace and good order." The opinion concluded with the remarkable observation that "the underlying fallacy of the plaintiff's argument ... [is] the assumption that the enforced separation of the two races stamps the colored race with a badge of inferiority. If this be so, it is not by reason of anything found in the act, but solely because the colored race chooses to put that construction upon it."[146]

By the end of the century the Supreme Court had done its best to obliterate the legal order envisioned by the sponsors of the Civil War amendments and statutes. In this regard the Court had joined the other branches of the federal government.[147] It was, as Justice Blackmun observed, "our Dark Age of Civil Rights."[148] Despite the hopes of the Reconstruction leaders, the federal government had not emerged as a significant force in protecting citizens from misconduct by state officials. The ingredients for the new legal order may have been in place, but more was needed to convert plans to reality. An important step in the transformation process was taken in 1908 when the Supreme Court decided *Ex parte Young*.[149] In that case the Court ruled that a federal district court had power to issue an injunction against a state official who was enforcing an unconstitutional state law. Today, such injunctions are commonplace and the principle established in *Young* may seem rather unremarkable. In 1908, however, the significance of the decision was tremendous, prompting Justice Harlan to warn in his dissent that *Young* would "work a radical change in our governmental system. It would inaugurate a new era in the . . . relations of the National and state governments."[150] To be sure, the decision armed the federal district court judges with a weapon to use against unconstitutional state conduct.

The hand of the lower federal court was further strengthened a few years later when the Supreme Court ruled in *Home Telephone and Telegraph Co. v. Los Angeles* that federal courts may use that weapon and enjoin official misconduct under the Fourteenth Amendment even when the misconduct also violates state law.[151] Moreover, such official action may be enjoined by the federal court without first awaiting a state court decision on whether the challenged conduct might also violate the state's own laws.

Young and *Home Telephone* did not inaugurate the new era overnight. In fact the decision prompted congressional responses designed to somewhat slow the pace of the change. Congress amended the judicial code to require that three federal judges (rather than the usual one judge) initially hear challenges to the constitutionality of state laws.[152] Subsequently, it passed the Johnson Act,[153] which deprived the district courts of power to enjoin state public utility rate orders and the Tax Injunction Act, which stripped the federal court of power to enjoin the collection of state taxes.[154] Despite these minor setbacks, *Young* and *Home Telephone* moved us closer to the new legal order contemplated by the sponsors of the amendments and laws adopted during Reconstruction, a legal order that recognized the primacy of the federal government in protecting constitutional rights.

The real breakthrough came with the decision in the school desegregation case, *Brown v. Board of Education*.[155] The Court shattered the "separate but equal" barrier erected by *Plessy*, proclaiming that "separate educational facilities are inherently unequal."[156] In so doing, it gave impetus to the federal courts as primary guardians of constitutional rights and to the civil rights injunction as the remedial tool for protection of such rights. *Brown*, of course, was not decided in a vacuum. It was the climax of a sustained legal battle by the National Association for the Advancement of Colored People against the very foundations of the *Plessy* doctrine.[157]

Moreover, the world outside the courtroom was rapidly changing and protection of civil rights was becoming a national political issue. In the aftermath of *Brown*, Congress was forced into action by the widespread resistance of state officials to the desegregation mandate.[158] During the decade following *Brown*, Congress passed perhaps the most important civil rights laws in our nation's history. In 1957, it enacted the first civil rights act since the Reconstruction period.[159] That act established the Civil Rights Commission, created a new Civil Rights Division in the Justice Department, and gave the Justice Department the power to bring voting rights cases on behalf of disenfranchised blacks. Seven years later Congress enacted the "most potent civil-rights bill in history."[160] The 1964 act prohibited discrimination by hotels, theaters, restaurants, and other places of public accommodation.[161] It outlawed discrimination by recipients of federal financial assistance and prevented employers from discriminating on the basis of race, creed, color, national origin, or religion in making employment decisions. The act also gave the attorney general additional enforcement powers and authorized the federal courts to hear cases brought by the government or by individuals.

The blatant resistance to *Brown* also eventually forced the national executive branch to use its powers against the unconstitutional conduct by state officials. The emphasis here should be on "eventually." President Eisenhower failed to provide the kind of leadership necessary to generate support for *Brown.* Indeed, he, "either by design or by obtuseness, comforted and dignified those who were ranged against the Court."[162] Shamefully, he at no time declared that *Brown* should be followed not only because it was a decision of the highest court but, more importantly, because it was right.[163] President Eisenhower was eventually forced to send federal paratroopers to Arkansas to force the admission of black children to Little Rock Central High School. "Even then, the President did not use the dramatic confrontation at Little Rock to say that lawlessness could not be tolerated in America any longer; even then, he did not follow up and call upon the country to move ahead with desegregation."[164]

Although at first also reluctant, President Kennedy assumed an active role in the civil rights movement. He provided federal protection to freedom riders who traveled throughout the South in an effort to focus national attention on the continuing segregation of the races and on the refusal of state officials to take any action.[165] Kennedy's confrontation with Alabama Governor George Wallace pushed him "beyond the limit of patience with the defiantly segregationist South."[166] In sharp contrast to Eisenhower, he took a strong stand against the segregationists, stating in a nationally televised speech: "We are confronted primarily with a moral issue. It is as old as the Scriptures and is as clear as the Constitution."[167] He then added:

If an American, because his skin is dark, cannot eat lunch in a restaurant open to the public; if he cannot send his children to the best public school available; if he cannot vote for the public officials who represent him; if, in short, he cannot enjoy the full and free life which all of us want, then who among us would be content to have the color of his skin changed and stand in his place? Who among us would then be content with the counsels of patience and delay? One hundred years of delay have passed since President Lincoln freed the slaves, yet their heirs, their grandsons, are not fully free. They are not yet freed from the bonds of injustice; they are not yet freed from social and economic oppression. And this nation, for all its hopes and all its boasts, will not be fully free until all its citizens are free.[168]

One week later President Kennedy sent Congress the bill that became the 1964 Civil Rights Act.

Protection of constitutional rights became a national issue in one other respect as well. During the late 1950s and early 1960s, we were engaged in a cold war with the Soviet Union and competed for the support of third world countries whose citizens were primarily nonwhite. To win this support we had to appear to be treating our own black citizens fairly. President Kennedy alluded to this dimension of the civil rights movement as well:

We preach freedom around the world, and we mean it. And we cherish our freedom here at home. But are we to say to the world—and much more importantly to each other—that this is the land of the free, except for the Negroes; that we have no second-class citizens, except Negroes; that we have no class or caste system, no ghettos, no master race, except with respect to Negroes?[169]

Others have been more direct in asserting a convergence at this time between the interests of the blacks and the interests of the nation as a whole. Professor Derrick Bell contended that *Brown* itself "cannot be understood without some consideration of the decision's value to whites, not simply those concerned about the immorality of racial inequality, but also those whites in policymaking positions able to see the economic and political advances at home and abroad that would follow abandonment of segregation."[170] Specifically, he noted that *Brown* helped to provide credibility to our struggle to win the "hearts and minds of emerging third world peoples."[171] Second, it offered much needed reassurance to black war veterans "that the precepts of equality and freedom so heralded during World War II might yet be given meaning at home."[172] Finally, by eliminating state sponsored segregation *Brown* helped pave the way for the industrialization of the South.

Brown, thus, can be viewed as both a cause and an effect of the nationalization of the civil rights movement. The decision plainly placed protection of constitutional rights in the national spotlight and on the agenda of both Congress and the presidency. So, too, it thrust the federal courts into an active role as guardians of those rights and, in so doing, gave "special prominence" to the injunction as the judicial tool for enforcement.[173] In the wake of *Brown*, federal courts became the focus for public law litigation involving policies related not only to schools, but also to such matters as conditions in prisons and mental institutions, police conduct, zoning, and reapportionment.[174] The injunction became the vehicle for enforcement of constitutional rights in these varying contexts. Victims of unconstitutional practices increasingly turned to the federal courts seeking imposition of injunctive relief.

A decision a few years after *Brown* served as an additional element in the transformation of the federal courts. It will be recalled that as part of the Civil Rights Act of 1871, Congress had passed Section 1983 authorizing damages and injunctions against persons who, acting under color of state law, deprive another of any right secured by the Constitution or U.S. laws. Like other aspects of the Reconstruction laws, that provision faded into obscurity shortly after enactment.[175] In 1961, however, the Supreme Court decided *Monroe v. Pape*, which revived Section 1983 as the chief statutory means for obtaining federal court relief against state officials engaged in unconstitutional conduct.[176] In *Monroe*, the Court concluded that Section 1983 could be used as the vehicle for challenging the constitutionality of actions taken by Chicago police officers who broke into plaintiffs' home, routed them from bed, made them stand naked, and ransacked every room. One of the very purposes of Section 1983, Justice Douglas wrote for the Court, was to provide a federal remedy against such deprivations:

It is abundantly clear that one reason the legislation was passed was to afford a *federal right in federal court* because, by reason of prejudice, passion, neglect, intolerance, or otherwise, state laws might not be enforced and the claims of citizens to the enjoyment of rights, privileges, and immunities guaranteed by the Fourteenth Amendment might be denied by state agencies.[177]

In *Monroe* the Warren Court gave new life to the Reconstruction concept that federal courthouse doors should be open wide to individuals seeking relief from unconstitutional actions by state officials.

For the Warren Court, opening the doors of the Supreme Court alone was not adequate to protect individuals from unconstitutional state conduct. Rather, the Warren Court underscored the need for a federal forum at the trial level as well, in part because the Supreme Court can review only a small number of cases each year.[178] But, in addition, the Warren Court recognized that appellate review is not an adequate substitute for a determination by a federal district court in the first instance. As that Court said: "Limiting the litigant to review here [in the Supreme Court] would deny him the benefit of a federal trial court's role in constructing a record and making fact findings. How the facts are found will often dictate the decision of federal claims."[179]

One final development during this period also contributed to the emerging role of the federal judiciary in guarding constitutional rights. In 1919 Reginald Heber Smith observed that denial of justice to those most needing protection is often not attributable to the substantive laws but rather is due to defects in the administration of the law. He wrote:

There is something tragic in the fact that a plan and method of administering justice, honestly designed to make efficient and certain that litigation on which at last all rights depend, should result in rearing insuperable obstacles in the path of those who most need protection, so that litigation becomes impossible, rights are lost, and wrongs go unredressed.[180]

One of the "procedural" difficulties was the inability of the poor to afford the legal expenses of any litigation that might be necessary to protect their rights. Those living at, or below, a subsistence level could hardly divert funds to payment of lawyer's fees. In the post-*Brown* period an effort was made to address this problem. As part of President Johnson's War on Poverty, the federal government created a national Legal Services Program that provided free legal assistance to the poor. The program grew out of the civil rights movement, and the young lawyers who joined the program held a strong commitment to social justice.[181] Much of their work involved "service cases," representing poor people with landlord–tenant, family, consumer, and welfare problems. They however, were also involved in law reform efforts directed at changing laws and practices that were unfavorable to poor people. In many instances the law reform litigation involved constitutional challenges that were brought against state officials in federal courts.[182] The Legal Services Program and the attorneys working for it, thus, are very much part of our story.

By the late 1960s the legal structure for protection of constitutional rights, first envisioned during Reconstruction, was firmly in place. Individuals were no longer forced into state court when challenging unconstitutional conduct by the state's own officials. Rather, these individuals now had—in fact, as well as theory—federal rights, federal remedies, and an available federal forum. Moreover, in some instances they could even obtain free legal assistance in bringing their cases. Finally, the very political, economic, and social climate in which such cases arose had been altered. The isolationism of the late nineteenth and early twentieth centuries had yielded to a "new spirit of nationalism" in which the notion of states as separate units seemed outmoded in many respects.[183] As Judge John Gibbons aptly observed: "In the global village, deference to local solutions for problems that transcend local interests is a quaint anachronism."[184] And, our experience with segregation painfully revealed that protection of constitutional rights was a problem that transcended local interests.

As we entered the Burger Court era it was well established that the federal court doors should be opened wide to those alleging denial of constitutional rights by state officials. The Burger Court, however, quickly revealed that it had a very different vision of the federal judiciary's role in protecting these freedoms and promptly began its efforts to dismantle the federal courts and resurrect state courts as guardians of our constitutional rights. As early as 1970, the Society of American Law Teachers issued a statement warning that the Burger Court was "making it harder and harder to get a federal court to vindicate federal constitutional and other rights."[185] As this story unfolds, it becomes clear that the authors of that statement could not have been more accurate in their assessment of the Burger Court's plan for closing off access to the federal courts.

Notes

1. Texas v. White, 74 U.S. (7 Wall.) 700, 725 (1869).

2. Abramson & Gutmann, "New Federalism: State Constitutions and State Courts" in A WORKABLE GOVERNMENT? THE CONSTITUTION AFTER 200 YEARS 109 (B. MARSHALL ed. 1987).

3. A. NEVINS, THE AMERICAN STATES DURING AND AFTER THE REVOLUTION, 1775–1789 117 (1924).

4. Id.

5. SOURCES OF OUR LIBERTIES 148–62 (R. PERRY & J. COOPER ed. 1952).

6. A. KELLY, W. HARBISON, & H. BELZ, THE AMERICAN CONSTITUTION: ITS ORIGINS AND DEVELOPMENT 41 (6th ed. 1983) [hereinafter cited as KHB].

7. Z. CHAFFEE, JR., HOW HUMAN RIGHTS GOT INTO THE CONSTITUTION 18–20 (1952).

8. Id. at 18–20. See Palmer, "Liberties as Constitutional Provisions" in W. NELSON & R. PALMER, LIBERTY AND COMMUNITY: CONSTITUTION AND RIGHTS IN THE EARLY AMERICAN REPUBLIC 55 (1987).

9. See R. PERRY & J. COOPER, supra note 5, at 311.

10. KHB supra note 6, at 90.

11. Id. at 162.

12. F. BARBASH, THE FOUNDING 161 (1987).

13. See infra text accompanying notes 20–23.

14. See THE FEDERALIST PAPERS 227 (R. Fairfield ed. 1966).

15. F. BARBASH, supra note 12, at 162.

16. See e.g., THE FEDERALIST No. 78 (Fairfield), supra note 14, at 226–33; THE FEDERALIST No. 80 (Fairfield), supra note 14, at 236–41.

17. See THE FOUNDER'S CONSTITUTION 137 (P. KURLAND & R. LERNER eds. 1987) (statement of Mr. Randolph) [hereinafter cited as KURLAND & LERNER].

18. See 3 J. STORY, COMMENTARIES ON THE CONSTITUTION §1583 (1833); THE FEDERALIST No. 81 (Fairfield), supra note 14, at 246.

19. 1 THE RECORDS OF THE FEDERAL CONVENTION OF 1787 124 (M. FARRAND ed. 1966).

20. KURLAND & LERNER, supra note 17, at 134.

21. 1 M. FARRAND, *supra* note 19.
22. *See* M. JENSEN, THE MAKING OF THE AMERICAN CONSTI-TUTION 50 (1964).
23. 1 M. FARRAND, *supra* note 19, at 125.
24. *See id.* at 104–5; M. JENSEN, *supra* note 22.
25. 1 M. FARRAND, *supra* note 19, at 229.
26. *See id.* at 227; M. JENSEN, *supra* note 22, at 50–51.
27. KHB, *supra* note 6, at 102–3.
28. *See* M. JENSEN, *supra* note 22, at 67–68.
29. U. S. CONST., art. VI.
30. *See* 1 M. FARRAND, *supra* note 19, at 243; M. JENSEN, *supra* note 22, at 68–110.
31. U. S. CONST., art. III.
32. *Id.*
33. *Id.*
34. F. BARBASH, *supra* note 12, at 169.
35. THE FEDERALIST No. 78 (Fairfield), *supra* note 14, at 232.
36. KURLAND & LERNER, *supra* note 17, at 247–48.
37. *Id.*
38. *Id.* at 247.
39. THE FEDERALIST No. 82 (Fairfield), *supra* note 14, at 253.
40. *Id.*
41. *Id.* at 254.
42. KURLAND & LERNER, *supra* note 17, 145–61.
43. 1 Stat. 73.
44. For a history of the Judiciary Act of 1789, *see* Warren, *New Light on the History of the Federal Judiciary Act of 1789*, 37 HARV. L. REV. 49 (1923).
45. The states'-rightists gained an additional victory as well. Much of their attack was directed at the grant of diversity jurisdiction, federal court power to hear a case between citizens of different states. Such jurisdiction was designed to protect an out of state citizen from local prejudices that might exist in state courts. The antifederalists resented the suggestion of any such bias and were concerned that the federal courts hearing these cases might create their own laws rather than apply state law. To make certain the federal courts would use state law in deciding the cases, Section 34 was added to the judiciary act. That section provides: "The laws of the several states, except where the Constitution, Treaties or Statutes of the United States shall otherwise require or provide, shall be regarded as rules of decision in trials at common law in the court of the United States in cases where they apply."
46. Warren, *supra* note 44, at 52.

47. *Id.* at 109.
48. *Id.* at 52.
49. U. S. CONST., art. IV, §4.
50. U. S. CONST., art. I, §9–10.
51. U. S. CONST., art. I, §9.
52. U. S. CONST., art. III, §2.
53. U. S. CONST., art I, §10.
54. U. S. CONST., art. IV, §2.
55. *See* generally, D. BRAVEMAN & W. BANKS, CONSTITUTIONAL LAW: STRUCTURE AND RIGHTS IN OUR FEDERAL SYSTEM 434–36 (1987).
56. See KHB, *supra* note 6, at 121.
57. One amendment that was not ratified provided that there should not be less than one representative for every 50,000 people; the other provided that any change in salaries of senators and representatives would not take effect until an election had intervened. *See id.* at 122.
58. 32 U.S. (7 Pet.) 243 (1833).
59. *Id.* at 246.
60. *Id.* at 249–50. The Fourteenth Amendment was ratified twenty-five years after *Barron* and serves as a limit on state power. Eventually the Supreme Court ruled that some of the provisions in the Bill of Rights are incorporated into the Fourteenth Amendment as limits on the states. *See e.g.,* Duncan v. Louisiana, 391 U.S. 145 (1968) (right to jury trial); Cantwell v. Connecticut, 310 U.S. 296 (1940) (First Amendment rights).
61. 1 C. WARREN, THE SUPREME COURT IN UNITED STATES HISTORY, 90–96 (2d ed. 1971).
62. 2 U. S. (2 Dall.) 419 (1793).
63. 1 C. WARREN, *supra* note 61, at 97.
64. *Id.* at 100.
65. Because the Presidential proclamation of ratification was delayed three years, the effective date given for the amendment is 1798. J. ORTH, THE JUDICIAL POWER OF THE UNITED STATES: THE ELEVENTH AMENDMENT IN AMERICAN HISTORY 20 (1987). There has been ongoing scholarly debate over the precise interpretation of the Eleventh Amendment. *See, e.g.,* Field, *The 11th Amendment and Other Sovereign Immunity Doctrines: Part One,* 126 U. PA. L. REV. 515 (1978); Fletcher, *A Historical Interpretation of the Eleventh Amendment: A Narrow Construction of an Affirmative Grant of Jurisdiction Rather Than a Prohibition Against Jurisdiction,* 35 STAN. L. REV. 1033 (1983); C. JACOBS, THE ELEVENTH AMENDMENT AND SOVEREIGN IMMUNITY (1972); J. ORTH, *supra;*

Tribe, Intergovernmental Immunities in Litigation, Taxation, and Regulation: Separation of Powers Issues in Controversies About Federalism, 89 HARV. L. REV. 682 (1976).

66. 5 U. S. (1 Cranch) 137 (1803).

67. The Court could have avoided the entire discussion of judicial review by treating the case as one of statutory interpretation and concluding that section 13 did not confer jurisdiction. See Van Alstyne, *A Critical Guide to Marbury v. Madison*, 1969, DUKE L. J. 1, 14–16.

68. 5 U. S. (1 Cranch) 137, 175 (1803).

69. *Id.* at 176.

70. *Id* at 177–78.

71. A. BICKEL, THE LEAST DANGEROUS BRANCH 3 (1962).

72. *See* note 67, *supra*.

73. A. BICKEL, *supra* note 71, at 16–17.

74. *See, e.g.*, A. BICKEL, *supra* note 71; J. CHOPER, JUDICIAL REVIEW AND THE NATIONAL POLITICAL PROCESS (1982); J. ELY, DEMOCRACY AND DISTRUST: A THEORY OF JUDICIAL REVIEW (1980); L. HAND, THE BILL OF RIGHTS (1958); Fallon, *A Constructivist Coherence Theory of Constitutional Interpretation*, 100 HARV. L. REV. 1189, 1194–1231 (1987) (reviewing the literature on the legitimacy of judicial review).

75. *See* G. GUNTHER, CONSTITUTIONAL LAW 30 (11th ed. 1985).

76. Fairfax Devisee v. Hunter's Lessee, 11 U. S. (7 Cranch) 603 (1813).

77. U. S. CONST., art VI.

78. 6 Va. 11, 15 (1815).

79. 14 U. S. (1 Wheat.) 304 (1816).

80. G. GUNTHER, *supra* note 75, at 33.

81. 1 C. WARREN, *supra* note 61, at 452.

82. 14 U. S. (Wheat.) 304, 338 (1816).

83. *Id.* at 343.

84. *Id.*

85. *Id.* at 344.

86. *Id.* at 347.

87. *Id.*

88. *Id.* at 347–48.

89. *Id.* at 347.

90. 19 U. S. (6 Wheat.) 264 (1821).

91. *Id.* at 386–88.

92. A. BICKEL, *supra* note 71, at 1.

93. *See* note 81, *supra*.

94. *See* KHB, *supra* note 6, at 167–68.

95. 1 Stat. 596.
96. *See* KHB, *supra* note 6, at 136.
97. *Id.* at 168.
98. 2 Stat. 89.
99. KHB, *supra* note 6, at 169.
100. *Id.* at 172.
101. 2 Stat. 132.
102. 3 Stat. 195.
103. *See* Frankfurter, *Distribution of Judicial Power Between United States and State Courts*, 13 Cornell L. Q. 499, 508–9 (1928).
104. *Id.* at 508.
105. For an excellent bibliography, *see* KHB, *supra* note 6, at 795–801.
106. *See* Farber & Muench, *The Ideological Origins of the Fourteenth Amendment*, 1 Const. Com. 235 (1984).
107. *Id.* at 276–77.
108. *Id.*
109. J. tenBroek, Equal Under Law 158 (1951).
110. *Id.* at 197. *See also* H. Hyman & W. Wiecek, Equal Justice Under Law 386–438 (1982).
111. *See* H. Hyman & W. Wiecek, *supra* note 110, at 319.
112. 14 Stat. 27.
113. J. tenBroek, *supra* note 109, at 201.
114. 16 Stat. 144.
115. 17 Stat. 13.
116. 18 Stat. 335.
117. 42 U. S. C. §1983.
118. Cong. Globe, 42d Cong., 1st Sess., App. 68 (1871) (Rep. Shellabarger).
119. *Ex parte* Virginia, 100 U. S. 339, 346 (1880).
120. Cong. Globe, 42d Cong., 1st Sess., 335 (1871).
121. Cong. Globe, 42d Cong., 1st Sess., 374 (1871).
122. *See generally*, Chapman v. Houston Welfare Rights Organization, 441 U. S. 600 (1979).
123. *See id.* at 608–9.
124. 18 Stat. 470. For an excellent history of these jurisdictional statutes, see Wiecek, *The Reconstruction of Federal Judicial Power, 1863–1875*, 13 Am. J. of Legal History 333 (1969).
125. M. Kammen, A Machine That Would Go of Itself 95–96 (1986).
126. Frankfurter, *supra* note 103, at 499.
127. Blackmun, *Section 1983 and Federal Protection of Individual*

Rights—Will the Statute Remain Alive or Fade Away?, 60 N.Y. U. L. Rev. 1, 6 (1985).

128. *Id.*
129. Mitchum v. Foster, 407 U. S. 225, 239 (1972).
130. 83 U. S. 36 (1873).
131. H. Hyman & W. Wiecek, *supra* note 110, at 475.
132. 83 U. S. 36, 81 (1873).
133. *Id.* at 77–78.
134. U. S. Const., art. VI.
135. *See* H. Hyman & W. Wiecek, *supra* note 110, at 477–78.
136. 83 U. S. (16 Wall.) 36, 82 (1873).
137. H. Hyman & W. Wiecek, *supra* note 110, at 478.
138. Blackmun, *supra* note 127, at 111.
139. *See* R. Kluger, Simple Justice 61 (1976).
140. *Id.* at 62.
141. *Id.* at 68.
142. *Id.*
143. 109 U. S. 3 (1893).
144. 163 U. S. 537 (1896).
145. *Id.* at 544.
146. *Id.* at 551.
147. See J. Orth, *supra* note 65, at 53–57.
148. Blackmun, *supra* note 127, at 11.
149. 209 U. S. 123 (1908).
150. *Id.* at 175.
151. 227 U. S. 278 (1913).
152. 28 U. S. C. §2281, (repealed P.L. 94–381 (1976)).
153. 28 U. S. C. §1342.
154. 28 U. S. C. §1341.
155. 347 U. S. 483 (1954).
156. *Id.* at 495.
157. *See generally*, R. Kluger, *supra* note 140.
158. *Id.* at 748–75.
159. 71 Stat. 634.
160. R. Kluger, *supra* note 140, at 757.
161. 78 Stat. 241.
162. R. Kluger, *supra* note 140, at 753.
163. *Id.*
164. *Id.* at 754.
165. *See* J. Williams, Eyes on the Prize (1987).
166. R. Kluger, *supra* note 140, at 756.
167. *Id.*

168. *Id.*

169. *Id.*

170. Bell, *Brown v. Board of Education and the Interest-Convergence Dilemma*, 93 HARV. L. REV. 518, 524 (1980).

171. *Id.* at 524.

172. *Id.*

173. O. FISS, THE CIVIL RIGHTS INJUNCTION 4–5 (1978).

174. *See* Chayes, *The Role of the Judge in Public Law Litigation*, 89 HARV. L. REV. 1281 (1976).

175. One commentator discovered only twenty-one cases brought under 42 U. S. C. §1983 between 1871 and 1920. Comment, *The Civil Rights Act: Emergence of an Adequate Federal Civil Remedy?*, 26 IND. L. J. 361, 363 (1951).

176. 365 U. S. 167 (1961).

177. *Id.* at 180.

178. England v. Louisiana State Board of Medical Examiners, 375 U. S. 411 (1964).

179. *Id.* at 416.

180. R. SMITH, JUSTICE AND THE POOR 15 (1919).

181. *See* E. JOHNSON, JUSTICE AND REFORM: THE FORMATIVE YEARS OF THE OEO LEGAL SERVICES PROGRAM (1974).

182. *See, e.g.,* Goldberg v. Kelly, 397 U. S. 254 (1970); Shapiro v. Thompson, 394 U. S. 618 (1969).

183. Gibbons, *Our Federalism*, 12 SUFFOLK U. L. REV. 1087, 1096 (1978).

184. *Id.* at 1119.

185. A Statement of the Board of Governors of the Society of American Law Teachers (Oct. 10, 1970).

Chapter 3
Crossing the Threshold

Plaintiffs in *Warth v. Seldin* were early victims of the Burger Court's plan to close the federal courts to those seeking relief from the unconstitutional action of state or local public officials.[1] That case involved a challenge to the exclusionary zoning practices of the town of Penfield, a suburb of the city of Rochester, New York. The metropolitan Rochester area, like others throughout the country, was rapidly becoming a segregated society in which the black citizens lived in a central city surrounded by virtually all-white suburbs. In 1970, for example, 95 percent of the black population in Monroe County (which included Rochester and Penfield) lived in the city, while less than a fraction of 1 percent lived in the suburban Penfield.[2]

In that year a housing study of Monroe County concluded that there was great need for low- and moderate-income housing units, and it stressed the responsibility of suburban towns to accept their fair share. It found that these towns had blocked attempts to build such housing in large part because of racial prejudice.

The complete rejection by suburban communities of all low and moderate income housing is testimony to the severity of the problem of prejudice involved. While many community groups and agencies—as well as individual citizens—have been working for open housing, their various efforts have proved insufficient. Racial prejudice and discrimination must be considered one of the most serious obstacles blocking the construction of low/moderate income housing where it is needed.[3]

Penfield town officials had been particularly adamant in their refusal to allow construction of low- and moderate-income housing units. Those who had submitted proposals for the building of such housing reported that the town (1) delayed action of the proposals for inordinate periods of time; (2) denied approval for arbitrary reasons; (3) failed to provide necessary supporting services; and (4) amended the zoning ordinance to make approval of such units nearly impossible.[4] Members of the Rochester Home Builders Association reported that they had been threatened by town officials and told that, if they pursue a lawsuit over the exclusionary zoning practices, they would be precluded from building even luxury housing in the town.[5] It was clear to all that the town officials were determined to maintain the economically and racially stratified housing market. In this regard, it must be stressed that the excluded people firmly believed that the town was pursuing its policies in order to restrict opportunities for not only poor people but, more specifically, black citizens and members of other minority groups.

Efforts to persuade the town to voluntarily abandon its exclusionary practices were unsuccessful. As a result, a lawsuit was brought in federal court against the town and the officials responsible for the restrictive zoning policies and practices. The case was brought pursuant to Section 1983, alleging that defendants were subjecting plaintiffs to the deprivation of rights protected by the Constitution and by federal civil rights laws designed to prohibit racial discrimination in housing practices.[6]

Various individuals and organizations brought the lawsuit. The individuals were persons of low or moderate income who maintained that they were excluded from Penfield because of their race and income level. They alleged that they had searched for housing in Penfield, but were unable to find affordable housing because of the town's exclusionary practices. Each described in detail the injury they suffered as a result of the town's policy of excluding poor people and members of minority groups. Andelino Ortiz, for example, was working in Penfield but was forced to live forty-two miles from his job because no low-income housing was available there. His harm was not limited to the burdensome commuting problems and costs. His family was forced "to accept as a way of life, poor schools for our children, reduced job opportunities, [and] inferior community services."[7]

Clara Broadnax, another plaintiff, sought housing in Penfield in order to escape an inner-city environment characterized by dilapidated, substandard housing, violence, and insufficient or nonexistent community services. She was unable to find suitable housing in the town, so she and her children were forced to remain in the city and to endure deplorable living conditions in housing that included, among other things, defective electrical wiring, rat and mice infestation, crumbling walls and foundations, broken doors, and holes in the roof.[8]

Plaintiff Rosa Sinkler stated that she looked for housing in Penfield because she wanted to raise her children in an integrated community and obtain the benefits of the town's community services. One of her most important concerns was the quality of the schools. The public school in her area had been rated as one of the lowest in terms of effective instruction. Penfield schools, on the other hand, rated quite high. The town's exclusionary practices, she alleged, prevented her children from participating in a quality public educational program.[9]

One final group of individuals included property owners living in the city of Rochester. They maintained that the town's refusal to permit construction of low- and moderate-income housing forced the city to provide such housing, much of which is tax abated. The city property owners alleged that as a result they had been required to pay higher property taxes.[10] Moreover, concentration of low- and moderate-income housing in the city produced a "density crush" and accompanying environmental problems for those living there.[11]

The organizational plaintiffs included Metro-Act, a nonprofit corporation founded in 1965 after the riots in the inner city of Rochester. One of its primary purposes was the pursuit of activities designed to secure open housing in the metropolitan area. Many of its members were white residents of the town of Penfield.[12] Metro-Act alleged that as a result of the town's practice, those members are losing the benefits of living in an integrated society: "We believe that it is to . . . [our] own children's benefit to learn and, in life to come to healthy terms with different races and ethnic groups."[13]

The housing council was comprised of seventy-one public and private groups that were actively participating in efforts to eliminate racial and economic discrimination in the housing market.[14] It was organized in response to a housing study that had been prepared for a special committee appointed under the authority of the city council and county board of supervisors. The study cited the need for a single organization to channel the fragmented and uncoordinated housing efforts into meaningful action. The housing council was established as that organization, having the purposes of combating community deterioration and eliminating racial and economic discrimination in housing. In the lawsuit the housing council alleged that Penfield's restrictive housing practices inflicted harm on its members in two respects. First, those housing council members engaged in the development and construction of low- and moderate-income housing were suffering economic harm resulting from the loss of profits. Second, other members were thwarted in their efforts to pursue specific activities designed to further the housing council's designated purposes.

Finally, the Rochester Home Builders, although not one of the original parties, intervened in the lawsuit on the side of the plaintiffs. The organization was a nonprofit trade association of persons and companies engaged in the construction of residential housing in the metropolitan Rochester area, including Penfield. During the previous fifteen years, its members had built nearly 80 percent of the private housing units in the area.[15] It maintained in the lawsuit that Penfield's practices prevented association members from constructing low- and moderate-income housing in that area. As a result, its members had lost business opportunities and suffered damage in the amount of $750,000.[16]

The *Warth* lawsuit included every conceivable group that had been injured by the town's discriminatory practices. Consequently, it was an excellent vehicle for testing the constitutionality and lawfulness of discriminatory housing practices that had become widespread throughout many communities. These practices had played a significant role in establishing what the Na-

tional Advisory Commission on Civil Disorder described as "two
societies: one predominately white and located in the suburbs
. . . and one largely Negro located in central cities."[17]
The district court would have to decide whether the Constitution and U.S. laws allowed such restrictive housing practices.
Plaintiffs firmly believed that the answer should be clear. Defendants' exclusionary policies denied plaintiffs equal protection
of the laws as guaranteed by the Fourteenth Amendment and
infringed on their freedom of association, protected by the First
and Fourteenth Amendments. Additionally, defendants conduct
interfered on racial grounds with the ability of the nonwhite
plaintiffs to make contracts for rental of housing in violation of
two civil rights laws passed as part of the Reconstruction effort.[18]
Plaintiffs were equally confident that the case could be brought
in federal court. Section 1983 authorizes lawsuits against persons, like the Penfield officials, who act with the apparent authority of state law to deprive others of rights protected by the
Constitution or U.S. laws. Indeed, *Monroe v. Pape*[19] settled that
proposition.[20] Moreover, Section 1983 specifically authorizes injunctive relief to prevent the ongoing deprivation of federal
rights. Finally, the jurisdictional statutes enacted during the Reconstruction period expressly granted federal courts power to
hear such cases.[21] This was precisely the kind of case in which
the federal court was placed between the people and the state
officials to guard the constitutional and other federal rights at
stake.
The district court, however, dismissed the case and the court
of appeals affirmed on the ground that the plaintiff lacked
"standing" to challenge the town's practices.[22] The plaintiffs then
asked the Supreme Court to review the case and to consider the
following issue: "Whether plaintiffs have standing to seek judicial review of Penfield's racially discriminatory and exclusionary zoning ordinance and defendants' zoning practices which
deprive plaintiffs of constitutional and statutory rights and cause
them to suffer economic damage, physical and emotional hardship, and loss of the social benefits of living in an integrated
community."[23] The Court agreed to hear the case.
It is important to emphasize what was not at issue. First, there
was no dispute over the factual issues. The standing question is

a threshold one decided very early in the proceedings. The case had been dismissed well before the trial and before the parties had any opportunity to conduct an extensive investigation into the facts. At that stage in the lawsuit, procedural rules required the Court to assume that plaintiffs' factual allegations were true and that the Penfield zoning laws and practice had the purpose and effect of excluding poor people and members of racial minority groups. So too, the Court was not being asked to decide whether the practices violated the Constitution and U.S. laws.

The only issue before the Supreme Court was the threshold one of whether these specific plaintiffs had the right to bring a lawsuit in federal court to challenge the officials' conduct. Could these individuals and organizations be allowed to enter the federal courthouse and have a federal judge hear their case? In technical terms, the precise issue was whether plaintiffs had "standing to sue."

The standing doctrine has been described as one of "the most amorphous concepts in the entire domain of the public law."[24] Supposedly it is concerned with the party seeking to get a complaint before the federal court and not the specific legal issues that will be decided in the case.[25] The standing doctrine focuses on "who" is a proper party to bring a lawsuit in federal court and is derived from article III of the Constitution. The framers rejected the suggestion that the federal courts should perform an advisory role or act as a council of revision. Instead, they provided in article III that the federal courts would have power to hear only "cases" or "controversies." These seemingly innocuous words have generated much litigation and thousands of pages of judicial opinions. The Court recently observed that, as an irreducible minimum, the words require a person bringing a lawsuit to satisfy a twofold test. The litigant must show (1) some kind of personal injury, and (2) that the injury can be traced to the conduct being challenged.[26] An individual who satisfies this test has "standing to sue" and can at least walk through the federal courthouse doors. A finding of standing, it must be stressed, does not guarantee that the plaintiff will eventually win the case. It simply gives the federal judge power to decide whether in fact defendants have acted illegally or unconstitutionally.

The standing doctrine is said to serve a number of purposes. First, it is designed to ensure that the dispute is presented in an adversary context and in a form capable of judicial resolution.[27] Courts operate best when they are presented with a real, live dispute between adverse parties who have a stake in the outcome. Judges, unlike legislators, do not have the freedom to search for whatever material they deem relevant to the resolution of a problem. Instead, for the most part, they must decide on the basis of the material submitted by the parties. It is generally believed that truly adverse parties have an incentive to vigorously present the legal and factual bases for their positions. The standing requirement is one way to ensure that the parties before the court are adverse, having something of consequence hanging on the result, and, thus, will vigorously pursue their claims.[28] In this manner, it assures that legal questions will be presented in a concrete factual context and not in the "rarefied atmosphere of a debating society."[29]

The doctrine serves a second and related purpose as well. When courts are confronted with truly injured individuals they are better able to ascertain the real impact of the challenged conduct. The "flesh and blood facts" of a case expose the actual consequences of the behavior that is the subject of the lawsuit.[30] Professor Felix Frankfurter warned that such concreteness is particularly necessary in constitutional cases. "Every tendency to deal with constitutional questions abstractly, to formulate them in terms of barren legal questions, leads to dialectics, to sterile conclusions unrelated to actualities."[31]

In the setting of a constitutional attack on a statute, the standing doctrine also allows some lag time between the enactment of the legislation and the judicial determination of the law's constitutionality.[32] While the courts await a truly injured party, there is an opportunity to observe the real life consequences of the law. The time between enactment and adjudication leaves room to ascertain the law's ability to accomplish its intended goals.

The standing doctrine not only makes room for the lag time, but also serves as a restraint on the federal judiciary in its relations with the other branches of the federal government and the state governments as well. Under *Marbury v. Madison* the federal judiciary assumes the role of umpire, determining the constitutionality of the actions of our officials.[33] Federal judges, appointed for life and insulated from direct political pressure, can invalidate the decisions and acts of our elected representatives. This far-reaching power is tempered somewhat by the judiciary's limited power to enforce its judgments. The federal judiciary in some respects remains the least dangerous branch of government because it has to rely on the other branches for enforcement. The judiciary's ultimate power lies in its moral force, the ability to persuade the people that its decisions are legitimate. If the courts too frequently hold unconstitutional the actions of politically popular elected officials, it may lose that moral force and its legitimacy. In some instances, therefore, it may be best for the federal courts to avoid deciding a constitutional case, to duck a tough issue. This allows time for further discussions of the issue among the branches of government and the people. As Professor Alexander Bickel explained:

The essentially important fact, so often missed, is that the Court wields a threefold power. It may strike down legislation as inconsistent with principle. It may validate, or ... "legitimate" legislation as consistent with principle. Or *it may do neither*. It may do neither, and therein lies the secret of its ability to maintain itself in the tension between principle and expediency.[34]

When the Court does neither and withholds a constitutional judgment, said Bickel, it does not abandon principle. "It seeks merely to elicit the correct answers to certain prudential questions that ... lie in the path of ultimate issues of principle."[35]

The standing doctrine is one of the devices used by the federal courts to avoid deciding a difficult constitutional issue. The court can postpone a decision by holding that the party bringing the lawsuit is not an appropriate one and that any determination of the underlying issue must await an individual who is injured in fact by the defendant's conduct. Justice Powell, who was often a spokesman for a majority of the Burger Court on the standing issue, perhaps best summarized the judicial self-restraint aspect of the standing doctrine:

We risk a progressive impairment of the effectiveness of the federal courts if their limited resources are diverted increasingly from their historic role to the resolution of public-interest suits brought by litigants who cannot distinguish themselves from all taxpayers or all citizens. The irreplaceable value of the power articulated by Mr. Chief Justice Marshall lies in the protection it has afforded the constitutional rights and liberties of individual citizens and minority groups against oppressive or discriminatory government action. It is this role, not some amorphous general supervision of the operations of government, that has maintained public esteem for the federal courts and has permitted the peaceful coexistence of the countermajoritarian implications of judicial review and the democratic principles upon which our Federal Government in the final analysis rests.[36]

Justice Powell firmly believed that relaxed standing rules would lead to a flood of lawsuits and increased government by judiciary. Such a result, he feared, would not only destroy the public confidence essential to the courts, but also the vitality critical to the representative branches of government.

Finally, it has been suggested that the standing doctrine serves the value of self-determination. It guarantees that a lawsuit is brought by someone with a personal stake in the outcome—"that is, by someone with personal and not merely external preferences about the outcome."[37] Moreover, in a related fashion the standing requirement ensures that those most affected by the challenged activity will be adequately represented.[38]

Although in the abstract the purposes of the standing doctrine appear reasonable, they are not beyond criticism. It is easy to overstate the notion that the standing requirement is somehow necessary to ensure that the lawsuit is brought by a truly interested party who will vigorously pursue the claims. One commentator concluded that "if plaintiff did not have the minimal personal involvement and adverseness which Article III requires, he would not be engaging in the costly pursuit of litigation.... The idle and whimsical plaintiff, a dilettante who litigates for a lark, is a specter which haunts the legal literature, but not the courtroom."[39]

Similarly, it is not clear that the doctrine does a particularly good job of enhancing the legitimacy of the federal courts. The theory that federal courts can preserve their moral force, their legitimacy, by sometimes avoiding a difficult constitutional issue ignores reality. When the court holds that the plaintiff lacks standing to sue, it does indeed avoid deciding the underlying constitutional question. Such a holding is a statement that the wrong party brought the lawsuit; it says nothing about whether the conduct is, or is not, constitutional. And, in theory, it allows further time for public debate and for ripening of the constitutional principle at stake. In practice, however, the public is unlikely to perceive the complexities of the standing doctrine and the limited meaning of a determination that "plaintiff lacks standing to sue." It is more likely that the public will view such a determination as a statement that the plaintiff lost and that the challenged conduct must, therefore, be constitutional. Despite the court's desire to avoid expressing a view on whether the challenged conduct is constitutional, it is perceived by the public as making precisely such a decision.[40]

Equally suspect is the suggestion that strict standing rules are needed to avoid a flood of litigation in the federal courts. Certainly, advocates of strict standing requirements have been unable to provide data supporting this concern and are forced to rely on mere speculation. Former Solicitor General (and dean of the Harvard Law School) Erwin Griswold testified before a congressional committee against a bill that would have relaxed the standing to sue requirements. In so doing, he nevertheless conceded that "there is no way to measure the impact of [the bill] on the badly overcrowded federal courts in terms of the volume of cases which will be brought there for decision. It may not be very many."[41] States that have enacted very liberal standing laws have not experienced any flood of cases. Nor has a flood occurred as a result of the federal statutes that authorize standing by a broad class of citizens in environmental cases. The substantial cost of litigation serves as an effective restraint on the number of people who will actually bring a lawsuit. Indeed Chief Justice (then Judge) Burger recognized this fact when he wrote regarding standing to participate in administrative proceedings:

The fears of regulatory agencies that their processes will be inundated by expansion of standing criteria are rarely borne out. Always a restraining factor is the expense of participation in the administrative process, an economic reality which will operate to limit the number of those who will seek participation; legal and related expenses of administrative proceedings are such that even those with large economic interests find the costs burdensome.[42]

In any event, there is a more fundamental objection to the notion that standing rules should be used to reduce the workload of the federal judiciary. Even assuming liberal standing rules would lead to a flood of cases, it does not follow that such a drain is a legitimate basis for closing the doors to the federal courthouse. As Justice Harlan said: "Judicial resources, I am well aware, are increasingly scarce these days. Nonetheless, when we automatically close the courthouse door solely on this basis, we implicitly express a value judgment on the comparative importance of classes of legally protected interests. And current limitations upon the effective functioning of the courts arising from budgetary inadequacies should not be permitted to stand in the way of the recognition of otherwise sound constitutional principles."[43]

Finally, it is not self-evident that the standing doctrine should be used to prevent a supposed shift of power from the elected branches to the nonrepresentative federal courts. The proponents of strict standing rules beg the question by raising the specter of "government by judiciary." Again, in the abstract, one might agree with the proposition that the operation of government is better left to the elected branches than the nonelected federal judiciary. Even the most ardent supporters of strict standing rules, however, concede that in some circumstances federal courts must be allowed to review the actions of elected officials. Justice Powell, for example, recognized that the "irreplaceable value" of judicial review "lies in the protection it has afforded the constitutional rights and liberties of individual citizens and minority groups against oppressive or discriminatory governmental action."[44] The real question then should focus not on the generalized fear of a reallocation of power, but rather on the appropriateness of seeking judicial assistance in the circumstances of a particular case. An examination of specific cases, rather than abstract propositions, more clearly reveals the bankruptcy of the Court's recent approach to standing.

Consider the *Warth* case, for example. The Supreme Court concluded that none of the plaintiffs had standing to challenge the town's exclusionary zoning practices. The individuals and organizations were told that they would not be given an opportunity to prove that the town had pursued policies that had the purpose and effect of excluding the poor and the nonwhite citizens of the metropolitan area. The federal courthouse doors were closed to these parties.

The Court's discussion of the standing of the poor and nonwhite individuals is especially revealing. Justice Powell, writing for the majority, did not deny that these individuals were suffering injury.[45] Nor could he justifiably make such a denial. These individuals alleged that they were living in substandard, racially segregated housing and were being deprived of the opportunity to live in Penfield and enjoy the benefits of that community. The majority, instead, held that these individuals failed to show a "causal relationship between Penfield's zoning practices and . . . [their] asserted injury."[46] The defect, asserted Justice Powell, was that those bringing the case did not allege any "particularized personal interest" in Penfield property and did not focus on any particular housing project that was still viable and that might house these plaintiffs.[47]

Obviously, plaintiffs were unable to make such allegations. These individuals were poor people who could not afford the expensive housing in the town. Moreover, although housing plans had been submitted in the past, none were still pending at the time of the lawsuit because town officials had successfully discouraged any such proposals. Indeed, the homebuilders' association had stated in court papers that town officials had threatened the associations' members with the loss of all business in the town if they participated in efforts to force the town to allow construction of low-income housing. There was no particular housing proposal that preceded the start of the lawsuit because, as plaintiffs alleged, the town had thwarted every attempt to build multiracial, low-income housing. In his dissenting opinion, Justice Brennan captured the absurdity of the majority's position:

The portrait which emerges from the allegations and affidavits is one of total, purposeful, intransigent exclusion of certain classes of people from the town, pursuant to a conscious scheme never deviated from. Because of this scheme, those interested in building homes for the excluded groups were faced with insurmountable difficulties, and those of the excluded groups seeking homes in the locality quickly learned that their attempts were futile. Yet, the Court turns the very success of the allegedly unconstitutional scheme into a barrier to a lawsuit seeking its invalidation. In effect, the Court tells the low-income-minority and building company plaintiffs they will not be permitted to prove what they have alleged—that they could and would build and live in the town if changes were made in the zoning ordinance and its application—because they have not succeeded in breaching, before the suit was filed, the very barriers which are the subject of the suit.[48]

The majority confronted plaintiffs with a "catch–22": plaintiffs lack standing to challenge a town's refusal to permit construction of low-income housing because no such housing is being constructed. As a town's practices become more clearly exclusionary, it becomes more difficult to find developers willing to incur the substantial expense of developing and proposing a project in that town. The town that can best discourage any low-income housing proposals, can best ensure that it will not be challenged in federal court for its practices. "Nothing in article III, in the canons of sound judicial administration, or in the judicial precedents, required so harsh and bizarre a result."[49]

It is certainly difficult to justify the result on the ground that the parties were not truly adverse. The lawsuit included every group adversely affected by the town's exclusionary practices. These groups together certainly had a stake in the outcome and would vigorously pursue the case against the town officials. Additionally, it was pure folly to suggest that the federal court could not grant relief that would remedy the discrimination. If plaintiffs had been allowed to proceed and had won, the federal court could have enjoined the town from engaging in practices that have the purpose and effect of excluding people because of their race or poverty. Additionally, the court could have directed the town to take affirmative steps to remedy the effects of past discrimination. The town, for example, could have been ordered to devise a housing plan to cure the effects of their unconstitutional practices. Such remedial relief was not uncommon and had been ordered in school desegregation cases[50] and other housing cases.[51]

What then explains the unnecessarily severe application of the standing doctrine? Justice Douglas, offered an explanation in his dissenting opinion. The majority, he suggested, was using the standing doctrine to close the federal courthouse doors and thus prevent a flood of cases. He responded: "Standing has become a barrier to access to the federal courts. . . . The mounting caseload of federal courts is well known. But cases such as this one reflect festering sores in our society; and the American dream teaches that if one reaches high enough and persists there is a forum where justice is dispensed. I would lower the technical barriers and let the courts serve that ancient need."[52]

Justice Brennan offered another explanation in a dissenting opinion joined by Justices White and Marshall. The majority, he argued, merely paid lip service to the proposition that the focus of the standing doctrine is limited to the question of "*who* is a proper party." Instead, the majority used the standing discussion to mask its disagreement with the underlying merits of plaintiffs' challenge. As Justice Brennan said, the majority opinion, "which tosses out of court almost every conceivable kind of plaintiff who could be injured by the activity claimed to be unconstitutional, can be explained only by an indefensible hostility to the claim on the merits."[53] He appreciated the complexity of the case and the grave "sociological and political ramifications."[54] Nevertheless, said Justice Brennan, "courts cannot refuse to hear a case on the merits merely because they would prefer not to."[55]

The majority in *Warth* was not only hostile to the merits, but also unwilling to allow the federal courts to serve as guardians of the federal rights at stake. Despite allegations that local officials were discriminating on the basis of race and poverty in violation of various constitutional and federal statutory provisions, the Court slammed shut the federal courthouse doors. The standing doctrine was a convenient tool for limiting access to the federal judiciary. At one point the majority tipped its hand and unmasked its real concern that federal courts should not be involved in such disputes. In a footnote Justice Powell wrote, "Citizens dissatisfied with provisions of such [zoning] laws need not overlook the availability of the normal democratic process."[56]

The message was clear—those denied constitutional rights by local officials should seek protection through the political process not the federal courts. Such a suggestion is disingenuous at best. How could Andelino Ortiz, Clara Broadnax, and Rosa Sinkler obtain any protection whatsoever through the political process? Because of the town's alleged discrimination they could not live in Penfield, and because they did not live there, they obviously had no access to the political process that elected the town officials responsible for the discriminatory practices. Moreover, even if these individuals had access to Penfield's political process, it is unlikely they could exert much influence. Indeed, presumably the town officials' practices reflected the majority's preference to maintain an exclusive suburban community.

Unfortunately, *Warth* does not stand in isolation, but rather is representative of the Burger Court's use of the standing doctrine to close federal courts to constitutional litigants.[57] The burden of the restrictive standing rules has not been evenly distributed; it has fallen most heavily on the poor, the disadvantaged, and members of minority groups who have historically been the victims of discrimination. There is a terrible irony because these groups cannot adequately protect themselves through the political process and are most in need of judicial protection.[58] Yet, the Burger Court closed the federal courts to the constitutional claims of these groups.

The Court's different treatment of the standing question in two environmental cases highlights both the inconsistent application of the standing rules and the selective use of those rules to exclude certain groups. The plaintiff in *United States v. SCRAP* was an association formed by law students to "enhance the quality of the human environment for its members, and for all citizens."[59] The association (SCRAP) filed a federal lawsuit challenging orders issued by the Interstate Commerce Commission (ICC), which allowed railroads to collect a 2.5 percent surcharge on freight rates. SCRAP alleged in the suit that, as a result of the ICC orders, its members would suffer "economic, recreational and aesthetic harm." SCRAP and its members were not in the business of hauling freight and, thus were not directly harmed by the rate orders. The line of causation from defendant's conduct to plaintiff's harm was described as follows: "A general rate increase would allegedly cause increased use of non-recyclable commodities as compared to recyclable goods, thus resulting in the need to use more natural resources to produce such goods, some of which resources might be taken from the Washington area, and resulting in more refuse that might be discarded in national parks in the Washington area [used by members of SCRAP]."[60] Although the Court conceded that the line of causation was "attenuated" it nevertheless held that SCRAP had standing to challenge the rate orders.[61]

So too in *Duke Power Co. v. Carolina Environmental Study Group, Inc.*,[62] the Court permitted a "series of speculations" to serve as a basis for standing.[63] Plaintiffs in that case were two organizations and forty individuals living near planned nuclear power facilities. They brought a lawsuit in federal court challenging the constitutionality of the Price–Anderson Act, which imposes a limitation on liability for nuclear accidents. A nuclear accident, of course, had not yet occurred; indeed, the power plants had not been constructed. Plaintiffs, nevertheless, alleged that operation of the plants would cause thermal pollution of the lakes and disrupt their enjoyment of these lakes. The Court agreed that the plaintiff would be injured by the operation of the proposed plants. The more difficult question, however, was whether these harmful effects could be traced to the challenged conduct, the limitation on liability imposed by the act. The Court found a substantial likelihood that the power company could not complete construction or maintain the operation of the plants but for the protection of the act. Accordingly, it concluded that the causation component of the standing test had been met. This prompted Justice Stevens to write: "The string of contingencies that supposedly holds this litigation together is too delicate for me. We are told that but for the Price–Anderson Act there would be no financing of nuclear power plants, no development of those plants by private parties, and hence no present injury to persons such as appellees; we are then asked to remedy an alleged due process violation that may possibly occur at some uncertain time in the future, and may possibly injure the appellees in a way that has no significant connection with any present injury."[64]

The majority's willingness to overcome the threshold standing barrier in *SCRAP* and *Duke Power* is difficult to reconcile with its determination in *Warth*.[65] The possibility that plaintiffs in *Warth* were harmed by the challenged conduct and would benefit from the relief was no more remote than the possibility that plaintiffs in *Duke Power* would enjoy less polluted air and water if the limitation on liability were removed. Nor was it any more remote than the possibility that SCRAP members would enjoy cleaner parks if the court enjoined the ICC surcharge on railroad freight. The different results on the standing issue cannot be adequately explained by an assessment of the likelihood that defendants' conduct in each case caused the injury and that judicial action could remedy that harm. The resolution of the standing questions can be explained only by the Burger Court's hostility to the underlying rights sought to be protected by the *Warth* plaintiffs. The issue in that case was not whether suburban sanctuaries should be destroyed, but whether they should be open to all without regard to race or poverty. Nevertheless the Burger Court might well have perceived the litigation as a threat to the environmental and property interests of the suburban residents. To avoid intruding on those interests it simply closed the courthouse doors in the face of the *Warth* plaintiffs.

If, as some argue, the function of the federal courts, particularly the Supreme Court, is to protect fundamental values, these standing cases raise serious questions regarding the Burger Court's conception of the values worthy of protection.[66] Indeed, the contrasting results lend further support to those who maintain that the Burger Court was predisposed to protect those values that it associated with the wealthy.[67] If, as others contend, the role of the federal courts is to assure broad participation in the political process and protect those who cannot protect themselves in that process, then the results in these standing cases are indefensible.[68] Whereas the plaintiffs in *SCRAP* and *Duke Power* had access to the appropriate decisionmaking bodies, the members of minority groups excluded from Penfield in *Warth* were unable to participate in any way at all in the town's political process.[69]

The Burger Court, thus, adopted restrictive standing rules and then selectively applied them depending on its view of the underlying issues in the case. It might be argued that in the short term the complexity and inconsistency of those rules may well increase, rather than diminish, the burden on litigants as well as the federal courts. The parties must spend considerable resources on the threshold standing issue. They must draft papers, prepare briefs and records, and appear for hearings and arguments in the trial and appellate courts. In *Warth*, for example, one of the organizational plaintiffs spent between $9,000 and $10,000 in unsuccessfully litigating its right to bring the lawsuit.[70] This amount did not include the cost of attorney time (which was donated). Nor do defendants escape the burden for they, too, must bear the expenses of litigating the standing issue. Because defendants in many of these cases are public officials represented by public attorneys, the taxpayer finances the legal sparring over the standing question.

The federal judiciary also pays a price. It is forced to direct its limited resources from resolution of underlying claims to examination of the standing matter. In some instances the additional burden is substantial. In *Duke Power*, for example, the district court held a four-day evidentiary hearing, a minitrial, just to resolve the standing question.[71] In another case, *Simon v. Eastern Kentucky Welfare Rights Organization*, the standing issue was resolved after litigation spanning over five years.[72] Similarly, the standing issue in *Evans v. Lynn* took four years and many appeals to resolve.[73] These examples confirm one commentator's observations:

In the final analysis, the time-consuming efforts of litigants to persuade judges that they and their claims deserve a hearing on the merits probably do more to aggravate than alleviate pressure on scarce judicial resources. In addition, the failure of one set of litigants to win review of their claims does not end the matter, but simply means that other litigants will attempt to frame the issue more effectively and succeed in circumstances in which their predecessors have failed.[74]

Over the long term, the Burger Court's restrictive rules and its less than evenhanded application of those requirements directly and indirectly force litigants out of the federal courts. In cases like *Warth*, the direct impact is obvious: the courthouse doors were closed. The indirect impact is a bit more subtle. The

Burger Court sent a loud and clear message: the federal courts will gladly entertain a defendant's request to dismiss a case on standing grounds. The Court practically invited such requests, and those being sued responded accordingly. Individuals seeking to challenge the constitutionality of official conduct can be reasonably certain that their opponents will be ready to assert the standing argument. Even if these individuals are found to have standing to sue, they will have spent large amounts on litigation of this preliminary matter. The fight over the standing issue may also take years to resolve, and during that period the individuals may be subjected to the deprivation of constitutional rights. Such individuals may well conclude that bypassing the federal courts completely is both cheaper and faster. They can bring their cases in state courts that are not bound by the same standing rules used in federal court.[75] As a result, whether directly or indirectly, the Burger Court's restrictive standing requirements close the federal courts to individuals who believe their constitutional rights are being denied by public officials.

Notes

1. 422 U.S. 490 (1975). I served as co-counsel to the plaintiffs when the case reached the Supreme Court.

2. *See* Brief for Amicus Curiae National Committee Against Discrimination in Housing at 3, *Warth* v. *Seldin*, 422 U.S. 490 (1975) (No. 73–2024).

3. *See* Brief for Petitioner at 6–7, Warth v. Seldin, 422 U.S. 490 (1975) (No. 73–2024).

4. *See id.* at 8.

5. *See id.*

6. Plaintiffs alleged a deprivation of rights secured by the First, Ninth, and Fourteenth Amendments to the Constitution of the United States and by various Civil Rights Acts, 42 U.S.C. §§ 1981 and 1982. *See Warth*, 422 U.S. 490, 493.

7. Affidavit of Andalino Ortiz at 375–76, *Warth*, (No. 73–2024).

8. *See* Affidavit of Clara Broadnax at 410–12, *Warth*, (No. 73–2024).

9. *See* Affidavit of Rosa Sinkler at 453–55, *Warth*, (No. 73–2024).

10. *See* Brief for Petitioner at 5–6, *Warth*, (No. 73–2024).

11. *See* Affidavit of Warth, Reichert, Vinkey, and Harris, *Warth*, (No. 73–2024).

12. *See* Affidavit of Robert J. Warth at 183, *Warth*, (No. 73–2024).
13. *Id.* at 184.
14. *See* Affidavit of John C. Mitchell at 173, *Warth*, (No. 73–2024).
15. *See* Intervenor Complaint at 147, *Warth*, (No. 73–2024).
16. *See* Brief for Petitioner at 15, *Warth*, (No. 73–2024).
17. Report of the National Advisory Commission on Civil Disorders 220 (1968).
18. *See* 42 U.S.C. §§ 1981, 1982 (1984).
19. 365 U.S. 167 (1961).
20. *See* discussion *supra* at chap. 2.
21. *See* 28 U.S.C. §§ 1331, 1343 (1984).
22. *See* 495 F.2d 1187 (2d Cir. 1974).
23. Brief for Petitioner at 2, Warth v. Seldin, 422 U.S. 490 (1975) (No. 73–2024).
24. Flast v. Cohen, 392, U.S. 83, 99 (1968) (quoting *Hearings on S. 2097 Before the Subcommittee on Constitutional Rights of the Senate Judiciary Committee*, 89th Cong., 2d Sess. 465, 467–68 (1966) (statement of Prof. William D. Valente)).
25. *See* in Flast, 392 U.S. at 99.
26. *See* Gladstone, Realtors v. Village of Bellwood, 441 U.S. 91, 99 (1978).
27. *See* Flast, 392 U.S. at 101.
28. *See* A. BICKEL, THE LEAST DANGEROUS BRANCH 115 (1962).
29. Valley Forge College v. Americans United, 454 U.S. 464, 472 (1982).
30. A. BICKEL, *supra* note 28, at 116.
31. Frankfurter, *A Note on Advisory Opinions*, 37 HARV. L. REV. 1002, 1003 (1924).
32. *See* A. BICKEL, *supra* note 28, at 69–70.
33. 5 U.S. (1 Cranch) 137 (1803).
34. A. BICKEL, *supra* note 28, at 69.
35. *Id.* at 70.
36. United States v. Richardson, 418 U.S. 166, 192 (1973) (Powell, J., concurring).
37. Brilmayer, *The Jurisprudence of Article III: Perspective on the "Case or Controversy" Requirement*, 93 HARV. L. REV. 297, 311 (1979).
38. *See id.* at 310.
39. Scott, *Standing in the Supreme Court—A Functional Analysis*, 86 HARV. L. REV., 645, 674, (1973).
40. *See* Gunther, The Subtle Vices of the *"Passive Virtues"—A Comment on Principle and Expediency in Judicial Review*, 64 COLUM. L. REV. 1, 7 (1964).

41. *Hearings on S. 3005 Before the Subcommittee on Citizens and Shareholder Rights and Remedies of the Senate Committee on the Judiciary and the Committee on Governmental Affairs*, 95th Cong., 2d Sess. 58 (1978) [hereinafter Hearings on S. 3005].

42. Office of Communication of the United Church of Christ v. F.C.C., 359 F.2d 994, 1006 (D.C. Cir. 1966).

43. Bivens v. Six Unknown Fed. Narcotics Agents, 403 U.S. 388, 411 (1970) (Harlan, J., dissenting).

44. United States v. Richardson, 418 U.S. 166, 192 (1973) (Powell, J., Concurring).

45. See Warth v. Seldin, 422 U.S. 490, 304–5 (1974).

46. *Id.* at 507.

47. *See id.* at 505–6.

48. *Id.* at 523.

49. L. TRIBE, AMERICAN CONSTITUTIONAL LAW 134 (2d ed. 1988).

50. *See, e.g.*, Swann v. Charlotte-Mecklenburg Bd. of Educ., 402 U.S. 1 (1970).

51. *See, e.g.*, Gautreaux v. Chicago Housing Auth., 503 F. 2d 930, (7th Cir. 1974); Hart v. Community School Bd. of Brooklyn, 698 F. Supp. (E.D. N.Y. 1974), *appeal dismissed*, 497 F.2d 1027 (2d Cir. 1974).

52. Warth v. Seldin, 422 U.S. 490, 519 (1975) (Douglas, J., dissenting).

53. *Id.* at 520 (Brennan, J., dissenting).

54. *See id.*

55. *Id.*

56. *Id.* at 508 n.18.

57. *See e.g.*, Los Angeles v. Lyons, 461 U.S. 95 (1983); Valley Forge College v. Americans United, 454 U.S. 464 (1982); Gladstone, Realtors v.Village of Bellwood, 441 U.S. 91 (1979); Duke Power Co. v. Environmental Study Group, Inc., 438 U.S. 59 (1978); Simon v. Eastern Ky. Welfare Rights Org., 426 U.S. 26 (1976); Schlesinger v. Reservists Comm. to Stop the War, 418 U.S. 208 (1974); United States v. Richardson, 418 U.S. 166 (1974); Linda R. S. v. Richard D., 410 U.S. 614 (1973).

58. *See generally*, J. ELY, DEMOCRACY AND DISTRUST (1983) (The courts essential role is to assure broad participation in the political process.).

59. 412 U.S. 669 (1973).

60. *Id.* at 688.

61. *See id.*

62. 438 U.S. 59 (1978).

63. *Id.* at 77–78.

64. *Id.* at 102–3 (Stevens, J., concurring).

65. *See generally*, Braveman, *The Standing Doctrine: A Dialogue Between the Court and Congress*, 31 CARDOZO L. REV. 64–68 (1980).

66. *See e.g.*, A. BICKEL, *supra* note 28, at 27.

67. *See, e.g.*, Tushnet, *"...And Only Wealth Will Buy You Justice"— Some Notes on the Supreme Court 1972 Term* 1974 WIS. L. REV. 177, 180.

68. *See e.g.*, J. ELY, *supra* note 58.

69. My quarrel is with the result in *Warth* and not *SCRAP* and *Duke Power. See* notes 59–65, *supra.*

70. *See Hearing on S. 3005, supra* note 41, at 23 (testimony of Victor Vinkey).

71. *See* Duke Power Co. v. Carolina Env't Study Group, Inc., 438 U.S. 59, 72 (1977).

72. *See, e.g.*, Simon v. Eastern Welfare Right Org., 426 U.S. 76 (1976).

73. 537 F. 2d 571 (2d Cir. 1975) (en banc) *cert. denied*, 429 U.S. 1066 (1977).

74. Yarbrough, *Litigant Access Doctrine and the Burger Court*, 31 VAND. L. REV. 33, 69 (1978).

75. The federal rules are derived from article III of the Constitution, which applies to the judicial power of the federal courts, not the state courts.

Chapter 4
Our Federalism and Injunctions

Those who satisfy the restrictive standing rules and are allowed through the federal courthouse doors have not cleared all the necessary hurdles. The standing doctrine is simply one of many obstacles erected by the Burger Court in the path of individuals seeking access to the federal courts to challenge the constitutionality of official conduct. An additional obstacle concerns the availability of injunctive relief.

An injunction is a court order directing a person to take certain action or to refrain from certain conduct. It has ancient roots in English practice. The English law courts were unable to grant effective relief in certain matters, and as a result, a practice developed that allowed individuals to petition the king directly, invoking his power to do justice. The petition was usually referred to the chancellor who could issue a decree directing a person to do, or not to do, a specific thing. Disobedience could be punished by imprisonment. The chancellors developed their own rules and practices separate from those existing in the law courts. As a general proposition, equitable relief—an injunction—was regarded as a privilege awarded in the chancellor's discretion and only when no adequate remedy was available in the law courts.[1]

This system of separating equitable proceedings and "actions at law" (those heard by the English law courts) was adopted in the American colonies and persisted through the first half of the nineteenth century. Slowly, however, reform occurred and today we have a union of equitable proceedings and actions at law. The same procedures apply to both with one notable exception. Jury trials are available in actions formerly designated "at law." A judge, however, without the aid of a jury, decides whether to grant injunctive relief.

Injunctions can take two forms. A *prohibitory* injunction restrains a person from engaging in certain conduct. The other form, a *mandatory* injunction, directs a person to take certain affirmative steps. The *Pennhurst* lawsuit, for example, involved both kinds of injunctions. The district court judge prohibited the county officials from recommending that an individual be committed to the institution and directed officials to stop the excessive use of physical restraints and drugs. Affirmatively, he ordered the defendants to provide suitable community living arrangements and community services for the Pennhurst residents.

Use of the injunction as a tool for correcting unconstitutional practices can be traced to the turn of this century. Interestingly enough, at that time the injunction was used as a means of breaking strikes and preventing labor organization.[2] In 1894, Eugene Debs and the American Railway Union organized a strike that tied up the railroads. The strike was enjoined, federal troops were sent to break it, and Debs was arrested. One year later the Supreme Court sustained the injunction and gave legitimacy to its use.[3]

In 1908 the Supreme Court decided *Ex parte Young*, which addressed the specific question of whether a federal district court had power to enjoin a state official from engaging in alleged unconstitutional conduct.[4] In that case shareholders of the Northern Pacific Railway Company brought a lawsuit in federal court against Edward Young (attorney general of Minnesota), members of the Minnesota Railroad and Warehouse Commission, and other shippers of freight. The shareholders alleged that various legislative acts and commission orders operated to deprive them of their property without due process in violation of the Fourteenth Amendment. The complaint sought an injunction restraining enforcement of the challenged provisions.

The federal district judge granted an injunction that prohibited the attorney general from bringing a state court proceeding to enforce the state laws. The attorney general, however, ignored the injunction and commenced a lawsuit in state court to enforce the laws against the Northern Pacific Railway Company. Subsequently, the federal judge conducted a hearing, concluded that the attorney general had violated the order, and held him in contempt of court. The judge directed the attorney general to pay a fine and committed him to the custody of the U.S. Marshall until the fine was paid.

In the Supreme Court, the attorney general argued that the district court did not have power to hear the original case and, thus, had no power to issue an injunction against him. Specifically, he relied on the Eleventh Amendment that prohibits the commencement of a lawsuit in the federal courts "against one of the United States by citizens of another state." Although the amendment refers only to suits brought against a state by a citizen of another state, the Court had previously held that federal courts lack power to hear suits against a state by citizens of the same state.[5]

Notwithstanding the Eleventh Amendment, the Supreme Court concluded that a federal district court has power to enjoin a state official from engaging in unconstitutional conduct. The Court created a legal fiction, reasoning that a state official is stripped of his official character when he acts in violation of the Constitution. The Court explained:

> If the act which the state Attorney General seeks to enforce be a violation of the Federal Constitution, the officer in proceeding under such enactment comes into conflict with the superior authority of that Constitution, and he is in that case stripped of his official or representative character and is subjected in his person to the consequences of his individual conduct. The state has no power to impart to him any immunity from responsibility to the supreme authority of the United States.[6]

The Court carved out an exception to the general ban on federal court power to hear cases brought against state officials. The importance of the exception cannot be overstated. It allowed the federal courts to play a key role in enforcing the Fourteenth Amendment that, by its very terms, is a limit on the states. It provides: "nor shall any State deprive any person of life, liberty or property, without due process of law; nor deny to any person within its jurisdiction the equal protection of the laws." The decision in *Ex parte Young* authorized the federal courts to use the injunction as a means for ensuring that the state complied with the important due process and equal protection clauses of the Fourteenth Amendment. Justice Harlan recognized the significance of the decision in his dissent. He observed that the principle adopted by the Court "would enable the subordinate Federal courts to supervise and control the official action of the States as if they were 'dependencies' or provinces. It would place the States of the Union in a condition of inferiority never dreamed of when the Constitution was adopted or when the Eleventh Amendment was made part of the Supreme law of the land."[7] His observations, of course, may have been a bit overstated. For one thing, he ignored the Reconstruction efforts to place the federal courts between the individual and states as protectors of constitutional rights. Nevertheless, he was correct that the decision would eventually inaugurate a new era in the American judicial system. It would allow realization of the dreams of the Reconstructionists.

The primacy of the injunction as a tool for obtaining state compliance with the Constitution did not arrive until the school desegregation case, *Brown v. Board of Education.*[8] In the two decades after *Brown*, school desegregation became one of the "prime litigative chores" of the federal courts, and the injunction was the typical remedy in these cases.[9] The school desegregation cases "not only gave the injunction a greater currency, it also presented the injunction with new challenges, in terms of both the enormity and the kinds of tasks it was assigned. The injunction was to be used to restructure educational systems throughout the nation."[10]

Brown paved the way for expanded use of the injunction outside the school context as well. The "public law litigation model," including its reliance on the injunction as a remedy, became increasingly important.[11] Under the traditional litigation model, a lawsuit is used to settle disputes between private parties. Professor Abram Chayes described the features of the traditional model as follows:

1. The lawsuit is *bipolar*. Litigation is organized as a contest between two individuals or at least two unitary interests, diametrically opposed, to be decided on a winner-takes-all basis.

2. Litigation is *retrospective*. The controversy is about an identified set of completed events: whether they occurred, and if so, with what consequences for the legal relations of the parties.

3. *Right and remedy are interdependent*. The scope of the relief is derived more or less logically from the substantive violation under the general theory that the plaintiff will get compensation measured by the harm caused by the defendant's breach of duty—in contract by giving plaintiff the money he would have had absent the breach; in tort by paying the value of the damage caused.

4. The lawsuit is a *self-contained* episode. The impact of the judgment is confined to the parties. If plaintiff prevails there is a simple compensatory transfer, usually of money, but occasionally the return of a thing or the performance of a definite act. If defendant prevails, a loss lies where it has fallen. In either case, entry of judgment ends the court's involvement.

5. The process is *party-initiated* and *party-controlled*. The case is organized and the issues defined by exchanges between the parties. Responsibility for fact development is theirs. The trial judge is a neutral arbiter of their interactions who decides questions of law only if they are put in issue by an appropriate move of a party.[12]

On the other hand, the focus of public law litigation is "not a dispute between private individuals about private rights but a grievance about the operation of public policy."[13] Its main features include:

1. The scope of the lawsuit is not exogenously given but is shaped primarily by the court and parties.

2. The party structure is not rigidly bilateral but sprawling and amorphous.

3. The fact inquiry is not historical and adjudicative but predictive and legislative.

4. Relief is not conceived as compensation for past wrong in a form logically derived from the substantive liability and confined in its impact to the immediate parties; instead, it is forward looking, fashioned ad hoc on flexible and broadly remedial lines, often having important consequences for many persons including absentees.

5. The remedy is not imposed but negotiated.

6. The decree does not terminate judicial involvement in the affair: its administration requires the continuing participation of the court.

7. The judge is not passive, his function limited to analysis and statement of governing legal rules; he is active, with responsibility not only for credible fact evaluation but for organizing and shaping the litigation to ensure a just and viable outcome.

8. The subject matter of the lawsuit is not a dispute between private individuals about private rights, but a grievance about the operation of public policy.[14]

In the post-*Brown* era, public law litigation flourished. Federal courts were asked to remedy unconstitutional state practices relating not only to schools, but also to prison conditions, mental institutions, police conduct, public employment practices, zoning, and reapportionment. Although each of these cases involved individuals with real injury, the immediate focus was the operation of public policy. The injunction was used as the mechanism for changing the unconstitutional policy and the federal district judge actively participated in the administration of the injunctive relief.

The *Pennhurst* litigation illustrates the public law model and the important role for the injunction. The named individuals were real victims of the inhumane conditions but the lawsuit was not aimed at simply benefiting them. It was brought as a class action on behalf of all patients and was designed to force the state to close Pennhurst and provide suitable treatment in a less restrictive environment for each of the patients. The district court relied on the injunction to provide this remedy and, through appointment of a special master, maintained ongoing supervision of the ordered changes.

The Supreme Court, of course, set aside the injunctive relief, and this aspect of the case reveals another component of our story. It highlights the fact that the Burger Court made public law litigation, particularly the injunction as a tool for correcting constitutional abuses by state officials, a "special target of attack."[15] The Court chipped away at the power of the federal district courts to enjoin state officials from unconstitutional conduct. The articulated concern of the Court was "federalism," maintenance of a proper respect for state sovereignty. But, often federalism was simply a guise, masking the Court's hostility to the underlying rights asserted in the cases and to the notion of federal courts as vehicles for reform.[16] Early in the Burger Court years it became apparent that a profound retreat was in the process. The Burger Court appeared to be moving toward the position taken by Justice Harlan in 1908 when he dissented in *Ex parte Young.* That view would remove the federal district courts from the business of protecting constitutional rights against state intrusion and, instead, place primary reliance on the state courts.

With hindsight it is now clear that the retreat signal was given early in the Burger Court period. Unknowingly, John Harris, Jr. became the symbol of the retrenchment.[17] Harris was indicted in California state court for violating the California Criminal Syndicalism Act. That law punished anyone who advocates, teaches, or aids "criminal syndicalism," which is defined as any doctrine advocating the commission of a crime, unlawful acts of force, or unlawful methods of terrorism as a means of accomplishing a change in industrial ownership or control, or effecting any political change. Harris' alleged crime was distributing leaflets advocating change in industrial ownership through political action.

After the indictment, Harris tried to have the state court dismiss the indictment on the grounds that the act violated his rights of free speech and press guaranteed by the First and Fourteenth Amendments. The California trial court, however, refused to dismiss the indictment. He then asked a state appellate court to prohibit the prosecution but that request was also denied. As a result, he was forced to file a complaint in federal court seeking to enjoin the district attorney of Los Angeles County from prosecuting him. In the federal court proceeding, Harris alleged that the act and pending prosecution chilled the exercise of his constitutional rights of free speech and press. The federal district court agreed with Harris, held that the act violated the First and Fourteenth Amendments, and enjoined the district attorney from further prosecution of the pending state proceeding.[18]

The district attorney appealed to the Supreme Court, and it heard oral arguments in the case on three separate occasions. Finally, on February 23, 1971, the Court rendered its decision, *Younger v. Harris*, holding that a federal district court should not enjoin a pending state criminal proceeding except under special extraordinary circumstances.[19] Such unusual circumstances, said the Court, might exist if there had been bad faith or harassment in the state's enforcement of its laws, or if there were other special factors such as prosecution under a state law that was patently unconstitutional. The Court concluded that no such special circumstances existed and reversed the lower court's order enjoining the district attorney from proceeding with the state court prosecution.

Harris was sent back to state court where he again petitioned for a writ dismissing the criminal prosecution.[20] On May 7, 1971, his request was denied and he appealed to the state intermediate appellate court. On December 16, 1971, five years after his indictment, Harris finally won. The state court concluded that it was bound to dismiss the indictment by a recent Supreme Court case holding unconstitutional Ohio's similarly worded criminal syndicalism Law.[21] Under the "compulsion" of that case, the California court ruled that California's statute was also unconstitutional and that Harris should be discharged from custody.[22]

The significance of Harris' unfortunate experience lies in the Supreme Court's sweeping noninterference policy. That policy was not compelled by the Constitution or federal law. Quite to the contrary, both the Constitution and relevant statutes supported the exercise of federal judicial power to enjoin an unconstitutional state prosecution. Harris' right to relief was based on the First and Fourteenth Amendments and, as a result his case "arose under" federal law. Article III expressly extends the judicial power of the United States to such cases.[23] Moreover, during the Reconstruction period, Congress had provided for federal court jurisdiction to hear cases brought to enforce constitutional rights, and those laws were still very much in force.[24] Congress had also authorized injunctive relief against public officials who deprive individuals of their constitutional rights. Indeed, Section 1983 expressly states that every person who, acting under color of state law, subjects another to the deprivation of a right secured by the constitution shall be liable in a "suit in equity."[25] And, *Ex parte Young* had paved the way for federal court power to order injunctive relief against state officials, notwithstanding the Eleventh Amendment.

The Anti-Injunction Act was the one likely obstacle preventing relief for Harris.[26] That act prohibits a federal court from granting an injunction to stay proceedings in a state court. The act, however, includes three exceptions, one allowing such injunctions where "expressly authorized by Act of Congress." Section 1983 is precisely such an act of Congress authorizing an injunction to stay proceedings in state court. As a result, the Anti-Injunction Act was not a bar to the award of an injunction restraining the state court prosecution of Harris.[27]

Nevertheless, as the Court ruled in *Younger*, well-established equitable principles justified the conclusion that a federal court should not enjoin pending state criminal prosecutions.[28] A request for an injunction is an appeal to the court's discretion. As such, even if the power to award the equitable relief exists, a judge is not required to exercise it. One of the basic doctrines of equity jurisprudence is that injunctive relief should not be awarded where there is an adequate remedy "at law." The purpose of this restraint is to prevent erosion of the role of the jury. To this day, the courts have maintained the ancient English practice of having judges rule on requests for injunction but allowing jurors to decide actions at law. The basic proposition restraining equity power within narrow limits also serves the purpose of avoiding a duplication of lawsuits where a single case would be adequate. These narrowing principles are especially appropriate when a party tries to enjoin a pending criminal prosecution. A criminal defendant, like Harris, could raise his constitutional claim as a defense in the criminal case and a jury could be involved in deciding the matter. Moreover, these issues could be resolved in a single case, avoiding the duplication of proceedings resulting from a second lawsuit to enjoin the first.

A second traditional equity principle supported the Court's conclusion in *Younger* as well. Equitable relief is traditionally authorized only in cases where the party seeking the injunction can establish some type of irreparable harm.[29] The harm suffered by Harris—the cost, anxiety, and inconvenience of defending against a single state criminal prosecution—is not irreparable in the special legal sense of that term. Harris was found not to be suffering any unusual irreparable injury because he could raise the constitutional defenses in the pending state court criminal case.

The Court in *Younger* could have based its noninterference policy on traditional equity rules. But, it was not content to rely on those rules alone. Instead, it invoked notions of "comity" and "federalism" and, in so doing, sent a signal that it was preparing the lower federal courts for a wide retreat from their position as protectors of constitutional rights. Comity, the Court said in *Younger*, encompasses a "recognition of the fact that the entire country is made up of a Union of separate state governments, and a continuance of the belief that the National Government will fare best if the States and their institutions are left free to perform their separate functions in their separate ways."[30] Such respect for state functions is a central tenet of "Our Federalism." Justice Black, author of the majority opinion, explained:

What the concept of ["Our Federalism"] does represent is a system in which there is sensitivity to the legitimate interests of both State and National Governments, and in which the National Government, anxious though it may be to vindicate and to protect federal rights and federal interests, always endeavors to do so in ways that will not unduly interfere with the legitimate activities of the States.[31]

Out of respect for the state courts, the Court concluded that a federal court should not enjoin a pending state criminal proceeding absent exceptional circumstances. Justice Black cautioned that Our Federalism does not mean "blind deference to 'State's Rights' any more than it means centralization of control over every important issue in our National Government and the courts."[32] Our Federalism, as described by Justice Black, is a two-way street and encompasses sensitivity to the legitimate interests of both the states and the federal governments.

Unfortunately, in the nearly two decades following *Younger*, the Burger Court lost sight of Justice Black's warning and converted *Younger* and its federalism principle into blind deference to the states. Relying on "sloganeering references" to Our Federalism, the Burger Court severely curtailed the ability of lower federal courts to prevent state intrusion on individual freedoms.[33] In an effort to close the lower federal courts to individuals injured by unconstitutional state conduct, the Burger Court extended *Younger* well beyond the limited boundaries of that case. *Younger* has been employed as a judicial vehicle for returning to the pre-Reconstruction scheme in which state courts were the primary protectors of constitutional rights, subject to Supreme Court appellate review.[34]

The Burger court revealed its willingness to convert Our Federalism into a general preference for state courts when it began extending the *Younger* policy to pending *civil* cases. In *Younger* itself, the Court relied heavily on a supposed long-standing policy against enjoining state court *criminal* proceedings. One commentator conducted an exhaustive review of prior cases and concluded that there was, in fact, no such well-settled policy and that in this regard *Younger* "perpetuates an old wives tale."[35] Whatever the accuracy of the Court's historical analysis, it is clear that the *Younger* opinion stressed noninterference with pending state criminal cases. The decision itself would not preclude a federal court injunction of state civil proceedings. Yet, the Burger Court extended *Younger* well beyond the criminal context and relied on Our Federalism as a basis for federal noninterference with pending state civil proceedings.

At first the Court tried to maintain the ties to the criminal context by applying the noninterference policy to pending state civil cases that were closely related to criminal prosecutions. *Huffman v. Pursue, Ltd.*, for example, arose from the efforts of a local sheriff and prosecutor to close a movie theater showing pornographic films.[36] These officials brought a civil proceeding in state court under Ohio's nuisance law. The state court ordered the closing of the theater and the owner, rather than appealing to the higher state court, brought a lawsuit in federal court alleging that enforcement of the nuisance statute resulted in the deprivation of constitutional rights. The owner requested the federal court to enjoin enforcement of the state law. The district court granted the request, holding that the state statute was an overly broad restraint on First and Fourteenth Amendment rights.

On appeal, however, the Burger Court reversed concluding that the federal district court should have applied the *Younger* standard and refrained from interfering with the state civil proceeding. The Court said that it was unnecessary to make any "general pronouncements" about the applicability of *Younger* to all civil cases. Instead, it applied the noninterference policy because the Ohio proceeding was "more akin to a criminal prosecution than are most civil cases."[37] The state was a party to the nuisance proceeding that was both in aid of, and closely related to, state criminal laws that prohibited distribution of obscene material. A federal court injunction, the Court reasoned, would disrupt the state's efforts to protect the interests embodied in those criminal laws.

Huffman suggested that kinship with criminal proceedings might be the basis for gauging the extension of *Younger* to civil cases. Subsequent decisions made clear that the line is not so easily drawn. In *Trainor v. Hernandez*, for example, plaintiffs requested a federal court to restrain state officials from attaching their property as part of a state civil action brought by state officials to recover fraudulently obtained welfare benefits.[38] In their federal lawsuit under Section 1983, plaintiffs maintained that the state attachment proceedings violated the Fourteenth Amendment due process clause. The federal district court refused to dismiss the case, ruling that *Younger* does not apply where the pending state proceeding is neither criminal nor quasi-criminal in nature. The Supreme Court, however, held that *Younger* does indeed apply and that the lower federal court should not have enjoined the attachment aspect of the state proceeding. In reaching this result the Court emphasized two factors: (1) the state proceeding was brought by the state in its sovereign capacity, and (2) the state lawsuit was brought to vindicate an important state policy, the fiscal integrity of the public welfare program.[39]

Most recently, the Court went even further and eliminated the requirement that the pending state proceeding be brought by the state in its sovereign capacity.[40] In 1984, Pennzoil sued

Texaco in state court claiming that Texaco had tortiously in-
duced Getty Oil Company to breach a contract to sell shares of
stock to Pennzoil. One year later a state court jury returned a
verdict in favor of Pennzoil for over $10 billion. Under a state
rule, in order to appeal, Texaco would have to post a bond in
the amount of the judgment, including interest and costs. The
amount of the bond would have been over $13 billion.

Texaco brought a Section 1983 lawsuit against Pennzoil in
federal court claiming that, among other things, the bond requirement violated the due process and equal protection clauses
of the Fourteenth Amendment. It asked the federal district court
to enjoin Pennzoil from taking any steps to enforce the state
court judgment. The district court found that Texaco could not
afford a multibillion dollar bond and concluded that the bond
requirement violated the Fourteenth Amendment by effectively
denying Texaco a right to appeal in state court. The lower court,
therefore, enjoined Pennzoil from attempting to enforce the
state court judgment pending the final resolution of the federal
lawsuit.

Once again the Supreme Court determined that the lower
federal court should have refused to hear the case. Although
Chief Justice Burger had retired, the new Rehnquist Court gave
every indication that it would willingly continue the Burger
Court tradition and use *Younger* to limit the role of the lower
federal courts in protecting constitutional rights. It is important
to note that the state proceeding was neither criminal nor quasi-
criminal. Moreover, unlike *Trainor*, the state was not a party to
the state proceeding. Nevertheless, the Court concluded that
Younger was applicable and requires noninterference. The Court
applied the hands-off policy because the state's interests in the
pending civil proceeding "were so important that exercise of the
federal judicial power would disregard the comity between the
states and the National Government."[41] The Court, however,
did a particularly poor job of identifying the state's important
interest in the state court case. The only interest identified by
the Court—the state interest in enforcing compliance with its
courts' judgments—exists in every case.[42]

As Justice Stevens observed in his concurring opinion, the
majority's approach in the *Pennzoil* case "cuts the *Younger* doc-

trine adrift from its original doctrinal moorings which dealt with the states' interest in enforcing their criminal laws."[43] A doctrine that was designed as a limit on federal court power to enjoin state criminal proceedings developed into one that prevents federal judicial interference with any state civil proceeding in which the state has an "important interest."

As far-reaching as *Pennzoil* may appear, it is not the most extreme example of the reach of the *Younger* noninterference policy. In *Pennzoil* at least one similarity to *Younger* remained: the federal district court was being asked to enjoin a pending state proceeding. In *Rizzo v. Goode* the Court suggested that federalism concerns may require that a federal court refrain from issuing an injunction even in the absence of any pending state case.[44] The plaintiffs in *Rizzo* requested injunctive relief against an alleged pattern of mistreatment of minority citizens by Philadelphia police and city officials. The lower federal courts found an unacceptably high number of incidents of police misconduct and a pattern of unconstitutional conduct. The district court issued an injunction requiring the officials to draft a comprehensive program for restructuring the procedures for handling police misconduct. The Supreme Court eventually reviewed the matter and held that the case should have been dismissed because plaintiffs lacked standing to sue, they failed to show any real threat of future harm to themselves. Additionally, the Court ruled that the past few incidents of police misconduct did not justify the broad equitable relief ordered by the district court. Finally, the Court observed that principles of federalism militate heavily against the grant of injunctive relief, even in the absence of any pending state proceeding. Federalism concerns, Justice Rehnquist wrote for the majority, have greatest weight in cases seeking injunctions of state criminal proceedings but "likewise have applicability where injunctive relief is sought ... against those in charge of an executive branch of an agency of state or local government ... "[45]

The *Younger* line of cases severely diminishes the power of the lower federal courts to prevent unconstitutional conduct. In the name of Our Federalism, the lower federal courts have been stripped of authority to use the injunction as a tool for protecting individuals who are being denied their constitutional rights by state officials. Like the standing doctrine, Our Federalism forces such individuals out of the federal courts and requires them to bring their cases, if at all, in state courts.

In its haste to clear the federal court of these cases, the Burger Court failed to adequately explain the precise federalism concerns threatened by exercise of federal judicial power. Professor Martin Redish discerned four possible justifications in the various opinions: (1) the desire to avoid suggesting that state court judges might be unwilling or unable to enforce constitutional rights; (2) the need to prevent interference with the state judicial process; (3) the desire to preserve the discretion of state executive officials; and (4) the need to avoid interference with state legislative policies.[46] He concluded that these rationales are "inconsistent or internally flawed" and do not justify the broad noninterference policy.[47]

The first justification—the fear of insulting state judges—does not support abdication of federal judicial power because it is difficult to assess the extent of any insult caused by a federal injunction. An insult would arise if the federal government prohibited state courts from deciding constitutional issues. "But as long as the federal government has permitted litigants to adjudicate their constitutional claims in state court, it is difficult to see how neutrally providing litigants the option of seeking a federal adjudication in any way insults state courts."[48] In any event, it is the individual litigant who decides to raise the constitutional issue in federal, rather than state, court. Thus, the decision to seek federal judicial help reflects the litigant's, not the federal government's, view of the expertise and competence of state judges.

The desire to avoid interference with the integrity of the state judicial process is certainly justifiable. Federal judicial interference with every aspect of a pending state case would lead to piecemeal litigation and undue delays in enforcement of state law. This concern, however, does not require the broad noninterference policy developed by the Burger Court. A federal injunction preventing any proceeding at all in the state court would be easy to administer and would not cause repeated intrusions or piecemeal litigation. Moreover, the need to avoid interference with the state judicial process cannot justify federal restraint in cases like *Rizzo* where there is no pending state case. Even more troubling is the third suggestion that the *Younger* line of cases is justified by the desire to preserve the discretion of state executive officers. In deciding whether specific executive conduct is unconstitutional, the federal court may well consider the expertise and discretion of the official. For example, in determining whether state prison officials have complied with constitutional requirements, the Supreme Court has considered the need for deference to the expertise of these officials. As a result, in the prison context the Supreme Court has upheld conduct that might be unconstitutional in other settings.[49] In the prison cases, to continue the example, the need for deference is one of the factors weighed in the assessment of the merits of the constitutional claim. The type of deference established by the *Younger* line is very different; it is, as Professor Redish stated, "procedural" in nature.[50] When the federal court relies on *Younger* to avoid issuing an injunction it does not decide whether the challenged behavior is constitutional. Instead the federal court tells the litigant that the claim was raised in the wrong place—it should have been raised in state court. *Younger* does not guarantee that the ultimate resolution of the constitutional issue will include a proper weighing of the need for deference to executive officials. It simply shifts the forum in which the determination is made.

So too, the *Younger* line of cases cannot be justified by the desire to avoid interference with the accomplishment of state legislative policies.[51] In deciding the constitutionality of state legislation, courts—state or federal—should and do take into consideration the state interests reflected in the law. State laws, for example, that regulate economic matters are usually found to be constitutional if they serve some conceivable state interest.[52] State laws that discriminate on the basis of gender will be evaluated to determine if they serve important governmental interests and are substantially related to those objectives.[53] The desire to avoid interference with state legislative goals, then, is very much a part of the constitutional decision. Under the *Younger* doctrine, however, the federal court is not deciding the constitutionality of the state law. It merely finds that the case should have been brought in the state court.

In one respect *Younger* may well lead to less interference with state legislative goals and the discretion of state officials. The *Younger* doctrine substitutes state courts for federal courts as the decisionmaker. State judges may be less willing to declare state laws and official conduct unconstitutional.[54] But, if that is the justification for *Younger*, it turns the entire federalism notion on its head and "is embarassingly inconsistent with what is probably the primary basis for *Younger* deference, namely the desire to avoid insulting state judges by questioning their willingness to protect federal rights."[55]

The Burger Court failed to offer adequate justification for its sweeping claims that notions of federalism justify the broad non-interference policy. Instead it relied on vague references to Our Federalism that presumably convey all that the reader is required to know. In addition, by extending *Younger* to civil cases, the Court simply disregarded significant differences between criminal and civil proceedings.

First, if federal intervention in a pending state case creates any offense to state interests, it is more likely to occur in the criminal context. A state decision to designate certain conduct as criminal provides some indication of "the importance it has ascribed to prompt and unencumbered enforcement of its law."[56] On the other hand, in a civil proceeding (such as *Pennzoil*) the state is not even a party. The Burger Court's application of Our Federalism to pending state civil cases or, as in *Rizzo*, where there is no state proceeding at all ignores Justice Black's observation in *Younger* itself: an injunction against unconstitutional state conduct that is not part of a criminal prosecution is the kind of relief "that raises no special problems."[57]

Second, in the criminal context, safeguards for the individual exist at all stages of the process. A criminal prosecution requires the completion of preliminary steps, such as arrest and indictment, designed to protect the individual from illegitimate prosecution. Moreover, in a criminal case the state must provide counsel to indigent parties and prove its case beyond a reasonable doubt. An individual in a state criminal case, thus, has some protection against improper prosecution. No similar safeguards exist in the civil context.

Finally, an additional difference between criminal and civil matters suggests that *Younger* is less justified in the latter setting. Individuals in state criminal proceedings may eventually have an opportunity to present federal claims to a federal district court. After exhausting appeals in the state judicial system, state criminal defendants, who are being held in custody in violation of the Constitution or U.S. laws, can file a postconviction proceeding in federal district court.[58] Criminal defendants have an opportunity to raise their federal claims before a federal district court and appeal through the federal system if they lose. No analogous remedy is available to parties to state civil proceedings. They can appeal through the state court system and then try to obtain Supreme Court review of any federal claims. But, state civil litigants, unlike criminal defendants, will have no opportunity for consideration of the federal claims by a federal district court. Supreme Court review is an inadequate substitute for an initial determination by a lower federal court. Such review is discretionary, and the Court might decline to hear a case. In fact, the Court only hears a very small number of the cases presented to it each year.[59] Moreover, as the Court said (prior to the Burger years), "Limiting the litigant to review here [in the Supreme Court] would deny him the benefit of a federal trial court's role in constructing a record and making fact findings. How the facts are found will often dictate the decision of federal claims."[60]

The most serious objection to the use of Our Federalism to close the federal courts to constitutional litigants, however, is not the absence of an adequate theoretical justification. Nor is it the failure to distinguish between civil and criminal cases. Rather, the most fundamental defect in the sweeping application of *Younger* is the complete lack of regard for the federal interest in allowing the cases to be heard in federal court. Indeed, as the Burger Court extended *Younger* from a doctrine of noninterference in pending criminal cases to one of noninterference with state officials generally (regardless of the pendency of a state case), it simply ignored the federal interest in having federal courts open to constitutional litigants. One searches in vain for any mention of the federal interest in the *Younger* line of cases. A doctrine that was initially sensitive to the legitimate interests of both state and federal governments became totally engrossed in only the former. And, as Justice Stewart observed, the federal–state balance became "distorted beyond recognition."[61]

If the Court had been less near-sighted it could easily have found significant federal concerns in these cases. It would have found, for instance, that Congress was well aware of the tensions created by federal court review of the constitutionality of state official conduct. To ease that tension, Congress had provided that as a general proposition federal courts should not interfere with pending state proceedings.[62] But, Congress had made an exception for cases brought under Section 1983 against state officials who use their power to subject individuals to the loss of federal rights.[63] In such circumstances, the lower federal courts could be open to ensure that federal rights are not suppressed by overzealous state officials. The individual, of course, is free to elect to raise any federal rights in a state court proceeding. Under Section 1983, however, Congress provided the alternate federal forum for those who believe they cannot adequately protect their federal rights in the state court.

In the absence of a pending state proceeding, Congress plainly contemplated that the federal courts would be wide open to individuals challenging the constitutionality of state official conduct. The very purpose of Section 1983 and the other Reconstruction laws was to open the "federal courts to private citizens, offering a uniquely federal remedy against incursions under the claimed authority of state law upon rights secured by the Constitution and laws of the Nation."[64] The significance of the Reconstruction laws was derived in part from the fact that they placed the federal courts between the people and the states as guardians of federal rights.[65] The post-*Brown* era revealed that protection of federal rights is a national matter transcending local interests, and the lower federal courts have an important role to play.

In the name of Our Federalism the Burger Court attempted to defeat the congressional scheme that emerged during the past century for the protection of constitutional rights and restrict the use of an injunction as a tool for securing such rights. As one critic persuasively argued, the Burger Court's federalism notions represent a return to the antinationalism of the past.

One suspects that at the core of this philosophy of government is nostalgia for a return to an earlier era; a conviction that by restricting the reach of national law the Court can insulate the status quo; that if matters were left to the states, people and institutions would again know their places.[66]

Our Federalism, like the standing doctrine, was manipulated by the Burger Court in order to eliminate the lower federal courts as guardians of constitutional rights. The Court used supposed—and poorly explained—federalism concerns to dismantle the congressional plan for protection of federal rights. In that effort to rid the federal courts of constitutional challenges to state action, the Burger Court simply forgot, as Justice Brennan observed, that "one of the strengths of our federal system is that it provides a double source of protection for the rights of our citizens" and that federalism "is not served when the federal half of that protection is crippled."[67]

Notes

1. *See generally* F. JAMES, JR. & G. HAZARD, JR., CIVIL PROCEDURE §1.4 (3d ed. 1985).
2. *See* O. FISS, CIVIL RIGHTS INJUNCTIONS 1 (1978).
3. *See In re* Debs, 158 U.S. 123 (1895).
4. 209 U.S. 123 (1908).
5. Hans v. Louisiana, 134 U.S. 1 (1889).
6. *Ex parte* Young, 209 U.S. 159–60 (1908).
7. *Id.* at 175 (Harlan, J., dissenting).
8. 347 U.S. 483 (1953).
9. O. FISS, *supra* note 2, at 4.
10. *Id.*
11. Chayes, *The Role of the Judge in Public Law Litigation*, 89 HARV. L. REV. 1281, 1282–83 (1976).
12. *Id.*
13. *Id.* at 1302.
14. *Id.* at 1282–83.
15. O. FISS, *supra* note 2, at 5.

16. CHAYES, *supra* note 11, at 1305.
17. *See* Younger v. Harris, 401 U.S. 37 (1971).
18. *See* Younger v. Harris, 281 F. Supp. 507 (C.D. Cal. 1968).
19. 401 U.S. 37 (1971).
20. *In re* Harris, 20 Cal. App.3d 632, 97 Cal. Rptr. 844 (1971).
21. Brandenburg v. Ohio, 395 U.S. 444 (1969).
22. *In re* Harris, 20 Cal. App.3d 632, 97 Cal. Rptr. 844, 846 (1971).
23. Article III states that the judicial power of the United States extends to "all cases in Law and Equity arising under this Constitution.
24. For the current jurisdictional statute *see* 28 U.S.C. §1331 (1983).
25. 42 U.S.C. §1983 (1983).
26. 28 U.S.C. §2283 (1983).
27. *See* Mitchum v. Foster, 407 U.S. 225 (1972).
28. *See* Younger v. Harris, 401 U.S. 36, 44 (1971).
29. *See id.* at 46.
30. *Id.* at 44.
31. *Id.*
32. *Id.*
33. Gibbons, *Our Federalism*, 12 SUFFOLK U.L. REV. 1087, 1117 (1978). The *Younger* decision has provoked extensive scholarly debate. *See e.g.*, M. REDISH, FEDERAL JURISDICTION: TENSIONS IN THE ALLOCATION OF JUDICIAL POWER 296–323 (1980); and articles listed in Maroney & Braveman, *"Averting the Flood": Henry J. Friendly, the Comity Doctrine, and the Jurisdiction of the Federal Courts—Part II*, 31 SYRACUSE L. REV. 469, 475 n.30 (1980).
34. *See* Zeigler, *A Reassessment of the Younger Doctrine In Light of the Legislative History of Reconstruction*, 1983, DUKE L.J. 987. *But see* Bator, *The State Courts and Federal Constitutional Litigation*, 22 WM. & MARY L. REV. 605 (1981).
35. Wechsler, *Federal Court, State Criminal Law and the First Amendment*, 49 N.Y.U. L. REV. 740, 868 (1974).
36. 420 U.S. 592 (1975).
37. *Id.* at 604.
38. 431 U.S. 434 (1977).
39. *See id.* at 444.
40. Pennzoil Co. v. Texaco, Inc., 481 U.S. 1 (1987).
41. *Id.* at 11.
42. *Id.* at 13.
43. *Id.* at 30n.2.
44. 423 U.S. 362 (1976).
45. *Id.* at 380.
46. Redish, *The Doctrine of Younger v. Harris: Deference in Search of a Rationale*, 63 CORNELL L. REV. 463, 465–66 (1978).

47. *Id.* at 477.

48. M. REDISH, *supra* note 30, at 299.

49. *See generally*, Bell v. Wolfish, 441 U.S. 520 (1979).

50. M. REDISH, *supra* note 33, at 300.

51. *Id.* at 301.

52. *See, e.g.*, Williamson v. Lee Optical, 348 U.S. 483 (1955).

53. *See, e.g.*, Craig v. Boren, 429 U.S. 190 (1976).

54. *See* ch. 7, *infra.*

55. M. REDISH, *supra* note 33, at 301.

56. Younger v. Harris, 401 U.S. 31, 55 n.2 (1971).

57. *Id.* at 47 n.4.

58. 28 U.S.C. §2254 (1983).

59. In the 1987–88 Term, 5,268 cases were on the Supreme Court docket but only 167 cases were argued and submitted. See 57 U.S.L.W. 3074 (July 26, 1988).

60. England v. Louisiana State Board of Medical Examiners, 375 U.S. 411, 416 (1964).

61. Hicks v. Miranda, 422 U.S. 332, 357 (Stewart, J., dissenting).

62. 28 U.S.C. §2283 (1983).

63. Mitchum v. Foster, 407 U.S. 225 (1972).

64. *Id.* at 239.

65. *See id.* at 242.

66. Gibbons, *supra* note 30, at 1117.

67. Brennan, *State Constitutions and Protections of Individual Rights*, 90 HARV. L. REV. 489, 503 (1977).

Chapter 5
Damages

Section 1983, which plays such a large part in our story, provides that persons who act under state law and subject others to the deprivation of federal rights shall be liable not only for injunctive relief but damages as well. In theory, together with its jurisdictional counterpart, that law opened the federal courts to damage suits against state and local officials who were depriving others of rights protected by the U.S. Constitution or by federal laws. In fact, for reasons discussed in chapter 2, Section 1983 lay dormant for years and its impact was rather insignificant. One commentator found only twenty-one lawsuits brought under Section 1983 between 1871 and 1920.[1] In the wake of *Brown v. Board of Education*, however, Section 1983 emerged as the vehicle for obtaining federal court injunctions against unconstitutional state conduct. So too, it eventually emerged as the principal vehicle for recovering damages in federal court lawsuits against state officials who violate the Constitution.

The watershed with respect to damage remedies was the Supreme Court's 1961 decision in *Monroe v. Pape*.[2] That lawsuit was brought in federal court against the city of Chicago and individual Chicago police officers who broke into the Monroe home, routed the family from their beds, made them stand naked, and ransacked every room. Mr. Monroe was then taken to the police station and detained for ten hours while he was questioned about a murder. The police did not take him before a magistrate or permit him to call his family or a lawyer. Subsequently, they released him without bringing any criminal charges.

Relying on Section 1983, the Monroes filed a lawsuit in federal court against the city and the individual police officers. The Monroes alleged that the officers had neither a search warrant nor an arrest warrant and thus had conducted the search and made the arrest in violation of the U.S. Constitution. They asked to recover their damages but the district court dismissed the case and the court of appeals affirmed.

Section 1983 permits recovery only against persons who act "under color" of state law. The question before the Supreme Court asked if the action of these defendants should be construed to be "under color" of state law. Defendants argued that a person acts "under color" of state law only when state law authorizes the challenged conduct. Under this interpretation, Section 1983 would create a federal remedy only in those instances where the state law permitted the challenged official conduct. Section 1983 would authorize no remedy in cases, such as *Monroe* itself, where the officials violated their own state law. The recourse for any injured party would be a lawsuit in state court claiming a violation of the state provisions.

The Supreme Court unequivocally rejected this restrictive reading of Section 1983. The purpose of Section 1983, the court said in *Monroe*, was to create a "federal remedy . . . supplementary to the state remedy, and the latter need not be first sought and refused before the federal one is invoked."[3] The phrase *under color* of state law refers to action taken with the apparent authority of state law. Quoting an earlier case construing similar language in a different statute, the Court said: "Misuse of power, possessed by virtue of state law and made possible only because the wrongdoer is clothed with the authority of state law, is action taken 'under color of' state law." In *Monroe* the police officers had acted under color of state law because they misused the power given them by state law. The Monroes, therefore, could bring a claim for damages against the officers in federal court.

Just as *Brown v. Board of Education* gave vitality to the federal court injunction as a remedy against unconstitutional conduct,

Monroe gave new life to the federal court damage remedy. A crude measure of the impact of *Monroe* has been derived from annual statistics on the business of the federal courts. In 1961, when *Monroe* was decided, fewer than 300 lawsuits were brought in federal court under all the various civil rights acts. Twenty years later, over 30,000 suits were brought in federal court under the various civil rights acts (chiefly Section 1983).[4] Although in many of these cases the parties sought injunctive relief and were consequently encouraged by *Brown*, in others the victims requested damages. *Monroe* provided these individuals with a powerful weapon for obtaining such a remedy from the federal court. Indeed, the award of damages in a Section 1983 case serves a number of purposes. First, it compensates the individual victim for any injuries. Second, a damage award might operate to deter future misconduct by officials. Finally, and not insignificantly, a damage award serves a symbolic and educative function: it affirms the importance of the constitutional right and the federal government's commitment to protection of those rights.[5] As a result, *Monroe* brought us one step closer to realization of the Reconstruction efforts.

In one respect, however, the decision was not as far-reaching as the Monroes had urged. Although the Court ruled that the Monroes could bring a Section 1983 action in federal court for damages against the police officers, it held that they could not sue the city of Chicago. Section 1983 authorizes lawsuits against every "person" who acts under color of state law to deprive others of federal rights. Relying on the legislative history, the Court concluded that a city is not a person for 1983 purposes and cannot be sued in federal court under the statute. This construction of Section 1983 limited its effectiveness. A jury might be more willing to award a money judgment against a governmental entity than against identifiable individual officials, such as police officers, who will claim they were just doing their job. Moreover, in some instances a victim may be unable to recover because the individual official may not have the resources to pay a substantial damage award. The governmental unit has a "deeper pocket" than the individual public officers and is in a much better position to pay any judgment. Finally, exposure to damage awards might encourage the governmental entity to take steps to ensure that the conduct will not be repeated in the future. In cases like *Monroe*, for example, the possibility of a damage award against Chicago itself might encourage the city to adopt better training programs, more carefully supervise its police officers, or fire those that acted unconstitutionally. In this way damage awards against the city might operate to deter future unconstitutional conduct.

Despite these policy considerations, *Monroe* ruled that a Section 1983 action could not be brought against the governmental entity and that the suit against the city was properly dismissed. Even with this limitation, however, *Monroe* was a milestone, allowing the Reconstruction plan adopted ninety years earlier to become a reality. In a very real sense *Monroe* opened the federal courts to damage suits against officials who use their power under state law to deprive others of constitutional rights.[6]

The Burger Court's limited vision of the federal court's role in protecting constitutional rights, however, did not contemplate the expansive opportunities presented by *Monroe*. As a result, in implementing its plan for closing the federal courts to litigants challenging the constitutionality of official misconduct, the Burger Court employed various devices that restricted the availability of damage actions under Section 1983. This aspect of our story is not completely bleak, to be sure, and includes a few successes for victims of unconstitutional conduct. But, even these successes have been tempered and may become hollow victories.

Damages against Local Governmental Units

Let us begin with the most significant success with respect to Section 1983 and access to the federal courts. Seventeen years after the *Monroe* decision, the Burger Court had an opportunity to reconsider the proposition that Section 1983 does not extend to suits against a local governmental entity. That opportunity arose in *Monell v. Department of Social Services*, a case challenging the constitutionality of a policy requiring pregnant employees to take unpaid leaves of absence even though such leaves were not required for medical reasons.[7] The suit was brought in federal court in New York City against the New York City Department of Social Services, the commissioner of the department, the Board of Education of the City of New York, the chancellor of the board, the city of New York, and its mayor. The employees sought injunctive relief and backpay. The district court determined that an injunction was unnecessary because, after the lawsuit was filed, the city and board had changed their policies so that no pregnant employee would have to take a leave unless she is medically unable to perform her job. Although the district court concluded that the previous policy was unconstitutional and that the employees were wrongfully forced to leave, it refused to award back pay as well. Any such award, reasoned the district judge, would ultimately come from the city of New York, and the city could not be sued under the *Monroe* decision.

The Supreme Court reversed that aspect of the case. It conducted a fresh analysis of the debates surrounding the 1871 Civil Rights Act and concluded that Congress meant to include local governmental bodies among those "persons" to whom Section 1983 applies. The Court, however, quickly qualified its holding. The local governmental unit cannot be sued under Section 1983 solely because it employs someone who subjects others to deprivation of rights protected by the Constitution. Instead, local governing bodies can be sued under Section 1983 only when "the action that is alleged to be unconstitutional implements or executes a policy statement, ordinance, regulation or decision officially adopted and promulgated by that body's officers."[8]

The Burger Court decision in *Monell* opened the door a crack to Section 1983 cases against local governmental units. But then the Court slowly began to narrow that opening. After *Monell*, the key to stating a Section 1983 claim against a local government body is to allege the existence of some official policy or custom. A city, for example, could not be held liable under Section 1983 for an isolated, unjustified shooting by a police officer.[9] On the other hand, the city could be held responsible in the event that an individual was injured by a police officer who acted pursuant to a city policy authorizing the unjustified use of force. Distinguishing random acts from policies or customs has proved to be a difficult task.[10] Indeed, the policy or custom requirement has generated a great deal of litigation in the lower federal courts and has produced sharp division among the Supreme Court justices.

In the cases after *Monell*, the Court has been unable to give useful guidance.[11] It has divided, for instance, over such a basic issue as the meaning of "policy." Chief Justice (then Justice) Rehnquist has relied on the definition in *Webster's Ninth New Collegiate Dictionary*: A policy is "a definite course or method of action selected from among alternatives and in light of given conditions to guide and determine present and future decisions."[12] Implicit in this definition is the notion that a policy connotes a rule of general applicability.[13] Justice Brennan, on the other hand, has opted for a definition that would include single decisions. He quoted *Webster's Third New International Dictionary*: A policy is "a specific decision or set of decisions designed to carry out such a chosen course of action."[14]

Moreover, it has split over the proper standard for determining which local officials have final policy-making authority and can subject the governmental unit itself to liability.[15] Suppose, for example, a county sheriff has discretion to hire and fire deputies but is not responsible for establishing county employment policy. If the sheriff fires a deputy in an unconstitutional manner, will the county itself be liable under Section 1983? Four Justices offered the following answer to the hypothetical:

The County Sheriff may have discretion to hire and fire employees without also being the county official responsible for establishing county employment policy. If this were the case, the Sheriff's decisions respecting employment would not give rise to municipal liability, although similar decisions with respect to law enforcement practices, over which the Sheriff *is* the official policymaker, *would* give rise to municipal liability. Instead, if county employment policy was set by the Board of County Commissioners, only that body's decisions would provide a basis for county liability. This would be true even if the Board left the Sheriff discretion to hire and fire employees and the Sheriff exercised that discretion in an unconstitutional manner; the decision to act unlawfully would not be a decision of the Board. However, if the Board delegated its power to establish final employment policy to the Sheriff, the Sheriff's decision *would* represent county policy and would give rise to municipal liability.[16]

This answer, as one might expect, did not clear up the confusion. In one of the latest pronouncements on the policy or

custom issue, Justice O'Connor (joined by Chief Justice Rehnquist, Justice White, and Justice Scalia) attempted to articulate
some "guiding principles."[17] First, a local governing body may
be held liable under Section 1983 only for acts that it has officially
sanctioned or ordered. Second, only those officials who have
final policy-making authority may by their actions subject the
governmental entity itself to liability. Third, the courts should
look to state law to determine whether a particular official has
final policy-making authority. Finally, the challenged actions
must have been taken pursuant to a policy adopted by the official
responsible for making policy in that area of the government's
business.

It is unlikely that this attempt to establish guiding principles
will clarify the matter. As Justice Brennan pointed out in his
concurring opinion (joined by Justices Marshall and Blackmun),
identifying official policymakers is not an easy task. Chief Justice
Rehnquist suggested that courts can identify policymakers by
referring to state statutory law. But, as Justice Brennan count-
ered, local governing bodies take myriad forms and, in many
instances, real and apparent authority may diverge. In others,
state statutory law will fail to disclose where policy-making authority rests. Justice Brennan was forced to conclude that the
"commendable desire" of the plurality to define more precisely
municipal liability "had led it to embrace a theory . . . that is both
unduly narrow and unrealistic, and one that ultimately would
permit municipalities to insulate themselves from liability for the
acts of all but a small minority of actual city policymakers."[18]

The use of the policy or custom requirement to limit liability
of local governing bodies for damages under Section 1983 is not
surprising. This effort is derived from the same source as that
to limit injunctive relief. The source is "Our Federalism," the
desire to avoid federal interference with local governments. As
one commentator recently wrote: "The very existence of the
official policy debate is a creation of Burger Court federalism.
It seems likely that the creator's imprint will ultimately push the
concept in a restrictive direction."[19]

In one respect, the limits on liability for damages are more
detrimental to the federal interests embodied in Section 1983
than the restrictions on injunctive relief. When the federal court

invokes Our Federalism to deny an injunction, it makes a procedural determination that the federal forum is inappropriate and that the request should be addressed to the state court. To be sure, as discussed in chapter 7, this procedural determination may have serious consequences for the enforcement of the underlying constitutional rights. Nevertheless, the state courts have power to hear Section 1983 claims and at least in theory can enjoin unconstitutional conduct.[20] In contrast, the limits on damage liability resulting from the "official policy" doctrine are not procedural in nature but affect the very reach of Section 1983. The Supreme Court's determination that Section 1983 can be used against a local governing body only when an official policy or custom is challenged applies whether the case is brought in state court or federal court. In the absence of an official policy or custom, a local governmental unit cannot be sued for damages under Section 1983 in any forum, state or federal. The victim might be able to sue the entity on the basis of state law, but such lawsuits would have to be brought in state court. The policy or custom requirement, then, is another door-closing mechanism. It deprives the victims of a right to recovery under federal law and forces them to sue the officials, if at all, in state court.

Damages against the State

Although uncertainty over the availability of Section 1983 damage actions against local governing bodies continues to exist, no similar uncertainty exists with regard to such damage actions against the states. The Burger Court made it quite clear that as a general proposition the federal courts will be closed to those seeking damages to be paid from a state's treasury. The foundation for this barrier is the Eleventh Amendment. It should be recalled that although the language of that amendment simply bars federal law suits against a state by citizens of another state, it has been read, in conjunction with article III, as a ban on lawsuits in federal court against a state even when brought by a citizen of the same state.[21] This construction of the language is said to be derived from the history surrounding the ratification of the amendment. It was added to the Constitution in order to overrule the Supreme Court's determination in *Chisholm v. Geor-*

gia.[22] The precise effect of the Eleventh Amendment has been the subject of much debate.[23] The Court wrote that the purpose of the Eleventh Amendment was to restore the original understanding that states, as sovereigns, were immune from lawsuits in federal court unless they consented to being sued there.[24] Although that interpretation may be a revision of history, it continues to govern Eleventh Amendment doctrine.[25]

There is one difficulty with this view because, if strictly applied, it would mean that unconsenting state officials could not be sued in federal court even when they violate the Fourteenth Amendment. Such a result is problematic because the Fourteenth Amendment serves as a limit on the states themselves providing that "no state shall" deny equal protection of the laws or deprive a person of life, liberty, or property without due process. If strictly applied, the Eleventh Amendment would prevent a federal court from telling state officials to bring their conduct in line with the commands of the Fourteenth Amendment. To avoid this possibility, the Court held in *Ex parte Young*, that state officials who act in violation of the Constitution be stripped of their official authority and may be enjoined from further unconstitutional conduct.[26] State officials, as a result, can be sued for injunctive relief in federal court (unless, of course, the other hurdles discussed in chapter 4 bar the lawsuit).

With respect to damages, however, the Burger Court was not willing to create any similar opening. To the contrary it has strictly applied the Eleventh Amendment to prevent lower federal courts from hearing attempts to recover damages from states that are violating the Constitution or U.S. laws. This rigid application forces victims of such state conduct out of federal courts and into state courts, which are not limited by the Eleventh Amendment.

An example will illustrate the door-closing impact. In *Edelman v. Jordan*, welfare recipients alleged that Illinois state officials were denying welfare benefits in violation of federal law and the Constitution.[27] The benefits were part of a federal welfare program administered by the states, but funded by both the state and federal governments. The welfare recipients asked the federal court to enjoin future violations and to award them retroactive payment of the wrongfully withheld benefits. The federal district court concluded that Illinois had indeed ignored the clear command of federal law in withholding the welfare benefits. It enjoined future violations and directed payment of the wrongfully denied benefits. The court of appeals affirmed, holding that in light of *Ex parte Young*, the Eleventh Amendment did not prevent the award of benefits. The Burger Court, however, reversed that part of the lower court order directing payment of retroactive benefits. It concluded that under *Ex parte Young*, a federal court has power to order injunctive relief compelling state officials to conform their conduct in the future with federal statutory and constitutional requirements. That case, said the Court, does not support the proposition that a federal court can direct a state to pay funds from its treasury. Such an order, said the Court, "stands on quite a different footing" and runs afoul of the Eleventh Amendment.

It is not obvious how an order directing retroactive payments is different from one directing future compliance. As Justice Douglas pointed out in his dissent, prospective injunctive relief ordering state officials to comply with federal requirements in the future may have a serious financial impact on the state. In *Edelman*, the injunctive relief, which required Illinois to process welfare applications more promptly, would cost the state additional money in the future. The majority conceded that prospective injunctive relief may have financial implications for states but nevertheless concluded that such implications are different from those created by a retroactive award of damages. It apparently believed that the state is better able to budget for future compliance.[28]

Whatever the precise differences between a federal court order directing prospective injunctive relief and one granting retroactive damages, it is clear that the former is permitted, whereas the latter is banned by the Eleventh Amendment. It may be conceded that federalism concerns in cases like *Edelman* are undoubtedly present. A federal court order directing payment of funds from a state treasury may have an impact on the state's ability to accomplish its own legislative goals. In its effort to protect the state interest, however, the Burger Court once again simply ignored the federal interest at stake. Illinois had deliberately disregarded the requirements imposed by federal law in processing welfare benefits. Those requirements reflected a national commitment to prompt payment of benefits to people living below a subsistence level. This commitment is certainly substantial and, at the very least, deserved mention before the Court yielded to whatever state interests may have existed.

In recent years the Court has been split over the precise purposes of the Eleventh Amendment. In one case, Justice Brennan (joined by Justices Marshall, Blackmun, and Stevens) argued in a dissenting opinion that the amendment should be read as simply a restriction on federal judicial power to hear cases between a state and citizens of another state, or foreign citizens.[29] Under this view, the amendment does not prohibit federal jurisdiction over other cases authorized by article III, such as those arising under federal law. Moreover, Justice Brennan observed that there is no reason to believe that the Eleventh Amendment went beyond this purpose and established a broad principle of state sovereign immunity from federal lawsuits. On the other hand, a majority of the Court has taken the position that the amendment embodies a principle of sovereign immunity derived from federalism concerns implicit in asking one sovereign to respond in the courts of another.[30]

Although this internal debate continues, the lesson of *Edelman* is easy to discern.[31] The federal courts are closed to individuals attempting to recover damages from states that have violated the federal constitutional or federal law. Such individuals must bring their lawsuit in state court or abandon their attempt to recover damages.

There are exceptions to this limit on the judiciary's power to award damages against a state. These, however, were narrowly construed by the Burger Court and did not significantly open the federal courts to lawsuits seeking damages from a state for its unconstitutional action. The Eleventh Amendment, for example, bans such lawsuits only against an unconsenting state. A state can be sued in a federal court, even for damages, if it consents to the lawsuit. Finding such consent, however, is a difficult task. The Burger Court ruled that a general waiver of sovereign immunity expressed in a state statute is not sufficient to subject the state to a federal lawsuit even though it operates to allow a suit against the state in state court. Rather, to constitute a waiver of the Eleventh Amendment immunity, a state statute must specify the state's intention to subject itself to a suit in federal court.[32] For reasons discussed in chapter 7, a state would prefer to litigate in its own courts, where it is more likely to prevail. Consequently, it is unlikely to enact a law expressly subjecting itself to a lawsuit in the federal forum.

A second exception is derived from the need to reconcile the Eleventh and Fourteenth Amendments. The prohibitions of the Fourteenth Amendment are directed at the states and serve as restrictions on state power. The amendment profoundly altered the relationship between the federal government and the states and, in so doing, limited the sovereignty of the latter. It not only contains self-executing restrictions (section 1), but also gives Congress enforcement power (section 5). As the Burger Court recognized, a long line of cases "sanctioned intrusions by Congress, acting under the Civil War Amendments, into the judicial, executive, and legislative spheres of autonomy previously reserved to the States."[33] The existence of such congressional power, however, raises the possibility of a conflict with the Eleventh Amendment. Suppose Congress, acting under its power to adopt laws enforcing the Fourteenth Amendment, enacts legislation allowing suits against states in federal court. It should be quickly added that such a supposition is not merely hypothetical. In 1972, for example, Congress amended the federal equal employment opportunity law to allow employment discrimination suits to be brought in federal court against states and state officials. The law authorized a federal court to award back pay and attorney's fees to a victim of the discriminatory employment practice. The losing state would have to pay this award from its treasury. Does the Eleventh Amendment protect a state from this kind of congressionally authorized lawsuit in federal court?

To its credit, the Burger Court concluded that the Eleventh Amendment does not preclude federal judicial power where Congress, acting under the Fourteenth Amendment, authorizes the lawsuit.[34] The principle of state sovereignty embodied by the Eleventh Amendment is necessarily limited by the enforcement provisions of the Fourteenth Amendment. The Court specifically stated: "We think that Congress may, in determining what is 'appropriate legislation' for the purpose of enforcing the provisions of the Fourteenth Amendment, provide for private suits against States or state officials which are constitutionally impermissible in other contexts."[35]

What the Court gave with one hand, however, it has limited with the other. It subsequently ruled that the congressional intention to lift the state's immunity must be "unmistakably clear." This requirement has been strictly enforced and prevented Douglas Scanlon from suing California in federal court for allegedly denying him employment because of his handicapping conditions.[36] Scanlon alleged that he had not been hired by a state hospital because he was blind in one eye and a diabetic. He sued under the federal Rehabilitation Act, which prohibits recipients of federal funds from discriminating against "otherwise qualified" handicapped persons in making employment decisions. The act expressly allows enforcement lawsuits to be brought in federal court. Nevertheless, although it was undisputed that California was a recipient of federal financial assistance, the Court held that Scanlon's lawsuit was barred by the Eleventh Amendment. It said: "A general authorization for suit in federal court is not the kind of unequivocal statutory language sufficient to abrogate the Eleventh Amendment. When Congress chooses to subject the States to federal jurisdiction, it must do so specifically."[37] The Rehabilitation Act, the Court concluded, does not expressly authorize lawsuits against states. California, therefore, could not be sued in federal court despite the fact that its receipt of federal financial assistance was conditioned by federal law on a promise to refrain from discrimination against handicapped persons like Scanlon.

The Court's recent unwillingness to imply a waiver of the state's immunity from a state's participation in federally regulated programs marks a distinct break with prior cases. In 1964, for example, the Supreme Court found that an injured employee of an Alabama-owned railroad could sue the state in federal court for damages under the Federal Employer's Liability Act (FELA).[38] It reasoned that Congress had lifted the state's Eleventh Amendment immunity by making FELA applicable to every railroad engaged in interstate commerce. The Court reached this conclusion notwithstanding the absence of any unmistakably clear language subjecting a state to suit in federal court. Twenty-three years later the Rehnquist Court, maintaining the door-closing tradition of its predecessor, made clear that such implied waivers were insufficient, and overruled the Alabama railroad case.[39]

Most significantly, the Court ruled that Section 1983 itself does not remove the Eleventh Amendment barriers because the law does not contain unmistakably clear language that Congress intended to subject states to lawsuits in federal court. That statute, it will be recalled, was enacted by Congress to enforce the prohibitions of the Fourteenth Amendment. Moreover, it expressly outlines an award of damages against officials who, acting under color of state law, subject others to the deprivation of rights secured by the Constitution or federal law. The Court concluded, however, that Section 1983 does not abrogate state immunity:

1983 does not explicitly and by clear language indicate on its face an intent to sweep away the immunity of the states; nor does it have a history which focuses directly on the question of state liability and which shows that Congress considered and firmly decided to abrogate the Eleventh Amendment immunity of the States.[40]

This determination slammed the federal courthouse doors in the face of victims of unconstitutional state conduct who seek recovery for their injuries from the state itself. Assume, for example, that the Pennhurst patients wanted to recover damages for the injuries suffered as a result of the Pennsylvania practices. They could certainly allege that the state officials were acting under color of state law. Moreover, they could further claim, as they did, that the deplorable conditions caused them serious injuries and violated rights secured by the Constitution. The patients appear to satisfy the requirements of Section 1983. Yet, because of the Court's recent construction of the Eleventh Amendment and Section 1983, the lower federal court could not direct the state or its officials to pay damages that might come from the state treasury. To be sure, the patients could ask the Court to order injunctive relief restraining future abuses. Such relief would be appropriate assuming it is based on federal law and does not run afoul of the Our Federalism doctrine discussed in chapter 4. But, such injunctive relief, although important, is incomplete because it does not compensate the patients for the injuries suffered as a result of the inhumane treatment over a period of years. Equally important, in the absence of a real threat of a damage award, the state has little incentive to correct any abuses. State officials can gamble because if they get sued and if they lose, at worst the federal court might direct them to change their conduct in the future.[41]

Damages against Officials in Their Personal Capacity

The limitations on damage awards discussed to this point, it should be noted, apply only to cases in which the plaintiff is attempting to obtain money from the government entity itself. The policy or custom requirement restricts the availability of damage awards against a local governing body. The Eleventh Amendment limits the ability of litigants to receive damages from the state. Neither restriction, however, prevents a federal court from entering a money judgment against the public official, rather than the entity, in his personal capacity. In such circumstances the official—not the entity—is liable.

Practical restrictions, of course, may limit the likelihood of receiving money judgments from public officials who violate the constitutional right of others. These cases can be heard by a jury, and jurors may be reluctant—some argue, properly so—to impose damage awards on police officers, teachers, prison guards, mental health officials, and the many other public officials trying to perform their jobs within the bounds set by the federal constitution.[42] Moreover, even assuming a jury makes such an award, the officials may not have sufficient funds to pay the judgment. In such circumstances the victim of the unconstitutional conduct is left with an empty victory.

Besides these practical considerations, legal barriers prevent the award of damages against governmental officials sued in their personal capacity. Historically, government officers were immune from personal liability for damages resulting from discretionary acts within the scope of their functions. This immunity was based on the following concerns: (1) the injustice of imposing liability on an official who is required to exercise discretion; (2) the danger that threats of liability would deter an official's willingness to perform the job decisively and with good judgment; and (3) the likelihood that imposition of personal liability would deter qualified people from seeking governmental jobs.[43]

These legitimate policies, and the resulting personal immunity of public officials, present special problems in the context of Section 1983 litigation. By its very terms, that law authorizes damage awards against public officials acting under color of state law to deprive others of constitutional rights, and its purpose was to provide a compensation scheme for victims of such unconstitutional conduct. A personal immunity from damages for public officials collides directly with the very language and purpose of Section 1983.

The Burger Court was forced to resolve this tension between the policies underlying the personal immunity of public officials and the language of Section 1983. It did so by importing much of the personal immunity doctrine into Section 1983 litigation. The language of Section 1983, of course, does not provide any immunity for public officers and appears to reject such protection. It states that persons who, acting under color of law, subject others to the deprivation of constitutional rights "shall be liable" to the injured party in an action at law (an action for damages). The "shall be liable" language is not qualified in any way whatsoever. The statute, for example, does not state "shall be liable except to the extent immune under the common law." Yet this is precisely the qualification read into the statute.

In developing a personal immunity doctrine for Section 1983 cases, the Burger Court did not write on a clean slate. Chief Justice Earl Warren had noted previously that the legislative record of Section 1983 offers no clear indication that Congress meant to abolish all common law immunities.[44] The Burger Court continued the common law approach of distinguishing among the various types of officials. Judges, prosecutors, and state legislators, for example, are provided an absolute immunity from damage liability for acts performed within the outer perimeter of their line of duty.[45]

The decision of *Stump v. Sparkman* highlights only too vividly the impact of such absolute immunity.[46] The facts there were not in dispute. Ora McFarlin, mother of Linda Sparkman, presented to Judge Harold Stump of the Circuit Court of DeKalb

County, Indiana, a document entitled "Petition to Have Tubal Ligation Performed on Minor and Indemnity Agreement." In this petition Mrs. McFarlin stated that her daughter was fifteen years old, was "somewhat retarded" (although she attended public school and had been promoted each year), and had been staying out overnight with older youths or young men. The mother stated in the petition that it would be in Linda's best interests if she underwent a sterilization procedure. In the document Mrs. McFarlin agreed to indemnify the doctor and hospital if they were sued in the future. Without notifying the daughter, appointing a legal respresentative, or conducting any kind of hearing at all, Judge Stump signed the petition approving the tubal ligation. Less than a week later, Linda entered the hospital, having been told she was to have her appendix removed. The tubal ligation was performed and she was released unaware of the true nature of her surgery. A child was sterilized without anyone taking the "slightest step to ensure that her rights were protected."[47]

Two years later, Linda married and her inability to become pregnant led to the discovery that she had been sterilized. She subsequently brought a federal lawsuit against the judge, her mother, her mother's lawyer, the doctor, and the hospital. She requested damages for the alleged violation of her constitutional rights. Although the district court held that Judge Stump was absolutely immune from damages, the court of appeals rejected the judge's assertion of absolute immunity and reversed. It held that absolute immunity does not apply when a judge has acted in the "clear absence of all jurisdiction." Judge Stump, the court of appeals concluded, had no power at all under state law to approve the tubal ligation. Second, even if he had power, it was an illegitimate exercise of that authority because of a complete failure to comply with elementary principles of due process.[48] The judge, therefore, could not shield himself from damage liability.

The Supreme Court reversed the court of appeals and agreed with the district court's determination that Judge Stump was absolutely immune from damages for his part in the scheme to sterilize Linda Sparkman. It found that the court of appeals employed an "unduly restrictive" view of the scope of Judge

Stump's jurisdiction and thereby erred in rejecting his absolute immunity defense. Because Judge Stump's court is one of general jurisdiction "neither the procedural errors he may have committed nor the lack of a specific statute authorizing his approval of the petition in question rendered him liable in damages for the consequences of his actions."[49] Moreover, the Court rejected any suggestion that the signing of the petition was not a judicial act and that, therefore, Judge Stump should be stripped of his immunity. The Court agreed that a judge can assert absolute immunity only for "judicial acts" but it found that his approval in this case was such an act because (1) the approval of a petition is a function normally performed by a judge, and (2) the parties dealt with him in his judicial capacity. Accordingly, the Burger Court concluded that Judge Stump is immune from damage liability "even if his approval of the petition was in error."[50]

Undoubtedly, there are sound reasons for the common law rule that judges cannot be sued for damages. As the Court observed in 1872, it is

a general principle of the highest importance to the proper administration of justice that a judicial officer, in exercising the authority vested in him, shall be free to act upon his own convictions, without apprehension of personal consequences to himself. Liability to answer to everyone who might feel himself aggrieved by the action of the judge, would be inconsistent with the possession of this freedom, and would destroy that independence without which no judiciary can be either respectful or useful.[51]

On the other hand, there are important reasons to provide compensation to those injured by unconstitutional official conduct. The difficulty lies in striking the appropriate balance between these competing policies. The court of appeals struck the balance by concluding that the judge's action had "no basis in law or equity and was therefore taken without jurisdiction. In the absence of jurisdiction, a judge is not entitled to judicial immunity in a suit for damages that resulted from his action."[52] The Supreme Court, in contrast, struck the balance in favor of shielding the judge from liability.

Members of the executive branch—unlike judges, prosecutors, and legislators—do not have an absolute shield from damage liability. These officials—such as police officers, bureaucrats, prison guards, state hospital officials, school officials, and even high executive officers (e.g., governors) have a "qualified immunity." In some circumstances they can be held personally liable for damages resulting from their unconstitutional conduct. The circumstances, however, are narrowly defined. These officials are shielded from personal liability for damages insofar as their conduct "does not violate clearly established statutory or constitutional rights of which a reasonable person would have known."[53] Victims of unconstitutional conduct can recover damages only from executive officials who violate such "clearly established" rights.

Proving that a right is clearly established is difficult at best, and the Court has not fully explained what it means by the phrase. It has not specified, for example, where one looks to determine whether a right is clearly established. Does one look to prior decisions of the Supreme Court? appellate courts? or district courts? More troubling, it has not explained just what is meant by a "clearly established right." Much of constitutional litigation involves a case-by-case balancing of interests and, unless there is a previous, factually similar case, it is hard to conclude that the right is clearly established.[54] By way of illustration, assume again that the Pennhurst patients sought damages from the hospital officials in their personal capacity. The district court found that the practices violated the patient's rights under the due process and equal protection clauses of the Fourteenth Amendment as well as their rights to be free from cruel and unusual punishment as secured by the Eighth and Fourteenth Amendments. Are these clearly established rights? To be sure, it is clearly established that a state may not deprive an individual of liberty without due process. But, what constitutes "due process" depends on a balancing of interests that may vary from case to case. Does due process require that a patient suffering from a mental illness be held in the least restrictive environment? If so, what is the "least restrictive environment" demanded by due process? These matters were not clearly established and, thus, would preclude the award of damages against the individual officials responsible for the serious harm to the Pennhurst patients. As a result, Section 1983 would be unable to fulfill its objective of ensuring compensation for victims of unconstitutional conduct. This hypothetical situation confirms the real world conclusion of the court of appeals for the Seventh Circuit that "qualified immunity typically casts a wide net to protect government officials from damage liability whenever balancing is required."[55]

One might well agree that the policies underlying the personal immunity rules are substantial. We need well-qualified public officials who are free to exercise their discretion without undue fear of being subjected to lengthy litigation and exposed to personal liability. Important considerations, however, justify the award of compensation to victims of the unconstitutional actions of public officials. Such compensation returns victims to the position they might have been absent the unconstitutional conduct. And, it serves as a deterrent against further abuses. The Burger Court struck the balance between these competing interests in favor of the public officials rather than the victims and thereby sacrificed the compensation purpose of Section 1983. Indeed, as others have observed: "Where the immunity is absolute, the sacrifice of the compensation objective is complete. Even where the immunity is qualified, the obstacle to recovery may be substantial."[56]

One might not object to the erection of personal immunity barriers if the victims had some other recourse for recovery of damages in the federal court, such as suits directly against the governmental entity.[57] But, as already discussed, the Burger Court closed the other avenues. The Eleventh Amendment prevents the federal court from directing state governments to pay damages, and the "policy or custom" requirement limits the availability of damages against local governing bodies. The picture in federal court is thus complete: Damages are (1) unavailable from the state itself (unless it consents to suit); (2) unavailable from those public officials shielded by absolute immunity; (3) difficult to obtain from local governmental units; and (4) difficult to obtain from those officials cloaked with a qualified immunity.

These doctrines seriously curtail the ability of the lower federal courts to stand between the states and the people as guardians of constitutional rights. Standing alone, they reduce the likelihood that a federal court will award damages for injuries resulting from constitutional abuses. These limits on damage awards, however, do not stand alone. Instead they are among other barriers preventing lower federal courts from awarding damages to victims of unconstitutional conduct.

Redefining the Constitutional Right

One such barrier was created by the Court's redefinition, and narrowing, of one of the constitutional rights often raised in Section 1983 cases, the right to due process of law. The Burger Court redefined that right in a way that restricts the federal court's consideration of a request for damages against state and local officials. The decision in *Parratt v. Taylor* illustrates this aspect of our story.[58] It is a decision that one commentator recently described as "among the most puzzling" of the last decade.[59] The specific facts may seem somewhat trivial. Taylor, an inmate at a Nebraska prison facility, alleged that because prison officials negligently failed to follow their own mail procedure, they lost a $23.50 hobby kit that he had ordered by mail. He maintained that the officials had deprived him of his property without due process in violation of the Fourteenth Amendment. The district court agreed with Taylor and awarded judgment in his favor, explaining:

This is not a situation, where prison officials confiscated contraband. The negligence of the officials in failing to follow their own policies concerning the distribution of mail resulted in a loss of personal property..., which loss should not go without address.[60]

Moreover, the district court held that the officials were not immune from damage actions of this kind. The court of appeals affirmed in a brief order.

The state then asked the Supreme Court to review the case. One might well sympathize with a concern about the use of judicial resources to resolve a $23 dispute. Of course, no one forced the state to pursue an appeal to the court of appeals and then seek Supreme Court review. In addition, the Supreme

Court is not required to hear all cases that come before it and had discretion to decline review of the case.[61] This rather trivial incident, however, raised important legal issues, attracting the attention of twenty-five states that filed "friend of the court" briefs urging reversal. And, that is precisely what the Supreme Court did. It held that although defendants had acted under color of state law to deprive Taylor of his property, they did not subject him to the deprivation of any constitutional right.

The Court, of course, recognized that the Fourteenth Amendment prevents a state from depriving an individual of his property "without due process." It concluded, however, that the state provided all the process that is due. Under state law, Taylor could bring a postdeprivation proceeding against the state in state court. This postdeprivation state remedy satisfied due process even though it contains no provision for punitive damages or a jury trial, both of which would be available in a federal lawsuit under Section 1983. Consequently, *Parratt* established the proposition that a negligent deprivation of property that is unauthorized by state law does not violate the Fourteenth Amendment if an adequate postdeprivation state remedy exists. Three years later, the Court extended the reasoning of *Parratt* and held that even an intentional taking of property by state officials does not violate the Fourteenth Amendment when the state provides an adequate postdeprivation remedy.

Parratt and the later case, *Hudson v. Palmer*, have troubling implications for the role of federal courts as protectors of constitutional rights.[62] The most disturbing feature of these cases is the way they appear to reject the majority opinion in *Monroe v. Pape* that Section 1983 was intended to supplement any state remedy. Indeed, *Parratt* and *Hudson* seem closer to Justice Frankfurter's dissenting opinion in *Monroe*. In *Monroe* Justice Frankfurter urged that Section 1983 damage actions should not be available to challenge unauthorized official conduct if the state provides its own remedy. That position was rejected by a majority of the Court that held that Section 1983 authorizes damage actions in federal court against officials even when the conduct also violates state law and a remedy is provided in a state forum.

Despite that rejection of the Frankfurter position, the Court in *Parratt* used language remarkably similar to phrases found in

Justice Frankfurter's dissenting opinion. The majority in *Parratt* observed that to accept the argument that the official conduct in that case violated the Fourteenth Amendment "would almost necessarily result in turning every alleged injury which may have been inflicted by a state official acting under 'color of law' into a violation of the Fourteenth Amendment cognizable under §1983."[63] The majority feared that it would be "hard to perceive any logical stopping place to such a line of reasoning" and would " 'make of the Fourteenth Amendment a font of tort law to be superimposed upon whatever systems may already be administered by the States.' "[64]

These words echo the concerns of Justice Frankfurter in *Monroe*. He feared that extension of Section 1983 to cases like *Monroe* "makes the extreme limits of federal constitutional power a law to regulate the quotidian business of every traffic policeman, every registrar of elections, every city inspector or investigator, every clerk in every municipal licensing bureau in this country."[65] He added that his narrow view of Section 1983 "recognizes the freedom of the States to fashion their own law of torts in their own way."[66]

Parratt gives new vitality to the Frankfurter position. To be sure, *Parratt* and *Monroe* technically focused on different issues. *Parratt* involved a construction of the Fourteenth Amendment, whereas *Monroe* interpreted the "color of law" language of Section 1983. Nevertheless, both dealt with the relevance of two facts: (1) the allegedly unconstitutional conduct also violated state law, and (2) the state law provided a remedy.[67] In *Monroe*, the Court ruled that these facts were irrelevant to its determination that a federal remedy existed. In *Parratt*, the Court found that these two facts were dispositive requiring dismissal of the federal lawsuit.

The issue in both *Monroe* and *Parratt* ultimately concerned (in Justice Frankfurter's words) "a basic problem of American federalism," the relation of the federal government to the states in the protection of constitutional rights.[68] In *Monroe* the Court rejected Frankfurter's narrow vision of the federal government's role. Two decades later in *Parratt*, however, the Burger Court appeared to embrace Frankfurter's view, finding that unauthorized official misconduct that results in the taking of an individual's property is not a matter for the federal courts. The federalism problem, as in other contexts, was resolved by the Burger Court against those seeking access to the federal courts to vindicate federal constitutional rights.

Parratt and *Hudson* represent at least a partial retreat from the determination in *Monroe* that federal courts are open to constitutional challenges regardless of whether the challenged conduct also violates state law or whether the state provides its own remedy.[69] The scope of that retreat, however, is still uncertain. These cases might be limited to circumstances where: (1) the challenged conduct is random and not authorized by state law; (2) the constitutional claim is based on procedural due process—a claim that the official took an individual's property without prior notice and opportunity to be heard; and (3) the state provides its own postdeprivation remedy. Under the narrow view of *Parratt* and *Hudson*, it could be argued, for example, that Monroe itself would still be decided the same way. The police conduct plainly was unauthorized and Illinois provided a remedy to the victims of such conduct. But, plaintiffs in *Monroe* did not base their claim on procedural due process; rather, plaintiffs claimed that the police searched their home and made arrests without first obtaining warrants as required by the Fourth and Fourteenth Amendments.

In their narrowest aspect, *Parratt* and *Hudson* replace the federal courts with state courts (or agencies) as the forum for awarding damages when there has been an unauthorized taking of property by public officials. The reasoning of the cases, especially their reliance on federalism concerns, however, is not easily confined to procedural due process cases. As Justice Blackmun warned, "*Parratt* and *Hudson* could be used to deny a Section 1983 action to anyone claiming a constitutional violation by an official unauthorized to act as he did, as long as the State provides a damages remedy after the fact."[70] Under the broad view of these cases, *Monroe* itself would be decided differently today. The police misconduct was not authorized by state law and Illinois provided its own damages remedy, so the federal court would be closed to the Monroe family.

Measure of Damages

The Burger Court found an additional way to limit the effectiveness of Section 1983 in providing compensation to victims of unconstitutional conduct. It did so by taking a limited view of the kinds of damages that may be awarded. Over the centuries a body of rules has developed to implement the basic principle that an individual should be compensated for injuries resulting from the denial of a right. These rules allow a court to award various forms of damages.[71] Perhaps the most common form is known as *compensatory damages* and permits an award of an amount that compensates the victim for actual losses or injuries, including mental and emotional distress resulting from the challenged conduct. A second form, *punitive* (or *exemplary*) *damages*, is not intended to compensate for loss but instead is designed to punish the wrongdoer for flagrant or malicious conduct and to deter similar conduct in the future. Punitive damages can be awarded in addition to any compensatory damages that might be assessed. A third kind of damages is known as *nominal damages*, a small sum awarded to a victim who has suffered no substantial injury or loss but nevertheless has had a right invaded. Finally, in some limited instances *presumed damages* are allowed to be assessed against the wrongdoer. These damages can be substantial in amount and are awarded without proof of any actual loss or injury. For example, certain forms of defamation are presumed to cause significant loss and injury, and damages can be awarded without establishing that in fact such loss or injury occurred.

In recent years, the Court has been asked to decide the extent to which these general rules on damages apply in cases brought under Section 1983 to recover for the deprivation of constitutional rights. For the most part the Court adopted the general rules as the starting point for determining the prerequisites for the award of damages in 1983 cases. It has concluded, for example, that an individual can receive compensatory damages for actual loss and injury, including mental and emotional distress caused by the denial of a constitutional right.[72] Moreover, it has allowed courts to order officials to pay punitive damages for flagrant unconstitutional conduct.[73] With respect to this latter form of damages, however, the Court added a significant qualification. It ruled that punitive damages may be awarded against officials, but they may not be awarded against a governmental entity.[74] The Court reasoned that an award of punitive damages against the entity itself would only punish the taxpayers who, of course, took no part in the misconduct. Moreover, the Court found that the deterrence rationale does not justify making punitive damages available against a governing body. It determined that there is no reason to suppose that corrective action, such as discharge of the offending official, would not be taken unless punitive damages are awarded against the entity. Allowing juries and courts to assess punitive damages against the official, said the Court, provides sufficient protection against the prospect of recurrent constitutional violations.

A difficult problem arises with regard to damages when an individual is denied a constitutional right but is unable to show any actual loss. In such circumstance, should a jury or court be free to award substantial damages to reflect the importance of the constitutional right? In *Carey v. Piphus*, for example, students alleged that they had been suspended from school without first being provided an adequate opportunity to be heard.[75] The lower courts found that the students had been denied procedural due process rights protected by the Fourteenth Amendment. The school officials did not challenge that determination on appeal to the Supreme Court, but instead asked the Court to review the court of appeals' ruling that a substantial nonpunitive amount could be awarded as presumed damages even if the students did not suffer any actual loss other than the denial of procedural due process. The Supreme Court agreed to review the case and subsequently ruled that the lower court had erred in permitting an award of such damages. It plainly rejected the suggestion that, as in defamation cases, the jury or court should be allowed to presume that injury flows from the denial of procedural due process. The Court observed that the doctrine of presumed damages has no application to procedural due process cases because it is unreasonable to assume that every departure from constitutionally mandated procedures is as likely to cause distress as the publication of certain forms of defamation. Moreover, the Court saw no particular difficulty in producing evidence that actual injury, such as mental distress, was caused by the denial of procedural due process. Accordingly, the Court concluded that "although mental and emotional distress caused by the denial of procedural due process itself is compensable under §1983,...neither the likelihood of such injury nor the difficulty of proving it is so great as to justify awarding compensatory damages without proof that such injury actually was caused."[76]

The Court did concede that, even in the absence of provable injuries, some monetary award is justifiable because of the importance of the right to procedural due process. It borrowed from the body of general rules relating to damages and held that a jury or court could assess nominal damages in the absence of proof of actual loss. The Court then returned the case to the district court for reconsideration in light of these principles and instructed that if the lower court finds no actual injury flowing from the denial of due process, it should award the students a nominal sum not to exceed one dollar.

In the absence of actual provable injuries, the conclusion that only a single dollar may be awarded to remedy the denial of due process has troubling implications for the effectiveness of Section 1983. First, it reduces the deterrent effect of lawsuits brought under that statute. Plainly, the prospect of an award of one dollar has little capacity to deter an official from future misconduct. Second, such a nominal award tends to trivialize the importance of the constitutional right by sending the message that the inherent value of procedural due process is a buck, at best. Finally, the limitation on damage awards may discourage the bringing of Section 1983 lawsuits in federal court. Individuals, like the students in *Carey*, may not be entitled to injunctive relief because they may be unable to show a substantial likelihood that they will be suspended in the future.[77] If they could show actual injuries flowing from the constitutional deprivation they could recover damages and would have good reason to bring the case. Without such provable injuries, the prospect of recovering one dollar provides little incentive for bringing a federal lawsuit. In addition, an individual who prevails on the constitutional claim but receives only a nominal amount nevertheless is entitled to recover attorney's fees and the costs of litigation.[78] It is unclear, however, whether litigants would be—indeed, should be—encouraged to bring a lawsuit just so their lawyers could recover fees.

Carey did not completely foreclose the chances of recovering presumed damages in Section 1983 cases. It dealt only with procedural due process cases and left open the possibility that cases involving other constitutional rights may be treated differently. As the Court said in Carey, "The elements and prerequisites for recovery of damages appropriate to compensate injuries caused by the deprivation of one constitutional right are not necessarily appropriate to compensate injuries caused by deprivation of another."[79]

Eight years later, however, the Burger Court closed that opening and the victim this time was Edward Stachura, a tenured school teacher in the Memphis, Michigan public schools.[80] Stachura taught a seventh-grade life science course, using a textbook that had been approved by the school board and that included a chapter on human reproduction. As part of the study of this material he showed the students pictures of his wife during her pregnancy and two films concerning human growth and sexuality, both of which had been approved by the principal. A number of parents complained about these teaching methods. Although the complaints were based largely on inaccurate rumors, the school board suspended Stachura without pay for the remainder of the school year.

Stachura brought a lawsuit in federal court under Section 1983 claiming a deprivation of liberty and property without due process in violation of the Fourteenth Amendment, as well as a denial of academic freedom as protected by the First and Fourteenth Amendments. He sought damages for these constitutional violations. The district court instructed the jury that it could award damages based on the value or importance of the constitutional rights. The district judge told the jury:

If you find that the Plaintiff has been deprived of a Constitutional right, you may award damages to compensate him for the deprivation. Damages for this type of injury are more difficult to measure than damages for a physical injury or injury to one's property. There are no medical bills or other expenses by which you can judge how much compensation is appropriate. In one sense, no monetary value we place upon Constitutional rights can measure their importance in our society or compensate a citizen adequately for their deprivation. However, just because these rights are not capable of precise evaluation does not mean that an appropriate monetary amount should not be awarded.

The precise value you place upon any Constitutional right which you find was denied to Plaintiff is within your discretion. You may wish to consider the importance of the right in our system of government, the role which this right has played in the history of our republic, [and] the significance of the right in the context of the activities which the Plaintiff was engaged in at the time of the violation of the right.[81]

The jury found the school officials and the board liable and awarded \$275,000 in compensatory damages and \$36,000 in punitive damages.

When the case reached the Supreme Court the sole issue was whether damages could be awarded based on the value of the right. Stachura urged that *Carey* did not control because his case involved not only procedural due process claims but also First Amendment rights. Relying on the opening in *Carey*, he argued that First Amendment cases should be treated differently and that the jury in such cases should be allowed to presume the existence of substantial damages flowing from the denial of First Amendment rights.

The Supreme Court, however, rejected that suggestion. *Carey*, it concluded, did not permit different resolution of the damage issue depending on the nature of the constitutional right at stake. The Court emphasized that in Section 1983 cases damages must be designed to compensate. "That conclusion simply leaves no room for noncompensatory damages measured by the jury's perception of the abstract 'importance' of a constitutional right."[82] The Court observed that damages based on the importance or value of a constitutional right are an "unwieldy tool for ensuring compliance with the Constitution."[83] Because there is no sound guidance concerning the monetary value to be placed on constitutional rights, it feared that if presumed damages were available, juries might award arbitrary amounts or use their discretion to punish unpopular defendants. Finally, the Court opined that presumed damages are not necessary to vindicate constitutional rights. Nominal, not presumed, damages are the appropriate means of vindicating those constitutional rights whose deprivation has not caused any provable loss or injury. The Court, therefore, returned the case to the district court for a new trial on the damage issue. The trial court could award compensatory and punitive damages but no damages based on the importance of the First Amendment rights.[84]

Conclusion

It should be stressed that when considered separately, each of the developments discussed in this chapter has some reasonable basis. The difficulty results from the cumulative impact of these various developments. First, individuals denied constitutional rights are not permitted to recover damages in federal court from the state itself. Second, they are not allowed recovery against a local governmental entity unless they can establish that the injuries were caused by an official policy or custom. Third, they will not be awarded damages against individual officials with absolute immunity, and are not likely to recover from those with qualified immunity, unless they meet the rather difficult task of showing that the officials violated a clearly established constitutional right. Fourth, those who overcome these hurdles may find that the amount of any damages is nominal, like the one dollar awarded the plaintiff in *Carey*. Finally, individuals denied property without due process may have no recourse at all in federal courts.

These various developments have seriously eroded the effectiveness of Section 1983 as a vehicle for compensating victims of unconstitutional conduct by state and local officials. Moreover, they have undermined the federal court's role in guarding constitutional rights and providing adequate remedies when violations occur. Indeed, "the prospect of Section 1983 as an effective scheme of compensation for official misconduct seems largely illusory."[85] Stripped of a federal remedy and a federal forum, the individual must resort to the state courts for relief from unconstitutional official conduct.

Notes

1. Comment, *The Civil Rights Act: Emergence of Adequate Federal Civil Remedy?* 76 IND. L. J. 361, 363 (1951).
2. 365 U.S. 167 (1961).
3. *Id.* at 183.
4. P. SCHUCK, SUING GOVERNMENTS: CITIZEN REMEDIES FOR OFFICIAL WRONGS 200 (1983).
5. *See* Whitman, *Constitutional Torts*, 79 MICH. L. REV. 5 (1980).
6. Section 1983 applies against persons who act under color of state law and, thus, does not apply to federal officials.
7. 436 U.S. 658 (1978).
8. *Id.* at 690.
9. *See* Oklahoma City v. Tuttle, 471 U.S. 808 (1985).
10. *See, e.g.*, Bandes, *Monell, Parratt, Daniels and Davidson: Distinguishing a Custom or Policy from Random Unauthorized Act*, 72 IOWA L. REV. 101 (1986); Mead, *42 U.S.C. Section 1983; Municipality Liability: The Monell Sketch Becomes a Distorted Picture*, 65 N.C.L. REV. 518 (1987).
11. *See, e.g.*, City of St. Louis v. Praprotnik, 108 S. Ct. 915 (1988); Pembaur v. Cincinnati, 475 U.S. 469 (1986); Oklahoma City v. Tuttle, 471 U.S. 808 (1988). Recently, the Court did eliminate one source of confusion. In *City of Canton v. Harris*—U.S.—(1989) (57 U.S. L.W. 4270, Feb. 28, 1989), it held that municipality liability under Section 1983 is not limited to instances where the policy itself is unconstitutional. Such liability can also be found when a valid policy is applied in an unconstitutional manner so long as the application can be attributed to the entity itself.
12. Oklahoma City v. Tuttle, 471 U.S. 808, 823 n.6 (1985).
13. Snyder, *The Final Authority Analysis: A Unified Approach to Municipal Liability Under Section 1983*, 1986 WIS. L. REV. 633.
14. Pembaur v. Cincinnati, 475 U.S. 469, 481 n.9 (1986).
15. *Compare* Pembaur v. Cincinnati, 475 U.S. 469 (1986) *with* City of St. Louis v. Praprotnik, 108 S.Ct. 915 (1988).
16. Pembaur v. Cincinnati, 475 U.S. 469, 483 n.12 (1986) (Justice Brennan joined by Justices Marshall, White, and Blackmun).
17. City of St. Louis v. Praprotnik, 108 S.Ct. 915, 925 (1988).
18. *Id.* at 928 (Brennan, J., concurring).
19. Brown, *Municipal Liability under Section 1983 and the Ambiguities of Burger Court Federalism: A Comment on City of Oklahoma City v. Tuttle and Pembaur v. City of Cincinnati—the "Official Policy" Cases*, 27 B.C.L. REV. 833, 909 (1986).

20. Maine v. Thiboutot, 448 U.S. 1 (1980).
21. Hans v. Louisiana, 134 U.S. 1 (1890).
22. 2 U.S. (2 Dall.) 419 (1793).
23. For an excellent, readable account of the history, *see* J. ORTH, THE JUDICIAL POWER OF THE UNITED STATES: THE ELEVENTH AMENDMENT IN AMERICAN HISTORY (1987).
24. Hans v. Louisiana, 134 U.S. 1 (1890).
25. *See* J. ORTH, *supra* note 23.
26. 209 U.S. 123 (1908).
27. 415 U.S. 651 (1974).
28. *Id.* at 666 n.11.
29. Atascadero State Hospital v. Scanlon, 473 U.S. 234, 247 (1981) (Brennan, J., dissenting).
30. Pennhurst State School and Hospital v. Halderman, 465 U.S. 89 (1984).
31. Welch v. State Department of Highways and Public Transportation, 107 S. Ct. 2941 (1987). For a sampling of the recent literature on the purposes of the Eleventh Amendment, *see* Amar, *Of Sovereignty and Federalism*, 96 YALE L.J. 1425 (1987); Brown, *State Sovereignty Under the Burger Court—How the Eleventh Amendment Survived the Death of the Tenth: Some Broader Implications of Atascadero State Hospital v. Scanlon*, 74 GEO. L.J. 363 (1988); Field, *The Eleventh Amendment and Other Sovereign Immunity Doctrines: Part One*, 126 U. PA. L. REV. 515 (1978); Fletcher, *A Historical Interpretation of the Eleventh Amendment: A Narrow Construction of an Affirmative Grant of Jurisdiction Rather than a Prohibition Against Jurisdiction*, 35 STAN. L. REV. 1033 (1983); Nowak, *The Scope of Congressional Power to Create Causes of Action Against State Governments and the History of the 11th and 14th Amendments*, 75 COLUM. L. REV. 1413 (1975).
32. Atascadero State Hospital v. Scanlon, 473 U.S. 234 (1985).
33. Fitzpatrick v. Bitzer, 427 U.S. 445, 455 (1976).
34. *Id.* In *Pennsylvania v. Union Gas Co.*,____U.S.____(1989), a majority concluded that Congress also has powers under the commerce clause to abrogate the state's immunity.
35. *Id.* at 456.
36. Atascadero State Hospital v. Scanlon, 473 U.S. 234 (1985).
37. *Id.* at 246. *Accord, Delmuth v. Muth*,____U.S.____(1989) (intent to abrogate must appear unequivocally in the text of the law).
38. Parden v. Terminal Ry. Co., 377 U.S. 184 (1964).
39. Welch v. State Dept. of Highways and Pub. Transp., 107 S.Ct. 2941 (1987).
40. Quern v. Jordan, 440 U.S. 332, 345 (1979). In *Will v. Michigan Department of State Police*,____U.S.____(1989), the Court held that states, and state officials sued in their official capacities, are not "per-

sons" within meaning of Section 1983. This means that Section 1983 actions cannot be brought against states and state officials even in state court.

41. The only financial incentive to changing the practices is derived from the possibility that the federal court might direct the states to pay the plaintiff's attorney's fees. The Civil Rights Attorney's Fees Award Act, 42 U.S.C. section 1988, has been interpreted by the Court to authorize a federal court to award attorney's fees against a state. Hutto v. Finney, 437 U.S. 678 (1978).

42. P. SCHUCK, *supra* note 4, at 59–81.

43. *See* Scheuer v. Rhodes, 416 U.S. 232 (1974).

44. Pierson v. Ray, 386 U.S. 547 (1967).

45. *See* Stump v. Sparkman, 435 N.J. 345 (1978) (judges); Imbler v. Pachtman, 424 U.S. 409 (1976) (prosecutors); Tenney v. Brandhove, 341 U.S. 367 (1951) (legislators).

46. 435 U.S. 349 (1978).

47. 552 F.2d 172, 176 (7th Cir. 1977).

48. *Id.*

49. 435 U.S. at. 359–60.

50. *Id.* at 364.

51. Bradley v. Fisher, 80 U.S. 335, 347 (1872).

52. 552 F. 2d 172, 176 (7th Cir. 1977).

53. Harlow v. Fitzgerald, 457 U.S. 800, 818 (1982).

54. *See, e.g.*, Anderson v. Creighton, 479 U.S. 808 (1987) (right to be free from warrantless search not supported by probable cause and exigent circumstances is clearly established; nevertheless, not clearly established that search of plaintiff's home was objectively unreasonable).

55. Benson v. Allphiss, 786 F.2d 268 (7th Cir.), *cert. denied*, 479 U.S. 848 (1986).

56. P. Low & J. JEFFRIES, CIVIL RIGHTS ACTIONS 43 (1988).

57. *See* P. SCHUCK, *supra* note 4, at 82–121 (arguing for greater immunity for officials and expanded liability for governmental bodies).

58. 451 U.S. 527 (1981).

59. Monaghan, *State Law Wrongs, State Law Remedies, and the Fourteenth Amendment*, 86 COLUM. L. REV. 979 (1986).

60. 451 U.S. 527, 531 (1981).

61. *See* 28 U.S.C. §1254.

62. 468 U.S. 517 (1984).

63. 451 U.S. at 544.

64. *Id.* citing Paul v. Davis, 424 U.S. 693, 701 (1976).

65. 365 U.S. 167, 242 (1961) (dissenting).

66. *Id.* at 245.

67. *See* Monaghan, *supra* note 59, at 979.

68. 365 U.S. at 222.

69. *See generally* Shapiro, *Keeping Civil Rights Actions Against State Officials in Federal Court: Avoiding the Reach of Parratt v. Taylor and Hudson v. Palmer*, 3 LAW & INEQUALITY 161 (1985).

70. Blackmun, *Section 1983 and Federal Protection of Individual Rights—Will the Statute Remain Alive or Fade Away?*, 60 N.Y.U. L. REV. 1, 25 (1985).

71. *See generally*, Memphis Community School Dist. v. Stachura, 477 U.S. 299, 305–313 (1986).

72. *See* Carey v. Piphus, 435 U.S. 247, 257 (1978).

73. Smith v. Wade, 461 U.S. 30 (1988).

74. City of Newport v. Fact Concerts Inc., 453 U.S. 247 (1987).

75. 435 U.S. 247 (1978).

76. *Id.* at 264.

77. *See* City of Los Angeles v. Lyons, 461 U.S. 95 (1983). The student might request an injunction directing the school officials to change school records. Carey v. Piphus, 435 U.S. 247, 252 (1978).

78. 42 U.S.C. §1988. *See generally* M. SCHWARTZ & J. KIRKLIN, SECTION 1983 LITIGATION: CLAIMS DEFENSES, AND FEES, 340–51 (1986).

79. 435 U.S. 247, 264–65 (1978).

80. Memphis Community School Dist. v. Stachura, 477 U.S. 299 (1986).

81. *Id.* at 302–3, 106 S. Ct. 2537, 2540–41 (1986).

82. *Id.* at 309–10.

83. *Id.* at 310.

84. Although the Court unanimously agreed that the case must be remanded for a new trial on damages, four Justices (Brennan, Marshall, Blackmun, and Stevens) were convinced that portions of the majority opinion might be read to suggest that damages are limited to out-of-pocket fees, monetary loss, and such injuries as mental anguish and harm to reputation. These four emphasized that although damages could not be awarded based on the importance of the right, the violation of a constitutional right may itself constitute a compensable injury. They did not elaborate on this distinction. 477 U.S. at 313–16 (Marshall, J., concurring).

85. P. Low & J. JEFFRIES, *supra* note 56, at 43.

Chapter 6
Rules of Preclusion

The developments discussed in the previous chapters close the federal courts and force victims of alleged unconstitutional state action into state courts. In some instances the door-closing impact is direct. In a case like *Warth*, for example, the federal court lacks power to hear the case because the plaintiff does not have standing to sue.[1] Similarly, if the federal court concludes that *Younger* and its notions of Our Federalism apply to a case, the litigant must turn to the state courts.[2] The federal court in those instances lacks power to grant the requested relief. When the Eleventh Amendment applies, the individual is again completely barred from obtaining relief in a federal court and must proceed, if at all, in state court.[3] So too, in cases like *Parratt*, the Court has redefined the constitutional right in such a way as to leave the individual no remedy other than a lawsuit in state court based on state law.[4]

In other instances the door closing is accomplished indirectly. Prior to a lawsuit it may not be clear whether the individual would be barred from the federal forum. The plaintiffs in *Warth*, for example, believed that they had satisfied the standing requirements, and four justices agreed. After the *Warth* decision, however, a victim of allegedly unconstitutional practices would have to assess the likelihood that resources may have to be spent in federal court on litigating the threshold question of standing.

Such an individual may well prevail on that question, but at a substantial cost. Moreover, while the standing issue is being fought over, enforcement of the underlying constitutional right is delayed. Discouraged by the prospects of the additional expense and the delay, the individual may forego the federal forum and file initially in state court.

The state courts, of course, may hear federal constitutional claims and it is not surprising that the number of such claims being brought in state courts under Section 1983 has increased in the past decade.[5] The doctrines discussed in the previous chapters encouraged this development, and the Supreme Court expressly ratified it by ruling that state courts have jurisdiction to hear Section 1983 cases.[6] Although the Court left open the question whether state courts must hear Section 1983 matters,[7] one commentator has recently reported that every state court system has agreed to hear these kinds of cases raising federal constitutional rights.[8]

Once in the state court the individual may be precluded from ever bringing his or her constitutional claim in a lower federal court. Indeed, part of the plan for closing the federal courts to these cases has included strict, some might say harsh,[9] application of preclusion rules and the full faith and credit statute.[10] This development by the Court has been the final nail closing the federal courthouse doors.

To fully appreciate the significance of this aspect of our story it is necessary to understand the rules of preclusion, which often baffle law students as well as lawyers. One federal judge observed that these rules are "universally respected, but actually not very well liked."[11] As the rest of this chapter reveals, this observation, made over forty years ago, no longer accurately portrays the Supreme Court's view. Rules of preclusion have now become a "rather prominent feature of our federal litigation landscape."[12]

These rules can be divided into two categories, those relating to *claim* preclusion and those relating to *issue* preclusion. Under claim preclusion, a final judgment on the merits bars relitigation of the same claim between the same parties in a subsequent lawsuit.[13] A losing party, of course, can appeal a judgment to a higher court and seek a reversal. The party, however, cannot begin a separate lawsuit and attempt to relitigate the claim. The first judgment is said to extinguish the plaintiff's claim.[14] For these purposes, a claim includes "all rights of the plaintiff to remedies against the defendant with respect to all or any part of the transaction, or series of transactions, out of which the action arose."[15] Under the modern view, what constitutes a transaction or series of transactions is determined "pragmatically, giving weight to such considerations as whether the facts [of the two lawsuits] are related in time, space, origin, or motivation, whether they form a convenient trial unit, and whether their treatment as a unit conforms to the parties' expectations or business understanding or usage."[16]

Consider the following illustration of the operation of claim preclusion. Assume that the patients in Pennhurst sue in state court alleging that state officials were violating state law by subjecting them to inhumane conditions and not providing treatment. Suppose the state trial court holds that no state law has been violated and dismisses the lawsuit. The patients could appeal to a higher state court arguing that the trial judge was wrong. If the patients, however, instead file a second lawsuit against the same state officials and again challenge the identical conditions on the same state law grounds, they will be precluded from litigating the second case by claim preclusion. The judgment in the first case precludes relitigation because the two lawsuits involve the same claim.

Now suppose that the same patients bring a second lawsuit against the same state officials but this time challenge the conditions on the basis of a law not raised in the first lawsuit. The second lawsuit, for example, might assert a violation of the state constitution. Claim preclusion would bar this second lawsuit as well even though the legal question presented was not raised or decided in the first case. The two cases are between the same parties and arise out of a single transaction, or series of transactions—the conditions at the hospital—and, thus, involve the same claim. As a result, the first judgment extinguishes the claim that includes all rights to a remedy, even those that were not asserted, but could have been in the first case. The effect of this aspect of claim preclusion is to force a party to raise in one lawsuit all bases for recovery against the defendant.

The second category of preclusion rules involves issue preclusion, which applies when the first and second lawsuit concern different claims but the same issue arises in both. Application of issue preclusion requires satisfaction of three requirements: (1) the issue to be precluded in the second case must be identical to the issue actually decided in the first case; (2) the determination of the issue in the first case must have been necessary to the judgment in that case; and (3) the party against whom issue preclusion is sought in the second case must have had a full and fair opportunity to litigate that issue.[17]

Once again an example may help illustrate the doctrine. Suppose in the first lawsuit the Pennhurst patients sue state officials in state court claiming that these officials failed to provide any treatment programs and thereby violated a state statute. Assume that the patients lose; the court decides that in fact the patients received treatment programs. The same patients bring a second lawsuit, this time not against the state officials but against local officials involved in the commitment process. They again attack the alleged absence of treatment programs, which was the subject of the first case. Technically, claim preclusion does not bar the second lawsuit because it is against a different party. Nevertheless, the patients may be precluded from relitigating the same factual issue of whether treatment programs were provided. That issue was actually decided and cannot be relitigated so long as its determination was essential to the prior judgment, and the patients had a full and fair opportunity to litigate it in the first case.

In the second case, the patients could assert other factual or legal contentions that were not asserted in the prior lawsuit against the state officials. Issue preclusion, unlike claim preclusion, only prevents relitigation of issues actually decided. It does not preclude litigation of those legal or factual issues not actually raised and determined in the first case.

Preclusion rules are based on the sound principle that litigation must come to an end, and the policies served by these rules are clear. First, they are intended to relieve parties of the cost and vexation of multiple lawsuits. Second, by preventing relitigation they conserve judicial resources and allow courts to address matters not previously heard. Finally, they remove the risk that a second court might reach a determination inconsistent with the first court. By preventing inconsistencies, the rules encourage reliance on judicial decisions.[18] Application of preclusion rules, thus, "is central to the purpose for which civil courts have been established, the conclusive resolution of disputes within their jurisdiction."[19] Modern procedural systems are designed to permit full development of the contentions of the parties.[20] Rules governing civil litigation include various provisions allowing parties to fully present whatever factual and legal theories rise out of the conduct being challenged. The rules permit notice pleading,[21] alternative (even inconsistent) positions,[22] liberal amendments to raise contentions previously omitted,[23] joinder of parties[24] and claims,[25] extensive discovery of evidentiary material,[26] and freedom to develop theories during the trial.[27] Such procedural rules have expanded the initial opportunity to fully litigate a case. Having been afforded that initial opportunity, the litigant is not entitled a second opportunity. At that point preclusion rules operate to deny the individual a second "day in court." In this way, the preclusion rules mediate the litigant's interest in obtaining a full opportunity to be heard and society's interest in the finality of judgments.

The difficulty with preclusion rules arise not in the abstract, but in their application in specific cases. For example, suppose the Pennhurst patients, discouraged about the prospects of having their case heard in federal court because of the developments previously discussed, sue in state court alleging that the conditions violate state law as well as the federal constitution. If they lose, can they begin a second lawsuit in federal court seeking to again litigate the federal constitutional issue? Or, assume that in the first case in state court they rely only on state law. If they lose, can they bring a second lawsuit in federal court based on the federal constitution?

Prior to the Burger Court era, the Supreme Court suggested that usual preclusion rules might not apply when an individual first litigates in state court and then brings a second case in federal court raising a federal constitutional issue. In *England v. Louisiana State Board of Medical Examiners*, the Court observed that an individual who actually raises the constitutional issue in the state court may not later raise the same issue in federal court.[28] Traditional issue preclusion rules would bar relitigation of the issue. The individual in those circumstances could appeal through the state court system and then attempt to obtain Supreme Court review of the highest state court's judgment.[29] That individual, however, has lost any right to bring the issue before a federal district court. On the other hand, an individual who presents only the state law issues to the state court and reserves the federal constitutional issue for federal court may subsequently litigate that federal question in the district court. In short, traditional claim preclusion rules would not apply in this context.

England rejected the application of claim preclusion because of the importance of allowing a litigant to gain access to a federal court to litigate a federal constitutional issue. The Court observed that the " 'right of a party plaintiff to choose a federal court where there is a choice cannot be properly denied.' "[30] Moreover, the Court stressed the right of access to a federal district court. It recognized that a state court litigant raising a constitutional question could seek review by the Supreme Court. That was the original plan under the Judiciary Act of 1789.[31] Such direct appellate review, however, is not an adequate substitute for initial district court consideration of the constitutional issue. As the court said in *England*: "Limiting the litigant to review here [the Supreme Court] would deny him the benefit of a federal trial court's role in constructing a record and making fact findings. How the facts are found will often dictate the decision of federal claims."[32] Accordingly, the Supreme Court concluded that the "possibility of appellate review by this Court of a state court determination may not be substituted, against a party's wishes, for his right to litigate his federal claims in the federal courts."[33]

England was technically limited to instances where an individual brings a case in federal court claiming a violation of both state law and the federal constitution and the federal court decides to abstain from deciding the case. Under such abstention, the federal court postpones any federal proceedings until the individual goes to state court.[34] The purpose of abstention is to allow the state courts to first rule on an unclear question of state law. Such clarification may lead to a decision for the plaintiff and remove the need to rule on the constitutional question.[35]

The concern in *England* was whether the plaintiff would be allowed to return to federal court to pursue the federal constitutional issue if he or she does not prevail on the state law issue in state court. In this context the Court determined that normal claim preclusion rules would not apply. The litigant can reserve the right to return to federal court for determination of the constitutional issue there so long as that issue was not presented to the state court.

At least one federal court concluded that the principle announced in *England* should apply more broadly than the abstention context. Before filing in federal court, the plaintiff in *Lombard v. Board of Education* had commenced two proceedings in state court to challenge his suspension and termination from a teaching position.[36] After losing in state court, he filed a lawsuit in federal court under Section 1983 alleging that the school board's actions violated his constitutional rights. The board moved to dismiss the federal action on the ground that it was barred by claim preclusion. The board had a rather strong argument, at least if traditional preclusion rules applied. The state cases and the federal case involved the same parties and rose out of the same series of transactions, Lombard's suspension and termination. They, therefore, presented a single claim. As a result, the state court judgments barred Lombard from litigating all legal theories that were actually raised or could have been raised in the state proceedings. The constitutional theories were in fact not raised in state court although they could have been and, consequently, under claim preclusion they could not be asserted in a subsequent lawsuit.

The court of appeals for the Second Circuit, however, refused to preclude Lombard from raising his federal constitutional theories in federal court. The court concluded that the doctrine of issue preclusion does apply in full force in a subsequent case brought in federal court under Section 1983. Consequently, a federal court litigant is prevented from relitigating a federal constitutional issue that was determined in a prior state court proceeding. *Claim* preclusion, however, does not apply, and a prior state court judgment does not bar federal court consideration of constitutional challenges that were not actually decided in the state court.

142   Protecting Constitutional Freedoms

The court offered two reasons for its exception to traditional
claim preclusion rules. First, relying on *Monroe v.
Pape*, the court reasoned that the remedy provided by Section 1983 was intended
to supplement any state court remedies.[37] To apply claim preclusion would overrule the "essence" of *Monroe*.[38] Second, an
individual challenging state action should have the option to
contest that action on state grounds in state court and on federal
grounds in federal court. In this manner a role is preserved for
the state courts as interpreters of their own law. But, at the same
time, the federal courts can perform the role envisioned by Congress when it enacted Section 1983.[39] That role was to serve as
"guardians of the people's federal rights."[40]

The Burger Court had a different vision of the federal court's
role, and its plan for closing the federal courts did not include
exceptions to preclusion rules. To the contrary, in a series of
cases the Court made clear that these rules could be used to close
the federal courthouse doors.[41] The Court's refusal to follow the
Lombard approach and allow exceptions was premised in part on
the full faith and credit statute that provides that state court
judicial proceedings "shall have the same full faith and credit in
every court within the United States . . . as they have by law or
usuage in the courts of such State."[42] This law has existed in
essentially unchanged form since 1790.[43] The Court interpreted
the statute as requiring a federal court to give a state court
judgment the same preclusive effect as it would be given by the
state court that rendered the judgment.[44]

Moreover, the Court expressly rejected the argument that
Congress intended Section 1983 to repeal the full faith and credit
statute or contravene general preclusion rules.[45] Justice Blackmun, joined by Justices Brennan and Marshall, argued vigorously for such an exception in Section 1983 cases. He urged that
when Congress enacted Section 1983 as part of the Reconstruction effort it "specifically made a determination that federal oversight of constitutional determinations through the federal courts
was necessary to ensure the effective enforcement of constitutional rights."[46]

A majority of the Court, however, was unpersuaded. It ruled
that the full faith and credit statute required a federal court to
give a state court judgment the same effect as the state would

give it. If the state court would apply traditional preclusion rules then the federal court must do the same.[47] The majority found nothing in the language or history of Section 1983 suggesting that Congress intended to create an exception when a litigant first goes to state court and then subsequently raises a federal constitutional issue in federal court.

The Court's approach is illustrated by *Migra v. Warren City School District*.[48] Ethel Migra had been employed by the Warren City School District as a supervisor of elementary education. In 1979, the board voted not to renew her contract. Migra sued in state court alleging that the board had breached a contract and that individual board members had wrongfully interfered with the employment contract. The state court ruled for Migra, ordered her reinstatement, and directed the board to pay compensatory damages.

Migra then began a lawsuit in federal court under Section 1983 contending that the board's actions had been intended to punish her because she had participated in the design of a desegregation plan opposed by board members. The federal complaint claimed that the board had violated the federal constitution by intruding on Migra's First Amendment rights, denying her equal protection of the laws, and depriving her of property without due process. These legal theories had not been asserted in the state court case. Nevertheless, the district court dismissed the federal action on the basis of claim preclusion, and the court of appeals affirmed. The Supreme Court agreed to review the case in order to decide whether a state court judgment should have claim preclusive effect in a federal court lawsuit brought under Section 1983 to remedy the deprivation of federal constitutional rights.

The Court had previously ruled that the full faith and credit statute and issue preclusion apply in Section 1983 cases.[49] A federal court could not allow relitigation of an issue that was determined in a state court if that state court would bar relitigation. Prior to *Migra* the Court had not addressed the question of whether claim preclusion should also apply in Section 1983 cases.

In *Migra*, the Court concluded that the full faith and credit statute and claim preclusion do indeed apply in federal cases under Section 1983 raising constitutional challenges. In so doing, the Court explicitly rejected Migra's argument that litigants should have the right to bring their state law theories in state court and their federal theories in federal court. "Although such a division may seem attractive from a plaintiff's perspective, it is not the system established by 1738 [the full faith and credit statute]."[50] That statute, the Court observed, not only reflects the need for finality in litigation, but also serves the additional function of promoting federalism values.[51] Our federal structure of government includes a dual system of state and federal courts. Within that structure, federal courts should avoid interfering with legitimate attempts by state courts to resolve disputes conclusively.

As a result, the Court concluded that Migra's case must be returned to the district court for a determination of Ohio's preclusion law. If Ohio would use claim preclusion to bar the second lawsuit, the federal court must do the same. In such circumstances Migra would be prevented from litigating her constitutional challenges in federal court despite the fact that no court—state or federal—had previously considered them.

Two years after the *Migra* decision, the Court extended the preclusion rules even further. In *University of Tennessee v. Elliott*, the Court considered whether a finding made by a state administrative agency should be given preclusive effect in a subsequent Section 1983 case brought in federal court.[52] Quite often, an individual will select an available administrative proceeding to pursue relief from illegal official conduct.[53] The administrative route is quick and less expensive than the judicial alternative. Frequently the individual is not even represented by a lawyer at such proceedings. In *Elliott*, the Court concluded that individuals who select the administrative route may confront preclusion difficulties if they subsequently bring a Section 1983 case in federal court. The Court held that "when a state agency 'acting in a judicial capacity . . . resolves disputed issues of fact properly before it which the parties have had an opportunity to litigate,' federal courts must give the agency's factfinding the same preclusive effect to which it would be entitled in the State's courts."[54]

The answers to the hypothetical questions posed earlier are now reasonably clear.[56] If the Pennhurst patients first sue in state court they cannot subsequently challenge the same conduct in federal court. If they raise the federal constitutional issues in state court, issue preclusion would bar relitigating those issues in federal court. Moreover, even if they fail to raise the constitutional issues in state court they will be barred from litigating them in federal court. Under claim preclusion the state court judgment precludes a subsequent lawsuit raising any issues that arise out of the conduct challenged in the state court case, regardless of whether those issues were actually presented in the first case. *Migra* requires the federal court to preclude a second lawsuit, if the state court would bar it.

The general principles underlying *Migra* may well be sound and unimpeachable. Unfortunately they have been applied in an inflexible and formalistic fashion to close the federal courts to constitutional litigants. The unfairness that results from mechanical application of the rather technical preclusion rules is perhaps best revealed by an account of one individual's decade-long attempt to obtain redress for a violation of her constitutional rights. The story that follows dramatically highlights the real world effect of the latest preclusion developments.[56]

This story began over a decade ago. In November 1974, a back ailment prompted Lorraine Gargiul to take an extended sick leave from her post as a tenured kindergarten teacher in the Liverpool School District.[57] Four months later, the district superintendent notified Ms. Gargiul that she should report to the district physician, Dr. Paul Day, for a physical examination. In reply, Ms. Gargiul informed the superintendent that she would be able to return to work on March 17, as stated in a certificate from her own doctor. She declined, however, to make an appointment with the district physician, explaining that she had always gone to female doctors and was unwilling to be examined by a male. Alternatively, she offered to be examined, at her own expense, by any female physician selected by the district or by a local medical society. The school board flatly rejected this offer and, effective March 17, 1975, suspended Ms. Gargiul without pay until the district's doctor could determine whether she was physically able to return to work. Ms. Gargiul continued to refuse to be examined by Dr. Day and, five months after the suspension, the board determined that there was probable cause to charge Ms. Gargiul with insubordination. A charge of incompetence as a teacher was added as well. In the meantime, Ms. Gargiul had appealed the board's suspension decision to the state commissioner of education. After a hearing, which was later described as "little more than a round table discussion,"[58] the commissioner dismissed the appeal, concluding that the board's action was not arbitrary because section 913 of the New York Education Law authorized a school board to require a teacher to submit to a medical examination.[59] This result was an excellent example of bureaucratic nonsense. The issue was not whether the board had the authority to require an examination, but whether it had been an arbitrary exercise of that authority to direct Ms. Gargiul to submit to an examination by a male physician. On an application to reopen the decision, Ms. Gargiul attempted to argue that the suspension violated her constitutional right to privacy. The commissioner denied her application, declining to address the merits of her constitutional claim because it had not been raised in the initial proceeding.[60]

In the time between the education commissioner's two rulings, Ms. Gargiul commenced two lawsuits, an action in federal court pursuant to Section 1983, and a proceeding in state court challenging the board's decision to suspend her without pay. In the federal lawsuit, she alleged that the board's policy of requiring a female to be examined by a male doctor violated the constitutional right of privacy. The parties agreed to postpone proceedings in the federal lawsuit until the outcome of all state proceedings. With the benefit of hindsight, this agreement to postpone the federal proceedings was a critical error for Ms. Gargiul. At the time, however, it reflected a reasonable judgment by Gargiul's lawyers. First, the state proceeding could resolve Gargiul's challenge more quickly and at much less cost to all parties than the federal lawsuit. Second, under the *Lombard* decision, Ms. Gargiul could reasonably have anticipated that if her state law theories failed in state court (and that court did not determine her federal constitutional challenges), she could return to federal court and litigate the federal issues there.

Her attempts to prevail in the state court were in fact unsuccessful. In the proceeding challenging her suspension without pay, she alleged that the board acted arbitrarily and, in addition, deprived her of property (i.e., pay) without a hearing.[61] The state court dismissed the proceeding on the ground that it was filed too late and a state appellate court affirmed on the same ground, concluding further that the suspension without pay had not violated any right to a hearing.[62] In light of *Lombard*, it is important to note that Ms. Gargiul did not raise—and the state court did not decide—whether the school board had violated Ms. Gargiul's right of privacy.

While these initial legal skirmishes were taking place, the school board convened a hearing panel to decide the charges of insubordination and incompetence. Two years after the suspension without pay (a period during which Ms. Gargiul remained unemployed), the panel reached its decision. On April 4, 1977, a majority found Ms. Gargiul guilty of incompetence, and recommended that she be dismissed. Perhaps because the panel was unwilling to sustain the charge of "insubordination" (for refusing to be examined by Dr. Day), it recommended that Ms. Gargiul receive backpay retroactive to March 17, 1975, the effective date of her suspension. One month after the panel's decision, the school board dismissed Ms. Gargiul on the ground of incompetency, but rejected the panel's recommendation to pay Ms. Gargiul for her two-year suspension. In the board's view, Ms. Gargiul's suspension for refusing to submit to a physical examination by Dr. Day had been entirely proper.

Ms. Gargiul challenged the 1977 decision to terminate her employment and withhold back pay in a second state court proceeding. The state court upheld the termination, but declined to address the merits of her claim for back pay—a claim rooted in her contention that the suspension for refusing to submit to a physical examination by a male doctor violated her constitutional right to privacy.[63] This constitutional claim could not be litigated, the court reasoned, because Ms. Gargiul had failed to appeal the state commissioner's earlier decision or join him as a party.[64]

Having exhausted the state judicial proceedings, Ms. Gargiul returned to federal court, amending her complaint to allege that the board's 1977 decision to terminate employment without pay violated her constitutional rights, just as the 1975 suspension.[65] On May 17, 1982, more than seven years after the initial suspension, the district court concluded that the amended complaint failed to state a claim for relief.[66] As Judge Roger Miner saw it, there simply was no constitutional right entitling a female teacher to refuse to submit to a physical examination by a school district's male physician.[67]

One year later, the second circuit reversed.[68] The court first concluded that under the *Lombard* rationale, Ms. Gargiul's constitutional challenge to her suspension was not precluded because it was never actually litigated and determined in the state court proceedings.[69] On the merits, the court ruled that the school board had indeed subjected the plaintiff to the deprivation of her constitutional rights.[70] The court held that the board's actions with respect to the suspension were "so unreasonable as to be arbitrary" and in violation of the due process clause.[71] Judge Oakes concurred on the ground that the board's insistence on Ms. Gargiul's submission to an examination by a male doctor violated her constitutional right to privacy.[72]

The school board was determined to establish its right to suspend a female teacher who refused to be examined by a male doctor. Accordingly, after losing in the second circuit, the board asked the Supreme Court to review the case. On February 21, 1984, the Supreme Court vacated the second circuit's judgment and remanded the case for consideration in light of the recent *Migra* decision.[73] The second circuit in turn remanded the case to the district court to determine whether New York would give the prior state court judgments preclusive effect in a subsequent action under Section 1983.[74]

On March 6, 1985, almost ten years to the day after the initial suspension, the district court ruled that Ms. Gargiul's constitutional challenge was barred by New York's claim preclusion law.[75] At this point, Ms. Gargiul contacted me and a colleague and asked if we would represent her on an appeal from the district court's order. We agreed for a number of reasons. First, like the second circuit, we were unable to fathom any legitimate reasons for the school board's insistence that Ms. Gargiul be examined by a male doctor. Second, the retroactive application of *Migra* to bar a challenge that had been allowed in the second circuit under *Lombard* seemed particularly inappropriate and harsh. Third, it was by no means clear that the district court had properly interpreted New York law to preclude the constitutional challenge. Finally, and most importantly, we were moved by the human impact of the application of claim preclusion doctrine that seemed terribly formalistic, even if correct. Ms. Gargiul was confused and distressed by the latest events. For ten years she had been embroiled in legal proceedings trying to recover from the shambles made of her professional life because she refused to yield to an utterly arbitrary policy. The second circuit finally had ruled in her favor and she believed her case was being returned to the district court for a determination of damages. Instead, her case had been dismissed, and she had not received a penny. Moreover, our best efforts to explain this stunningly swift turnabout met with no success. She was particularly baffled—not surprisingly—by the notion that her federal case could have been dismissed because of the prior state judicial proceedings. Repeatedly we were asked "had not the second circuit concluded that her constitutional rights had been violated," and "had not the state courts declined to address this matter on the merits?"

We were not optimistic about the prospects of a reversal. To be sure, we firmly believed that retroactive application of *Migra* was inappropriate under the standard announced in *Chevron Oil Co. v. Huson*.[76] There, the Supreme Court identified the three factors to consider in determining whether a Supreme Court decision should be applied only prospectively in a civil case. First, the decision must establish a new principle of law by overruling clear past precedent on which litigants may have relied. Second, the court must examine the purpose of the new rule and determine whether retroactive application would further or retard that purpose. Finally, the court must consider whether retroactive application would produce substantial inequitable results.[77]

Application of the *Chevron Oil* factors appeared to support Ms. Gargiul's contention that *Migra* should not be given retroactive effect in her case. First, *Migra* established a new principle of law overruling clear precedent in the second circuit. Until *Migra*, it was firmly established in that circuit that a prior state court proceeding does not bar federal court consideration of constitutional claims that were not determined by the state court. Indeed on Ms. Gargiul's first appeal to the second circuit, the court had ruled that the case fell within the *Lombard* doctrine and that she was not barred from litigating her substantive due process challenge.[78] The Supreme Court itself had expressly recognized that *Migra* established a new rule of law in the second and third circuits.[79]

In addition, a refusal to apply *Migra* retroactively in the rather unique context of Ms. Gargiul's case would not disserve the policies underlying that decision.[80] The principle concern of *Migra* is comity, the desire to maintain proper respect for the state courts. Ms. Gargiul acted in a manner that was consistent with this concern. She postponed her federal proceedings, presented her claim to the state court, and invited that court to decide the merits. The state court declined to reach the merits for procedural reasons that have no application to federal actions under Section 1983. If the federal court had addressed the merits of Ms. Gargiul's due process claim it would not have undermined the integrity of the state court proceedings.

The Court observed in *Migra* that the full faith and credit statute also reflects the desire to avoid vexatious litigation and to conserve judicial resources. There could be no serious contention that the federal action was vexatious, because it was filed in 1976, well before the state proceedings, and Ms. Gargiul agreed to stay the federal proceedings while she pursued her claim in state court. Nor would judicial resources have been squandered if the district court subsequently addressed the merits of the claim. Extensive resources had already been devoted to the case, and the second circuit had previously held that Ms. Gargiul had stated a claim for relief. The only remaining issue concerned the extent of her damages.

Finally, retroactive application of *Migra* would produce the most inequitable result. Throughout the years, Ms. Gargiul conducted the litigation in a manner consistent with the preclusion rules established for the second circuit. She filed the federal lawsuit and then agreed to stay the proceeding, confident that she could return to federal court if the state court failed to address the merits of her substantive due process claim. To bar her return because of a subsequent change in preclusion rules would be unfair, to say the least. The nonretroactivity doctrine was designed to avoid precisely this kind of injustice.[81]

Even apart from the retroactivity issue, we believed that as a matter of federal law application of claim preclusion in these circumstances was inappropriate. The Supreme Court had ruled that special circumstances may warrant an exception to the command of the full faith and credit statute.[82] Moreover, preclusion does not attach if the state court proceedings did not provide a full and fair opportunity to litigate.[83] The exact contours of these two exceptions have not been defined. Nevertheless, Ms. Gargiul's case arguably fell within both.[84] As intriguing as these questions of federal law were, it seemed to us, as we thought about how the case should be presented to the second circuit, that the court would not have to reach them because defendants had failed to meet their burden of establishing that New York law would bar Ms. Gargiul's constitutional challenge to the school board's 1977 refusal to provide back pay for the suspension period.[85] As one might have guessed, there was not a single state case directly on point. There were, however, cases that appeared to support the propositions that (1) the first state court judgment upholding the 1975 suspension would not operate as a bar because the 1977 decision was a separate transaction;[86] (2) the second state court judgment would not operate as a bar because it was decided on procedural grounds;[87] and (3) neither state court judgment would operate as a bar in a federal suit against public officials sued in their individual, rather than official, capacities.[88]

Our pessimism, quite frankly, was not based on any perceived flaw in the legal arguments. Rather, it was a product of practical considerations. Ten years of litigation before a variety of state and federal tribunals provided the court of appeals with a powerful incentive to affirm the dismissal of Ms. Gargiul's complaint and bring the case to a long-overdue close. Our fears proved well-founded. On May 14, 1986, a divided second circuit ruled that under New York law, Ms. Gargiul's federal challenge was barred by claim preclusion.[89] Additionally, the court held that *Migra* could be given retroactive effect and that the case did not fall within any exception to the full faith and credit statute.[90]

Ms. Gargiul's eleven-year battle was over.[91] She had paid a substantial price for her commitment to a principle. Her suspension without pay, dismissal, and subsequent inability to find another teaching position were all triggered by her refusal to be examined by a male doctor. To this day, it is difficult to imagine any legitimate basis for either the board's rather draconian response to Ms. Gargiul's simple request or the investment of considerable taxpayer resources in defending its conduct. In any event, after eleven years, the school board had prevailed. Ms. Gargiul was not the only loser. Our legal system, too, had not fared well. The courts had somehow contrived to require hundreds of hours—purportedly in the interests of conserving resources and preserving respect for their judgments—to snuff out a valid constitutional claim on grounds having nothing to do with its merits.

Ms. Gargiul's unhappy fate vividly illustrates the potential difficulties created by *Migra*'s interpretation of the full faith and credit statute and the rules of preclusion. Inflexible and formalistic application of *Migra* can produce unfair results. Overburdened courts may easily be seduced to reduce their caseloads by a rigid application of prelcusion rules. One can of course imagine other even more efficient measures to accomplish the same objective. For example, a scheme could be designed that randomly dismisses with prejudice a specified number of lawsuits pending for more than a year. Such a scheme would undoubtedly put an end to those cases at much less cost than our present system, but it plainly would not comport with our notions of fairness.[92] Application of the *Migra* rule to promote the finality of judgments should be no less sensitive to fairness considerations.

In joining those who urge a flexible case-by-case application of *Migra*,[93] I am mindful of Judge Jon Newman's recent call for a rethinking of the concept of fairness in the litigation process.[94] Judge Newman (who also happened to author the majority opinion in *Gargiul*) has suggested that the undesirable aspects of the litigation process—costs and delays—stem from a narrow concept of fairness, an "emphasis on perfecting results in the case at hand."[95] He has urged that fairness be thought of more broadly:

First, we must learn to evaluate the fairness of each step in the litigation process not only in the narrow context of its own discrete contribution to the result, but in the broader context of its incremental value in promoting fairness compared to the inevitable risks of an unfair outcome. Second, we must include in our assessment of fairness not only fairness of result in the dispute at hand, but fairness in the broader context for all who use and wish to use the litigation process. Third, we must think about fairness of result not only in the familiar context of losses compensable within the legal framework, but in the broader context of all similar losses that occur across the whole spectrum of human activity.[96]

The strict application of preclusion rules is undoubtedly consistent with Judge Newman's broader vision of fairness. By removing cases from the litigation process, we reduce the delays and costs for those who wish to use that process. Under Judge Newman's proposal, it is thus possible to conclude that the *Gargiul* court reached a fair result.[97] Ms. Gargiul's dispute had been in the system for over a decade. If the court had held that the federal action was not barred, the case would have been remanded for a hearing on damages producing added costs for the school board. Moreover, the litigation system itself would have paid a price—additional time allocated to a decade-old matter. And the costs would have been increased because of the inefficiencies created by the need to rely on somewhat stale evidence.[98] Finally, there was even a suggestion in the majority opinion that—notwithstanding the previous panel's decision[99]— the constitutional violation was not all that clear.[100] Thus, the incremental value in promoting fairness to Ms. Gargiul may not have outweighed the overall perceived unfairness.

Even under Judge Newman's proposal, however, fairness to the individual litigant is not ignored.[101] He would probably not endorse a random system of dismissing cases despite the benefits accruing to the opponent and to the entire system from such ruthless caseload reduction. We are, thus, left with the question of whether, and to what degree, considerations of fairness to the individual litigant should impact the application of preclusion rules. In Ms. Gargiul's case, for example, can it really be irrelevant that she had conducted the entire litigation in a manner consistent with the then existing preclusion rules?

The Supreme Court has not yet clearly ruled on the contours of any federal law exceptions to the command of the full faith and credit statute. It has said that preclusion will not attach if the litigant did not have a "full and fair opportunity" to litigate the issue or claim in the state forum.[102] On one occasion, the Court described this exception as a narrow one, holding that a prior judgment "need do no more than satisfy the minimum procedural requirements of the fourteenth amendment's due process clause in order to qualify for the full faith and credit guaranteed by federal law."[103] On another occasion, however, the Court explained the full and fair opportunity exception in more sweeping terms, concluding that "redetermination of issues is warranted if there is reason to doubt the quality, extensiveness, or fairness of procedures followed in prior litigation."[104]

In addition to the requirement that the litigant had a full and fair opportunity to litigate, the Court has suggested that various other considerations must be satisfied before a federal court must give preclusive effect to a state court judgment.[105] Issue preclusion, for example, may not be appropriate when controlling facts or law have changed significantly,[106] or when a claimant has been forced to litigate in state court because of the abstention doctrine.[107] As with the full and fair opportunity exception, however, the Court has not precisely defined the other conditions that might serve as exceptions to the full faith and credit statute.

Migra mentions only one exception to the requirement that a federal court apply the claim preclusion rules of the state court that rendered the first judgment.[108] When a federal court abstains from deciding a constitutional issue until the state court first addresses state law issues,[109] the plaintiff is free to reserve the right to a federal forum for the federal claim by informing the state court of an intention to return to federal court to litigate the federal claims.[110] Other than this reference, *Migra* is noticeably silent on any case-by-case exceptions.

Gargiul highlights the need for case-by-case exceptions to preclusion rules and the command of the full faith and credit statute. To be sure, courts should not ignore the rules and allow the exceptions to swallow the general proposition that federal courts must look to state law to determine the preclusive effect of state judgments. In many instances, the state itself may recognize exceptions to general preclusion rules, and a federal court, in applying them, would simply be following the mandate of the full faith and credit statute. In addition, however, as a matter of federal law, the federal courts should be free to conclude in an individual case that special circumstances warrant a finding that application of state preclusion rules would be unjust.[111]

The *Gargiul* litigation illustrates an additional potential harm flowing from a rigid application of the full faith and credit statute. Quite simply, formalistic application of the statute may undermine the very federalism principles supposedly furthered by that provision. The threat to federalism appears in two guises.

First, the statute forces the federal court to ascertain state preclusion rules in some instances when no such rules are directly on point.[112] Federalism tensions are created whenever a federal court must make "estimates" about what a state court would do in the circumstances of a specific case.[113] As Justice Frankfurter warned in an analogous context, "no matter how seasoned the judgment of the district court may be, it cannot escape being a forecast rather than a determination."[114] In that situation the federal court is making a "tentative answer which may be displaced tomorrow by a state adjudication.... The reign of law is hardly promoted if an unnecessary ruling of a federal court is thus supplanted by a controlling decision of a state court."[115]

In *Gargiul*, the court was forced to reach a tentative answer— more pointedly, was forced to guess—about whether New York would hold that the previous state proceedings were a bar to a subsequent civil rights action under Section 1983. No state court previously had addressed this precise issue. The New York courts, of course, have developed a body of general rules related to claim preclusion, but it is by no means obvious that these genral rules apply in determining the claim preclusive effect in a subsequent civil rights action brought pursuant to Section 1983 to redress a constitutional deprivation.[116] A New York court, for example, might apply an exception. Or, it might adopt as a matter of state law the *Lombard* rationale holding that because Section 1983 was intended to supplement other state remedies, the prior judgment would not bar litigation of constitutional issues that were not actually determined in the first proceeding.[117]

"Educated guesses" by federal courts about how the states might apply their preclusion rules to civil rights actions are extraordinarily difficult. In guessing about the very same preclusion question presented in *Gargiul*, courts in the second circuit have reached conflicting results.[114] Similarly situated litigants have thus been treated differently by federal courts struggling to discern state law. This injustice only compounds the injury to federalism.

The threat to federalism appears in a second guise as well. Our federalism is premised on proper respect for state functions, particularly administration of a judicial system that can give effect to underlying substantive policies.[119] After *Migra*, a civil rights claimant must make a difficult decision whether to invoke a state's judicial or administrative procedures, and thereby face a heightened risk of precluding a subsequent federal action, or to forego the state procedure entirely by going directly to federal court. *Migra* may thus encourage avoidance of state judicial proceedings. Similarly, *Elliott* encourges avoidance of state administrative proceedings.

Ms. Gargiul's case illustrates this irony of *Migra*. With the benefit of hindsight, it is clear that Ms. Gargiul erred in consenting to stay her federal court proceeding in order to give the state courts an opportunity to correct any official misconduct. If she had avoided the state courts altogether she would have been able to litigate her constitutional claims in a federal forum, and in light of the second circuit's initial decision would have prevailed.

Of course, to formulate such a bypass strategy, litigants must be familiar with the various forum selection alternatives and the risks of preclusion associated with each.[120] Quite often, however, litigants are unaware of the traps and do not consult a lawyer until after an administrative proceeding has been concluded, and for good reason. The administrative route is quick and much less expensive than the judicial alternative. Moreover, although aggrieved individuals may be aware of the availability of an administrative remedy, they are not likely to be informed of the consequences of pursuing that alternative. Having selected the administrative route, litigants may thus have set a "preclusion trap" at the very outset of the proceedings.[121]

Finally, because of the developments discussed in previous chapters, many litigants will not have a real option of bypassing the state forum and selecting a federal court. These individuals are forced into a state forum and once there will not have an opportunity to bring their federal constitutional claim to a federal court. Unless the Court relaxes the preclusion rules they will suffer the same fate as Lorraine Gargiul. The doors to the federal district court will be closed tight.

Like Ms. Gargiul, they will be able to appeal through the state court system and then seek review in the U.S. Supreme Court.[122] That Court, however, hears only a very small fraction of the cases in which review is sought.[123] Moreover, the Supreme Court is bound by the factfinding made by the trial court; it does not independently make factual determinations. These litigants thus will have been deprived of any factfinding by a lower federal court. The importance of the trial judge's role in making findings of facts cannot be ignored. Indeed, Justice William O. Douglas commented:

Judges are not fungible; they cover the constitutional spectrum; and a particular judge's emphasis may make a world of a difference when it comes to ruling on evidence, the temper of the court room, the tolerance for a proffered defense, and the like. Lawyers recognize this when they talk about "shopping" for a judge.[124]

In cases where they apply, the preclusion rules together with the other door-closing developments return us to the scheme for protecting federal constitutional rights that existed under the Judiciary Act of 1789. The aggrieved individual begins the lawsuit against the state or local officials in state court and enters the federal judicial system only by review in the Supreme Court, if it is granted. The preclusion rules keep the doors of the lower federal courts tightly closed.

Notes

1. Warth v. Seldin, 422 U.S. 490 (1975); see ch. 3.
2. Younger v. Harris, 401 U.S. 37 (1971); see ch. 4.
3. See chapter 5.
4. Parratt v. Taylor, 451 U.S. 527 (1981); see ch. 5.

5. *See* S. STEINGLASS, SECTION 1983 LITIGATION IN STATE COURTS 1–3 (1988).
6. Maine v. Thibotet, 448 U.S. 1 (1980).
7. *Id.* See also Martinez v. California, 444 U.S. 227, 283 n.7 (1980). Generally, state courts cannot discriminate against federal claims. *See* McKnell v. St. Louis & S. F. Ry, 292 U.S. 230 (1934).
8. S. Steinglass, *supra* note 5.
9. *See* Braveman & Goldsmith, *Rules of Preclusion and Challenges to Official Action: An Essay on Finality, Fairness, and Federalism All Gone Awry*, 39 SYRACUSE L. REV. 599 (1988); Smith, *Full Faith & Credit and Section 1983: A Reappraisal*, 63 N.C.L. REV. 59 (1984).
10. The full faith and credit statute, 28 U.S.C. §1738, provides in pertinent part:

Acts, records and judicial proceedings or copies thereof...shall have the same full faith and credit within the United States and its Territories and Possessions as they have by law or usage in the courts of such States, Territory or Possession from which they are taken.

11. Riordan v. Ferguson, 147 F.2d 983, 988 (2d Cir. 1945) (Clark, J., dissenting).
12. Braveman & Goldsmith, *supra* note 9, at 599.
13. *See generally*, Restatement (second) Judgments §27 (1982).
14. *Id.* at 24.
15. *Id.*
16. *Id.*
17. See Allen v. McCurry, 449 U.S. 90, 94–95 (1980).
18. *Id.* at 94.
19. Montana v. United States, 440 U.S. 143, 153 (1979).
20. *See* F. JAMES, JR. & G. HAZARD, JR., CIVIL PROCEDURE 588–590 (3d ed. 1985).
21. *See, e.g.*, Fed. R. Civ. P. 8.
22. *Id.*
23. *See, e.g.*, Fed. R. Civ. P. 15.
24. *See, e.g.*, Fed. R. Civ. P. 19,20.
25. *See, e.g.*, Fed. R. Civ. P. 18.
26. *See, e.g.*, Fed. R. Civ. P. 26–37.
27. *See, e.g.*, Fed. R. Civ. P. 15(b).
28. 375 U.S. 411 (1964).
29. 28 U.S.C. §1257.
30. England v. Louisiana State Board of Medical Examiners, 375 U.S. 411, 415 (1964) (*quoting* Wilcox v. Consolidated Gas Co., 212 U.S. 19, 40 (1909)).
31. *See* discussion, *supra*, at ch. 2.

32. England v. Louisiana State Board of Medical Examiners, 375 U.S. 411, 415 (1964).

33. *Id.* at 417.

34. Railroad Comm'n. of Tex. v. Pullman Co., 312 U.S. 496 (1941).

35. *See* Colorado River Water Conservation Dist. v. United States, 424 U.S. 800, 814 (1976).

36. 502 F.2d 621 (2d Cir. 1974), *cert. denied*, 420 U.S. 976 (1975).

37. 365 U.S. 167 (1961).

38. Lombard, 502 F.2d at 635.

39. *Id.* at 635–636.

40. Mitchum v. Foster, 407 U.S. 225, 242 (1972).

41. *See, e.g.*, University of Tenn. v. Elliott, 478 U.S. 788 (1986); Parsons Steel, Inc. v. First Ala. Bank, 474 U.S. 518 (1986); Marrese v. American Acad. of Orthopedic Surgeons, 470 U.S. 373 (1985); McDonald v. West Branch, 466 U.S. 284 (1984); Migra v. Warren City School Dist. Bd. of Educ., 465 U.S. 75 (1984); United States v. Stauffer Chem. Co., 464 U.S. 165 (1984); Kremer v. Chemical Const. Corp., 456 U.S. 461 (1982); Federated Dep't Stores, Inc. v. Moitie, 452 U.S. 394 (1981); Allen v. McCurry, 449 U.S. 90 (1980); Montana v. United States, 440 U.S. 147 (1979); Parklane Hosiery Co. v. Shore, 439 U.S. 322 (1979).

42. 28 U.S.C. §1738.

43. Allen v. McCurry, 449 U.S. 90, 96 n.8 (1980).

44. *Id.*

45. *Id.* at 97. The Court expressly rejected the argument that *England* demonstrates the impropriety of giving preclusive effect to a state court decision. *England* is limited to instances where the plaintiff brings a case in federal court and that court then abstains to allow a state court to resolve unclear questions of state law. In such circumstances, the litigant may reserve the federal issue by informing the state court of the intention to litigate that issue only in federeal court if he does not prevail in the state forum. *Id.* at 101 n.17.

46. *Id.* at 109 (Blackmun, J., dissenting).

47. *See* Migra v. Warren City School District Board of Education 465 U.S. 75 (1984) (claim preclusion); Allen v. McCurry, 449 U.S. 90 (1980) (issue preclusion).

48. 465 U.S. 75 (1984).

49. Allen v. McCurry, 449 U.S. 90 (1980).

50. Migra, 465 U.S. at 84.

51. *Id.*

52. 478 U.S. 788 (1986).

53. In *Patsy v. Board of Regents*, 457 U.S. 496 (1982), the Court held that a party need not exhaust state administrative remedies before

bringing a Section 1983 action in federal court. Under *Elliott*, however, a party who does first invite a state administrative process may later be precluded from relitigating issues in a subsequent federal court lawsuit.

54. University of Tennessee v. Elliott, 478 U.S. 788, 799 (1986). *See also* Zanghi v. Incorporated Village of Old Brookville, 752 F.2d 42 (2d Cir. 1985).

55. *See supra* at 209.

56. Much of the following is taken from an article that I and a colleague wrote about a case in which we were involved. *See* Braveman & Goldsmith, *supra* note 9. The *Syracuse Law Review* holds the copyright to this article but has kindly given its permission to reprint the material.

57. For a detailed summary of the facts, *see* Gargiul v. Tompkins, 704 F.2d 661 (2d Cir. 1982).

58. *Id.* at 667.

59. 15 N.Y. Educ. Dep't. Rep. 360 (1976).

60. *Id.* at 520.

61. See Gargiul v. Board of Education, 54 A.D.2nd 1085, 389 N.Y.S.2d 504, 505 (4th Dep't. 1976), *lv denied*, 41 N.Y.2nd 802 (1977).

62. *See, id.* at 1087, 389 N.Y.S. 2d at 506.

63. *See* Gargiul v. Board of Educ., 69 A.D.2d 986, 416 N.Y.S.2d 119 (4th Dep't), *lv. denied*, 48 N.Y.S.2d 606 (1979).

64. *See id.* at 986, 415 N.Y.S.2d at 120.

65. *See* Gargiul v. Tompkins, 535 F. Supp. 795, 797 (N.D.N.Y. 1981).

66. *See id.*

67. *See id.* at 798.

68. *See* Gargiul v. Tompkins, 704 F.2d 661 (2d Cir. 1983).

69. *See* Gargiul, 704 F.2d at 666.

70. *See id.* at 667–69.

71. *See id.* at 668.

72. *See id.* at 669–70.

73. *See* Tompkins v. Gargiul, 465 U.S. 1016 (1984).

74. *See* Gargiul v. Tompkins, 739 F. 2d 34 (2d Cir. 1984).

75. *See id.*

76. 404 U.S. 97 (1971).

77. *See id.* at 106–7.

78. *See* Gargiul, 704 F.2d at 670.

79. *See* Migra, 465 U.S. at 83 n.6.

80. *See id.* at 84.

81. *See* Chevron Oil, 404 U.S. at 108; England v. Louisiana State Bd. of Med. Examiners, 375 U.S. 146, 422 (1964).

82. *See* Haring v. Prosise, 462 U.S. 306, 313–14 n.7 (1983) (citing Montana v. United States, 440 U.S. 147, 155 (1979)).

83. *See* Kremer v. Chemical Const. Corp., 456 U.S. 461, 480–81 (1982); Allen v. McCurry, 449 U.S. 90, 95 (1980).

84. Two "special circumstances" suggested that the New York court judgments were not entitled to preclusive effect. First, the state courts had declined to consider Ms. Gargiul's substantive due process claim on the ground that she had failed to exhaust other state remedies. But the Supreme Court has held that state exhaustion requirements do not apply to federal civil rights claims. *See* Patsy v. Board of Regents, 457 U.S. 496 (1982); Monroe v. Pape, 365 U.S. 167 (1961). Second, the result of the state court proceedings had been to give preclusive effect to an unreviewed, informal decision of the commissioner of education that was not a "judicial proceeding" under the ambit of title 28, section 1738. *See* 28 U.S.C. §1738 (1982). *Cf.* University of Tennessee v. Elliott, 478 U.S. 788 (1986) (quasi-judicial state administrative proceedings entitled to preclusive effect as a matter of federal common law, not section 1738).

Finally, because the state courts had refused to consider the substantive due process claim when it was presented to them, it did not seem that Ms. Gargiul had been provided the requisite full and fair opportunity to litigate. *See* Robinson v. Ariyoshi, 753 F. 2d 1468 (9th Cir. 1985) (plaintiff denied full and fair opportunity to litigate constitutional issues where they were presented on petition for rehearing but state court did not consider them); Kovats v. Rutgers, 749 F. 2d 1041 (3d Cir. 1984) (plaintiff not precluded by state court judgment where state court declined to decide the merits of the issue presented on the procedural ground that plaintiff's exclusive remedy lay with arbitration).

85. The burden of establishing the elements of preclusion is on the party asserting the doctrine. *See* Capital Tel. Co. v. Pettersonville Tel. Co., 56 N.Y.2d 11, 18, 436 N.E.2d 461, 464, 451, N.Y.S.2d 11, 14, (1982); J. MOORE 1B MOORE'S FEDERAL PRACTICE, ¶ 0.408[1], at 293 (1984).

86. *See, e.g.*, O'Brien v. City of Syracuse, 54 N.Y. 2d 353, 445 N.Y.S.2d 687, 429 N.E. 2d 1158 (1981), Nunez v. 164 Prospect Park W. Corp., 92 A.D.2d 540, 459 N.Y.S.2d 105 (2d Dep't 1983).

87. *See, e.g.*, Schanbarger v. Commissioner of Social Serv., 99 A.D.2d 621, 472 N.Y.S. 175 (3d Dep't 1984).

88. *See, e.g.*, Roy v. City of August, 712 F. 2d 1517, 1521–22 (1st Cir. 1983). In fact, the second circuit agreed that a state judgment in a suit against public officials sued in their official capacity would not bar a later lawsuit against those officials in their individual capacities. *See* Gargiul, 790 F.2d at 272. Nevertheless, the court held that a remand was unnecessary, reasoning that as a matter of law defendants would

be immune because their conduct did not violate clearly established rights. *See id.* at 273. As the dissent pointed out, this issue had not been addressed by the district court. *See id.* at 279 (Oakes, J., dissenting).

89. *See* Gargiul, 790 F.2d at 272.

90. *See id.* at 274.

91. Ms. Gargiul did file a petition for rehearing *en banc*, which was also denied.

92. *See* Logan v. Zimmerman Brush Co., 455 U.S. 411 (1982).

93. *See, e.g.*, Smith, *supra* note 9.

94. *See* Newman, *Rethinking Fairness: Perspectives on the Litigation Process*, 94 YALE L.J. 1643 (1985).

95. *Id.* at 1643–44.

96. *Id.* at 1647.

97. *See id.*

98. An evidentiary hearing on remand would have focused on the individual defendant's good faith defense, whether they reasonably should have known they were violating clearly established constitutional rights. *See* Harlow v. Fitzgerald, 457 U.S. 800, 818 (1982). Evidence relating to this issue was ten years old.

99. *See* Gargiul v. Tompkins, 704 F.3d 661 (2d Cir. 1983).

100. *See* Gargiul v. Tompkins, 790 F. 2d 265, 273 (2d Cir. 1986).

101. *See* Newman, *supra* note 94, at 1646.

102. *See supra* note 83.

103. Kremer v. Chemical Const. Corp., 456 U.S. 461, 481 (1982).

104. Montana v. United States, 440 U.S. 147, 164 n.11 (1979).

105. *See* Haring v. Prosise, 462 U.S. 306, 313 n.7 (1983).

106. *See* Montana v. United States, 440 U.S. at 162.

107. *See id.* at 163.

108. *See* Migra, 465 U.S. at 85.

109. *See generally* Railroad Comm'n. Co. v. Pullman, 312 U.S. 496 (1941).

110. *See* England v. Louisiana State Bd. of Med. Examiners, 375 U.S. 411 (1964).

111. *See* Restatement (second) Judgments §26, 28 (1982) (recommended exceptions to issue and claim preclusion).

112. *See* Marrese v. American Academy of Orthopedic Surgeons, 470 U.S. 373 (1985) (state law measures the preclusive effect of a state court judgment in a subsequent lawsuit involving federal antitrust claims within the exclusive jurisdiction of the federal courts).

113. *See generally* M. REDISH, FEDERAL JURISDICTION; TENSIONS IN THE ALLOCATION OF JUDICIAL POWER 185–89 (1980) (discussion of federalism tensions created by Erie R.R. v. Tompkins, 304 U.S. 64 (1938).

114. Railroad Comm'n v. Pullman, 312 U.S. 496, 499 (1941).

115. *Id.* at 500.

116. *See, e.g.*, O'Brien v. City of Syracuse, 54 N.Y.2d 353, 429 N.E.2d 1158, 445 N.Y.S.2d 687 (1981).

117. This possibility is not idle speculation. Recently, the New York Court of Appeals demonstrated its sensitivity to the policies underlying Section 1983 by concluding that a longer statute of limitations applies in those actions than in other proceedings against public officials. 423 Salina St., Inc. v. City of Syracuse, 68 N.Y.2d 474, 503 N.E.2d 63, 510 N.Y.S.2d 507 (1986).

118. *See* Davis v. Halpern, 813 F.2d 37 (2d Cir. 1987); Giano v. Flood, 803 F. 2d 769 (2d Cir. 1986); Davidson v. Capuano, 792 F.2d 275 (2d Cir. 1986). These three cases each held that under New York law, damages were not available in an article 78 proceeding and that New York would thus not give a judgment rendered in such a proceeding claim preclusive effect in a later civil rights action for damages. Yet, in *Gargiul*, decided only fifteen days before *Davidson*, the majority took the opposite view. *See Gargiul*, 790 F.2d at 272 ("However, damage claims in an Article 78 proceeding may . . . be asserted against individuals in their official capacity.") *see also* Saumell v. New York Racing Ass'n, 600 F. Supp. 819 (E.D.N.Y. 1985) (damages could be recovered under New York law in article 78 proceedings).

119. *See, e.g.*, Pennzoil Co. v. Texaco, Inc., 481 U.S. 1 (1987); Fair Assessment in Real Estate Ass'n v. McNary, 454 U.S. 100 (1981); Judice v. Vail, 430 U.S. 327 (1977).

120. In suits against state—rather than local—officials sued in their official capacity, the Eleventh Amendment bars any relief based on state law theories (*see* Pennhurst State School & Hospital v. Halderman, 465 U.S. 89 (1984)), as well as damages based on federal law theories (*see* Edelman v. Jordan, 415 U.S. 65 (1974)), unless the state waives its immunity. The forum selection decision, thus, has serious consequences for the kind of relief that might be available.

In instances where the Eleventh Amendment prevents consideration of state law theories, the litigant could bifurcate the claim, bringing a separate lawsuit in state court raising those theories there. *See* Pennhurst, 465 U.S. at 122. This, of course, would lead to additional expense. Moreover, if a judgment were rendered first by the state court, it would have preclusive effect in the federal action. Issue preclusion might bar relitigation of those factual and legal issues actually determined by the state court. *See* Kremer v. Chemical Const. Corp., 456 U.S. 461 (1982). And, because the federal issues could have been raised in the state proceeding, claim preclusion might bar litigation of the federal issues in federal court if they are part of the same claim asserted in state court. *See* Migra v. Warren City School Dist. Bd. of Educ., 465 U.S. 75 (1984); Smith, *Pennhurst v. Halderman: The Eleventh Amendment, Erie and Pendent State Law Claims*, 34 BUFFALO L. REV. 227, 275–88 (1985).

121. *See* University of Tenn. v. Elliott, 478 U.S. 788 (1986).

122. 28 U.S.C. §1257.

123. In the 1987–88 Term, 5,268 cases were on the Supreme Court docket, but only 167 cases were argued and submitted. *See* 57 U.S.L.W. 3074 (July 26, 1988).

124. Chandler v. Judicial Council, 398 U.S. 74, 137 (dissenting opinion).

Chapter 7
Institutional Character

The developments examined in this book highlight an underlying theme in the Supreme Court's recent jurisprudence: a preference for state court adjudication of federal constitutional challenges to state conduct. To be sure, claims that state or local officials are violating the federal constitution continue to be brought in federal court. Nevertheless, in recent years the Supreme Court has used the various doctrines discussed in earlier chapters to clear the federal court dockets of cases against state and local officials. The Court has embraced the notion that litigants should rely on state courts when they seek to attack the constitutionality of state or local practices. Under this scheme for protecting rights the lower federal courts play a limited role and, as in the pre-Reconstruction days, the state courts once again become the primary protectors of federal constitutional rights.

The critical issue—one that has provoked much debate—is whether it really makes any difference if a state, rather than a federal, court hears these cases.[1] Before examining that issue, it is imporant to mention that this question and the surrounding debate are distinct from the important question of whether rights are better protected by a court or a legislative body.[2] So too, they can be considered independent of the current interest in using state constitutions to protect rights.[3] Whatever the resolution of those matters, individuals will continue to need the assistance of some court to redress the deprivation of federal constitutional rights by state or local officials.

Does it matter in any significant way that the Supreme Court has closed the federal courts so long as the state courts are open to claims of unconstitutional state conduct? I maintain that it does indeed matter for a number of reasons. First, as a general proposition state and federal courts, particularly at the trial level, are not equally willing and able to protect federal constitutional rights. Second, Congress, not the Supreme Court, has authority to assign jurisdiction to the federal courts and is better able to weigh the competing factors associated with that task. Third, protection of federal constitutional rights continues to be a national issue that transcends local interests. Finally, the decision to close the federal courts to certain classes of cases reinforces perceptions of unfairness and unequal treatment.

Parity between State and Federal Courts

Underlying the developments examined here is the Supreme Court's assumption that state and federal courts are equally competent to decide constitutional issues and equally sympathetic to a litigant's claim that state or local officials are violating the Constitution. The Supreme Court has "repeatedly and emphatically" rejected any suggestion that the state courts might be less competent or sympathetic.[4] Relying on the state judge's obligation under the supremacy clause to uphold the Constitution,[5] the Court has stated: "We are unwilling to assume that there now exists a general lack of appropriate sensitivity to constitutional rights in the trial and appellate courts or the several States. State courts, like federal courts, have a constitutional obligation to safeguard personal liberties and to uphold federal law."[6] And, the Court is plainly confident in the state courts' ability to do so.

Some have attempted to empirically test the Supreme Court's premise that state and federal courts are equally willing and able to protect constitutional rights.[7] Such studies are qualitative in nature, examining whether one judicial system is better than the other as guardians of these rights. An initial problem is defining what one means by "better." Professor Burt Neuborne, who has written extensively on the "myth of parity" between federal and state courts,[8] views the better forum "as the one most likely to assign a high value to the protection of the individual, even the unreasonable or dangerous individual, against the collective, so that the definition of the individual right in question will receive its most expansive reading and its most energetic enforcement."[9] In short, the better forum is the one more likely to rule for the individual and against the state or local officials. This, of course, does not presuppose that the better forum will always find for the individual. Rather, it defines the better court as the one more likely to assign a high value to individual freedom. Professor Neuborne's definition of "better" has been criticized by others, who argue that the Constitution protects not only individual freedom, but other values as well, especially federalism values.[10] State courts, they suggest, may be better able to protect these constitutional interests.

The dispute over the definition of quality may, as one commentator recently wrote, ultimately "dissolve into a dialogue about the underlying purposes of the Constitution and world views about the desirable content of constitutional decisions."[11] That dialgoue, although important, need not be resolved here. It is clear that the Supreme Court is using the Neuborne definition of quality when it asserts that state and federal courts are equally sensitive to, and competent to decide, federal constitutional claims. It thus becomes necessary to examine the accuracy of the Court's premise, using its own qualitative definition.

The empirical studies have yielded conflicting results on this issue. One study reviewed the outcome of constitutional cases in state and federal courts and concluded that "there is scant evidence of systematic hostility to federal constitutional rights in state courts."[12] A separate study questioned the conclusions of the first and, based on its own data, found that the lawyers involved in the process believe that federal judges have greater expertise on federal law issues and are more sympathetic to claims based on federal law.[13]

The various studies have not—and probably cannot—settle the question of the relative competence and sympathies of state and federal judges. As a result, much of the debate has rested on "human insight rather than on empirical evidence or scientific measurement."[14] On this intuitive level, many arguments are advanced to support the proposition that federal courts are more willing and able to protect constitutional rights, and that parity is a myth.[15] One argument is derived from the differences in the process for selecting judges.[16] The federal judiciary is appointed, not elected, and granted both lifetime tenure and guaranteed salaries. In contrast, most state court judges are elected, or appointed for fixed terms.[17] Although many of the states have adopted nonpartisan election processes for selecting judges,[18] only four grant life tenure to their judges.[19] As a result, federal judges are better insulated from majoritarian pressures and the influences of the elected branches of government. Such insulation allows the federal judiciary greater freedom to protect the rights of the politically weak or unpopular.

As highlighted by the recent failed nomination of Judge Bork to the Supreme Court, the appointment of federal judges is certainly not free from political considerations. It has been reported that President Theodore Roosevelt once observed that " 'a judge of the Supreme Court is not fitted for the position unless he is a party man, a constructive statesman, . . . keeping in mind his relations with his fellow statesmen who in other branches of the government are striving to cooperate with him to advance the ends of government.' "[20] Since 1888, over 90 percent of the federal judicial appointments on all levels have adhered to the party of the president making the appointment.[21] A recent study concluded that the Reagan administration maintained this tradition, packing the federal court system with politically conservative judges.[22]

Nevertheless, once appointed these judges can perform without fear of losing their jobs. In this respect, federal judges stand on very different footing than their state counterparts. Chief Justice Rose Bird of California can certainly testify to this difference. In 1986, she and two of her colleagues were ejected from the California Supreme Court because of voter hostility to views expressed in their opinions.[23] Justice Richard Neely of West Virginia would also be an excellent witness on the political sensitivity of state court judges. He recently constructed an argument for the nationalization of product liability law, and premised the argument in part on the susceptibility of state court

judges to local political pressure. State judges, he feared, were
so responsive to local political pressure that they could not be
trusted to develop sound principles relating to liability for unsafe
products.[24]

As a general proposition, state court judges are more suscep-
tible to the political pressures that operate in favor of the very
state laws or official conduct that become the subject of constitutional challenges. One need not be a lawyer or judge to appreciate the significance of this aspect of the story. For example,
individuals (such as those in *Warth v. Seldin*) who challenge the
constitutionality of exclusionary zoning laws may well perceive
that they will fare better before the politically insulated federal
judge than before a state judge who may have to face the very
voters favoring perpetuation of exclusionary suburbs. Similarly,
the patients at Pennhurst may correctly believe that a federal
judge would be more willing to order changes costing millions
of dollars than a state judge who may have to answer to the
state's taxpayers. When constitutional litigation involves a challenge to some manifestation of the majority's will, it seems especially inappropriate to close the federal courts and direct the
victims to the state courts. Even ardent supporters of cut backs
on federal court jurisdiction concede the appropriateness of federal court enforcement on behalf of the politically weak.[25]

The second argument for the superiority of the federal court
as guardians of constitutional rights is based on the assumption
that federal judges as a group are more competent than their
state counterparts to decide constitutional claims.[26] The relatively small federal judiciary tends to attract highly qualified
applicants and the selection process concentrates on legal talent
to a much larger extent than the state selection processes. Additionally, the federal courts tend to have more highly qualified
law clerks and lower caseloads, allowing careful attention to legal
issues.

It is difficult to assess the significance of these generalizations
about the quality of judges. Some of the differences are less
pronounced at the appellate level where state judges may be just
as qualified as federal appellate judges, and may have the time
and ability to devote to constitutional issues.[27] Moreover, at least
one commentator has urged that even at the trial level recent

appointments to the federal bench may have focused more on ideology and less on quality of the appointees.[28] Perhaps more significant are the differences in "mind set" between state and federal judges. Professor Neuborne argued that federal judges have greater expertise in the area of federal constitutional law and are imbued with a sense of mission in the enforcement of constitutional rights.[29] They work in an "ivory tower" insulated from the more cynicism-breeding constitutional cases found on the state court dockets. State judges often may be asked to decide what some might characterize as technical constitutional questions in the context of the sordid facts of a criminal case. In *Allen v. McCurry*, for example, the state court had to decide federal constitutional issues in a criminal case brought against a heroin dealer who shot and seriously wounded two police officers.[30] State judges see such cases on a regular basis and, not surprisingly, may become a bit hardened toward alleged constitutional violations. On the other hand, federal judges see the constitutional issue one step removed from the setting in which it arose. In *Allen*, the issue was presented not as part of a criminal case but in a civil lawsuit against the police officers who allegedly violated various constitutional provisions.

Justice Brennan captured quite nicely one aspect of the difference in mind set between a state and federal judge. Before his appointment to the Supreme Court, Justice Brennan sat on the New Jersey Supreme Court. In describing why the move from Trenton to Washington was difficult, he stressed the shift in perspective:

My state court responsibility, while it included jurisdiction over federal questions and federal-state conflicts, was inevitably colored by that fact that I was, after all, a state judge. My federal court responsibility, on the other hand, demands a national perspective—although, of course, a national perspective which recognizes the fundamental proposition that, as our Court has said, "the preservation of the States, and the maintenance of their governments, are as much within the design and care of the Constitution as the preservation of the Union and the maintenance of the national government."[31]

One final argument for the superiority of the federal judiciary as guardians of constitutional rights is based on differences between procedures in state and federal courts.[32] To the lay individual the rules of procedure may appear confusing and complex, designed simply to serve the gaming aspect of litigation. The soundness of these criticisms is not the issue here. Whatever their nature, "everyone now acknowledges that the rules of procedures employed to adjudicate disputes... have a major impact on how the substantive principles of law operate in practice."[33] Our story should not underestimate the importance of procedural differences between state and federal systems and the impact of those differences on the protection of rights.

Consider, for example, the class action procedures. The federal rules allow cases to be brought on behalf of all persons similarly affected by a challenged practice.[34] This class action device is a method for providing access to the courts for many who could not otherwise afford the cost of a lawsuit. The interests of the class members are represented in the lawsuit and each of the class members can share in the judgment. The class device has the added benefit of facilitating enforcement of the underlying rights. Public officials may be reluctant to adopt a policy when it may lead to liability not simply to the few who bring lawsuits but also to the many affected by the policy.[35] As a result the class action rule became an important instrument on behalf of those challenging official conduct, and the federal courts were receptive to use of that device.[36]

The state courts, on the other hand, are less familiar with the class action device and in some instances less willing to allow its use against governmental officials.[37] Consider the problem facing welfare recipients who are being denied benefits in violation of the federal constitution or federal law. Due to the Court's door-closing decision in *Edelman v. Jordan*, welfare recipients must sue in state court to recover wrongfully withheld benefits.[38] However, New York state courts, for example, are reluctant to allow class actions against state officials.[39] Consequently, only those few recipients able to bring a lawsuit will recover their benefits, while the majority of aggrieved individuals obtain no relief whatsoever.

This is precisely what happened in *Barton v. Lavine*.[40] Congress amended the Social Security Act to require states to use revised budgeting techniques in determining family welfare grants. These revised techniques would result in increased welfare grants to a family unit. Although Congress provided that the amendments "shall be effective on and after January 1, 1973," New York took the rather remarkable position that Congress really meant the amendments to become effective at some later date. As late as August 1974, families in New York were being denied the increased benefits. Ms. Barton sued the state welfare officials claiming that the state policy violated federal law and was invalid under the supremacy clause of the Constitution. Because she was seeking retroactive benefits, she brought the case in state court. She asked that court to treat the case as a class action on behalf of the thousands of recipients adversely affected by New York's illegal conduct.

The state courts agreed that New York officials were violating federal law. Indeed, the highest state court observed that the federal law could scarcely be more unambiguous about the effective date. The state courts, however, refused to allow the case to proceed as a class action. Thus, Ms. Barton, as well as the handful of other individuals who filed lawsuits, obtained relief. Thousands of others did not sue, perhaps because they were unaware of the change in the law or because they could not find a lawyer to represent them. They did not recover a penny. It was estimated that 11 percent of the families in New York receiving federal welfare benefits were adversely affected by the policy and that they were underpaid $10 million as a result of the New York officials' conduct.

Failure to allow class certification in cases like *Barton* encourages official disregard of obligations imposed by the Constitution and federal law. State officials are free to adopt even absurd positions knowing full well that any subsequent lawsuit will provide relief to only a small number of individuals. In *Barton*, for example, the welfare officials were unsuccessful in the lawsuit but nevertheless effectively prevailed in altering the intended reach of the federal law.

Some federal courts, like state courts, have restricted the availability of class actions, ruling that class certification is unnecessary when public officials are sued for injunctive relief.[41] That ruling, however, has been limited to cases requesting injunctive relief, and applied only when the officials assure the court that all persons affected by the challenged conduct will receive the benefit of the judgment.[42] That limit on class relief in federal courts does not apply in cases like *Barton* where damages are requested. For the most part, federal courts have been more generous in allowing cases to proceed as class actions. Ms. Barton, of course, could not have taken advantage of the more favorable federal procedure. If she had sued the officials in federal court she would have been unable to recover the wrongfully withheld benefits; that is the disturbing lesson of *Edelman*. Having been closed out of the federal forum and forced into the state court, she was deprived of the more effective class action procedure. Consequently, the court ordered relief was limited, and the underlying right was nonexistent for the vast majority of welfare families.

The conclusion that state and federal courts are not equally willing and able to protect constitutional rights, however, is best confirmed not by factors relating to competency and sympathies of the judges, or comparisons of procedures. Rather, the best confirmation is the very conduct of state officials who appear as defendants in federal lawsuits. If parity existed, state courts owuld be as likely as federal courts to invalidate official conduct. With regard to outcome, it would make little difference whether a case is decided by a state or federal judge. State officials, however, apparently do not subscribe to the notion that it matters little whether they are sued in state or federal court. Those sued in federal court regularly request dismissal of the federal lawsuit, arguing that the door-closing developments prevent the federal court from hearing the case and require that it be brought in a state forum. In this manner, the officials express a preference to litigate in the state courts. It seems fair to assume that such a preference is based on a perception that they have a better chance of winning in the state courts and that state court prejudice in favor of state laws, state officials, and state administrative process will operate to their advantage. As a committee of the Association of the Bar of the City of New York stated: "While the matter is not subject to final statistical proof or generalizations immune from exceptions, it is a fact demonstrated by experience of almost any government or private litigator that the state courts, and especially the lower state courts, are inclined to be much more deferential to state statutes and state political officials than are federal judges."[43]

Theories of relative competence and sympathies of judges, together with real life experience, expose the myth of parity. As a general proposition state and federal courts are not equally willing and able to protect federal constitutional rights. Nevertheless, the Supreme Court continues to pay lip service to the notion of parity. It should be stressed that the Court's references to the equal ability and sympathies of state judges in this context is nothing but lip service. One commentator persuasively argued that the Supreme Court adopted the door-closing devices not because of parity but because of disparity between the two court systems.[44] The Court expressed its clear preference for state court resolution of constitutional claims precisely because the state courts are likely to be more sympathetic to the state's interests. In short, "the Court allocates cases to state court because it prefers that any advantage go to the state rather than to the individual with a constitutional claim."[45]

It is important to stress that generalizations about the relative competence and sympathies of state and federal judges are not immune from exceptions. Those involved in constitutional litigation are well aware of individual state court judges, at all levels of state court systems, who are more sympathetic and better qualified to decide constitutional questions than certain federal judges. Some have even argued that in light of the Reagan appointments to the lower federal courts, individuals challenging the constitutionality of official conduct would now have a better chance of winning in state court.[46] Whatever the actual impact of these appointments, it should be emphasized here that individual differences exist among judges on both the state and the federal levels.[47]

Ultimately then, the difficulty with the doctrines discussed in previous chapters arises because they do not leave room for choice between the state and federal judicial systems. Usually we allow the individual to select the forum for litigation and we respect the forum choice so long as the court has power over the kind of case and over the defendant.[48] The victim of alleged unconstitutional conduct might conclude that the likelihood of prevailing is greater in state court, and bring the case there. In other instances the litigant might conclude that the general propositions are accurate and that the federal court would be more competent or sympathetic to the constitutional claims. In such circumstances the litigant would reasonably prefer the federal forum. The door-closing doctrines rob the litigant of that choice, forcing the case to be brought in a state court that may be less competent or sympathetic.

It has been urged that permitting the litigant to choose the forum would serve three important purposes.[49] First, it would maximize the opportunity for protecting constitutional rights by allowing the litigant to select the forum likely to be the most sympathetic. Second, allowing the ligitant to choose between state and federal courts would enhance individual autonomy. Such autonomy may not be the only goal to be served in designing jurisdictional rules, but it is at least one goal that should be respected. "Unless there are reasons for not doing so, litigants should be allowed to make as many choices as possible about the proceedings."[50] In this way we show respect for individual dignity and increase the likelihood that individuals will be satisfied and feel that they have been treated fairly. Finally, permitting litigants to choose the forum may in fact further federalism principles. "Although the term federalism connotes states' rights and had been used primarily by conservatives to impede the federal protection of individual liberties, in a much more neutral sense federalism refers to the existence of two sovereigns with governing authority over the same area."[51] Litigant choice would enhance this neutral form of federalism by creating a role for both the state and the federal courts in protecting constitutional rights.

Congressional Power to Determine Jurisdiction

The Court's door-closing decisions are troubling not only because they deprive litigants of choice and may force them into a less favorable forum, but also because they erode congressional power to determine the kinds of cases heard by the federal courts. The Constitution gives Congress power to establish lower federal courts and invest them with jurisdiction over the kinds of cases listed in article III.[52] The Supreme Court, and the lower federal courts, have a duty to respect the congressional determination regarding allocation of cases to the federal courts. Over 160 years ago, Chief Justice Marshall warned in this regard that the Court has "no more right to decline the exercise of jurisdiction which is given, than to usurp that which is not given. The one or the other would be treason to the Constitution."[53]

Congress has plainly expressed its will with respect to constitutional challenges to official action. Section 1983, and its jurisdictional counterpart, reflect a congressional judgment that federal courts, including the lower ones, should have power over such cases. It bears repetition that the very purpose of Section 1983 was to open "the federal courts to private citizens, offering a uniquely federal remedy against incursions under the claimed authority of state law upon rights secured by the Constitution and laws of the Nation."[54] It placed the federal courts between the people and the states as "guardians of the people's federal rights."[55]

There are many instances in which the Court has ignored Chief Justice Marshall's warning and the fundamental proposition that power to assign cases to the federal courts resides in Congress.[56] The door-closing developments are among the prime examples of judicial usurpation of congressional power to allocate work to the federal judiciary. By impeding access to the lower federal courts, the Supreme Court has in effect dismantled the scheme adopted by Congress for enforcement of federal constitutional rights.

This dismantling has supposedly been designed to ease the tension that necessarily exists in our federal system of government. It has occurred in the name of "federalism" and "comity," the respect that federal courts must pay to state courts. It is perhaps not completely facetious to observe that through judicial fiat the civil rights jurisdictional statutes have been amended to state: District courts have original jurisdiction over constitutional cases "provided that they shall not exercise such power when comity and federalism so require."

In relying on federalism to dismantle the congressional plan for enforcement of constitutional rights, the Court has ignored the basic principle that federalism is a two-way street. As Justice

Black described it, Our Federalism represents a "system in which there is sensitivity to the legitimate interests of *both* State and National governments."[57] Noticeably absent from the Court's recent door-closing decisions is any discussion whatsoever of the federal interest in having the case heard in the federal court. So too, the decisions are disturbingly silent on the precise harm that might occur to the state interests if the federal court exercised the power granted by Congress. The Court relies on rhetoric rather than analysis, and avoids any discussion of the state and federal interests. In so doing, it simply disregards the congressional judgment that there is a significant federal interest in providing a federal forum for litigation of federal constitutional rights.

To be sure, some federalism concerns may be implicated by a federal court challenge to the constitutionality of state action. Federalism tensions are created by the very existence of dual court systems with overlapping power. For example, it would be quite disruptive of state court proceedings and a state's interest in efficient enforcement of its criminal laws to allow defendants in a criminal case to run across the street to the federal court every time a federal constitutional question arose in the state proceeding. Some balancing of interests is necessary. The discussion in previous chapters has suggested, however, that the Court has not engaged in any weighing of state and federal interests. The question, moreover, is not simply how best to strike the balance, but who is in the best position to weigh the respective interests of the state and federal governments. Should the Court engage in any such balancing of interests, or is Congress more competent to perform that task?

The Supreme Court has held in another context that Congress is better able to weigh federalism concerns, and that the courts should defer to the congressional judgment. That context involved the scope of congressional power to regulate interstate commerce. The constitutional grant of such power to Congress has been interpreted quite broadly.[58] In 1976, however, the Court decided *National League of Cities v. Usery*,[59] a case that, in the words of the dissenters, repudiated principles "settled since the time of Chief Justice John Marshall."[60] The majority in *National League* struck down amendments to the Fair Labor

Standards Act (FLSA), which imposed minimum-wage and max-
imum-hour provisions on state and local governments. The Court
conceded that the amendments were within the scope of congressional power to regulate interstate commerce. Nevertheless, it
concluded that Congress' commerce powers are limited by principles of federalism and cannot be used to enforce provisions
against the states in "areas of traditional governmental functions."[61] The Court reasoned that to allow Congress such authority would impair the states' integrity and ability to function
in our federal system.

Less than a decade later the Court again confronted the issue
raised in *National League*. The precise question in *Garcia v. San
Antonio Metropolitan Transit Authority* was whether Congress could
impose minimum-wage and overtime provisions on transportation systems owned and operated by municipal governments.[62]
Under *National League*, Congress would lack such power if municipal ownership and operation of mass transit systems are traditional governmental functions. The *Garcia* Court reexamined
National League and ruled that the traditional governmental
function test is unworkable. More important, it held that the
National League must be overruled because it misperceived the
proper roles of Congress and the Court in assessing federalism
interests.

Garcia did not question the basic proposition that the states
occupy a special position in our constitutional system and retain
a significant measure of sovereign authority. But, the majority
added, "to say that the Constitution assumes the continued role
of the States is to say little about the nature of that role.... The
power of the Federal Government is a 'power to be respected'
as well, and the fact that the States remain sovereign as to all
powers not vested in Congress or denied them by the Constitution offers no guidance about where the frontier between state
and federal power lies."[63] That frontier, the Court said, should
not be determined by courts and judicially created "freestanding
conceptions of state sovereignty."[64] Rather, the framers intended
that the role of the states would be protected by the structure
of the federal government itself and through the political process. "It is no novelty to observe that the composition of the
Federal Government was designed in large part to protect the

States from overreaching by Congress."[65] The Constitution preserves a significant role for the states in the selection of the president and the national legislature. Representatives and senators are allotted on the basis of state lines as are the electors who select the president. This process for selecting the national government ensures that state interests will be protected at the national level.

Professor Herbert Wechsler best summarized the political safeguards of state interests when he wrote:

The national political process in the United States—and especially the role of the states in the composition and selection of the central government—is intrinsically well adapted to retarding or restraining new intrusions by the center on the domain of the states. Far from a national authority that is expansionist by nature, the inherent tendency in our system is precisely the reverse, necessitating the widest support before intrusive measures of importance can receive significant consideration, reacting readily to opposition grounded in resistance within the states. Nor is this tendency effectively denied by pointing to the size and scope of the existing national establishment. However useful it may be to explore possible contractions in specific areas, such evidence points mainly to the magnitude of unavoidable responsibility under the circumstances of our time.

It is in light of this inherent tendency, reflected most importantly in Congress, that the governmental power distribution clauses of the Constitution gain their largest meaning as an instrument for the protection of the states. Those clauses, as is well known, have served far more to qualify or stop intrusive measures in the Congress than to invalidate enacted legislation in the Supreme Court.[66]

The Court concluded in *Garcia* that the federal political process will protect the states quite effectively. That process has built-in safeguards to ensure that Congress will not promulgate laws that are unduly burdensome on the states. As a result, "state sovereign interests are more properly protected by procedural safeguards inherent in the structure of the federal system than by judicially created limitations of the federal power."[67]

Garcia provides guidance about how the frontier between state and federal judicial power should be determined as well. The states relinquished part of their sovereignty by including article

III in the Constitution, and giving Congress power to establish and assign jurisdiction to lower federal courts. It should be recalled that the framers did not work out the details regarding the allocation of power between the state and federal courts. The compromise that produced article III left the details to future congresses.[68] In this context, as well as others involving the exercise of congressional power, the states could protect their interests through the political process.

And, indeed, they have used the federal political process to protect those interests. As described in chapter 2, for example, the states initially refused to give the federal courts power to hear cases arising under the Constitution and federal law, retaining such authority for themselves. Similarly, after the Supreme Court decided *Chisholm v. Georgia*, which allowed states to be sued in federal court by out of state citizens, the Constitution was amended to overrule that decision. So too, the states reacted to *Ex parte Young*, which allowed federal injunctions against state officials, by having Congress enact laws limiting the use of the injunction. As these examples reveal, the federal political process has been quite effective in guarding the states from the federal judiciary.

Congress rather than the Supreme Court is vested with the authority to determine where the frontier between state and federal judicial power lies. In exercising that authority Congress has paid, and will continue to pay, full attention to the interests of the states; that is the inherent nature of the national political process. It certainly considered those interests when it enacted Section 1983 and the jurisdictional statutes allowing 1983 cases to be brought in federal court.[69] The Supreme Court, therefore, is on particularly weak ground when it closes the lower federal courts in the name of federalism. To be blunt, the court should not impose its views of the proper distribution of judicial power between the states and the national government. That is the business of Congress, which is institutionally more competent to perform the job.[70]

Protection of Constitutional Rights: A National Concern

The door-closing decisions are significant and disturbing for a third reason. By placing primary responsibility for enforcement of federal constitutional rights in the hands of state judges, they suggest that protection of these rights is no longer a national concern. The decisions do not attempt to explain the basis for such a suggestion, and for good reason. Protection of federal constitutional freedoms remains a national challenge, transcending local interests. It is not too simplistic to observe that surely the scope of a federal constitutional right should not depend on whether the right is asserted in Mississippi or New Jersey.

If we look past the Court's empty slogans about federalism and consider instead the actual reasons for our federal structure, we find little support for the proposition that enforcement of federal constitutional rights should be left to the state courts.[71] One reason people frequently offer in support of a federal form of government is that it insures that government will be "close to the people." Citizens will be more likely to participate in a government that is in close proximity to where they live and work. Local governments, thus, will be more in tune with the interests of local citizens.

This first reason may justify local control over many apsects of our dialy lives. It does not, however, justify turning over the job of guarding federal constitutional rights to local judges. On the contrary, this aspect of federalism reveals the need for a national role in protecting federal constitutional rights. Quite often, the litigant in constitutional cases is challenging some manifestation of the majority's will. The people, through their local officials, made a decision. A problem arises because the decision may violate a constitutional provision designed to protect individuals from the majority's determination. In such instances it is precisely because federal judges are less sensitive to the demands of the majority—less in tune with local interests—that they are superior guardians of the federal constitutional rights.

For similar reasons a second justification for a federal system does not support the door-closing developments. Related to the idea of keeping government close to the people is the argument that federalism protects individual liberty. In theory, diffusion of governmental power protects the individual by guarding against concentration of power in any single branch or level of government. This basis for our federal system has been the subject of debate and criticism. Before Charles Fried assumed the role of solicitor general, he questioned whether localism fosters liberty: "It seems to me that, with respect to liberty, the choice between centralism and localism is at best a standoff.... Small towns and small units can be as tyrannical as larger political institutions.... Those who look to local control as a kind of bulwark of individual liberty should be somewhat cautious."[72]

There is much evidence to support Fried's observation that localism does not necessarily foster liberty. As discussed in chapter 2, the Civil War amendments were ratified because states were not adequately guarding individual freedom. Similarly, Congress enacted Section 1983 to fill the void created by the states' refusal to enforce federal rights. Moreover, the federal courts emerged as guardians of constitutional rights because localism failed in this respect. In more recent years the states' failure to protect individuals has prompted Congress to enact extensive civil rights measures covering such matters as employment, housing, and voting. It is important to note that many of these measures protect citizens not only from the acts of private individuals and entities but also from discrimination by local and state governmental units themselves.[73] In these circumstances there is a sound basis for caution when examining the relationship between federalism and liberty.

However the general debate about federalism and liberty might be resolved, it seems unlikely that local judicial oversight is the best way to protect federal constitutional rights. Again, in this regard, state judges are often too close to the people and too responsive to local pressures. They lack the independence, insulation, and national perspective needed to guard the freedom guaranteed by the Constitution.

A third argument for our federal form of government is based on efficiency concerns. Some matters can be handled more efficiently at the local level. Judicial protection of federal constitutional rights, however, may not be one of those matters. As a general proposition, state courts are certainly no less burdened than the federal courts. It has been reported that the waiting period for a civil trial in the state courts has grown significantly, whereas the queue in the federal trial courts has grown only a little.[74] More important, for the reasons previously discussed, federal courts are institutionally more competent to handle constitutional litigation.

Finally, Our Federalism is said to foster social and economic experimentation by the states. In the frequently quoted words of Justice Brandeis, "It is one of the happy incidents of the federal system that a single courageous State may, if its citizens choose, serve as a laboratory; and try novel social and economic experiments without risk to the rest of the country."[75] This aspect of federalism may well justify state court consideration of federal constitutional questions. On some matters state courts have taken the lead and articulated new constitutional doctrine that was subsequently adopted by the Supreme Court, or gave more protection than the Supreme Court was willing to give.[76] Justice Brennan readily concedes the important influence of state court decisions on his own opinions. In a speech to the conference of chief justices, he stated that his opinions in such areas as reapportionment, obscenity, freedom of religion, and the rights of criminal suspects "have drawn much from trail-blazing state court opinions."[77]

The experimentation rationale for a federal structure supports the proposition that state courts should be open to federal constitutional cases. It does not justify the conclusion, however, that the federal courts must be closed to such matters. Under the congressional plan—before it was dismantled by the Court—both state and federal courts would be open to hear constitutional challenges to the behavior of public officials. Victims of such conduct should select the forum and might well pick a state court on the belief that the particular state court system will be more sympathetic to the federal claim. The litigant might also facilitate state experimentation by suing in state court on the basis of a state rather than a federal constitutional provision. In a number of instances state courts have interpreted their own constitution to provide greater protection for individual rights than provided by the U.S. Constitution.[78]

There is plenty of room for experimentation under this plan without requiring federal court abdication of a role in protecting rights. In this regard Justice Brennan concluded:

Every believer in our concept of federalism, and I am a devout believer, must salute this [state constitutional] development in our state courts. Unfortunately, federalism has taken on a new meaning of late. In its name, many of the door-closing decisions described above have been rendered. Under the banner of the vague, undefined notions of equity, comity and federalism the Court has condoned both isolated and systematic violations of civil liberties. Such decisions hardly bespeak a true concern for equity. Nor do they properly understand the nature of our federalism. Adopting the premise that state courts can be trusted to safeguard individual rights, the Supreme Court has gone on to limit the protective role of the federal judiciary. But in so doing, it has forgotten that one of the strengths of our federal system is that it provides a double source of protection for the rights of our citizens. Federalism is not served when the federal half of that protection is crippled.[79]

There is continued need for the "federal half of that protection." A national court system was adopted in order to insure the uniform application and supremacy of federal law. In the early years of our country such uniformity and supremacy could be attained through Supreme Court review of state court decisions. As a practical matter these purposes can no longer be achieved in this fashion; there are too many cases. The Supreme Court can review only a tiny fraction of the cases involving federal law. The lower federal courts have become "necessary components of the national judiciary."[80] In the words of one commentator:

As the federal caseload has grown the role of lower federal courts has undergone change. Today the lower federal courts are more than mere federal trial forums for cases falling within the Article III jurisdictional grant. First, in those instances where the Supreme Court makes a pronouncement of nation-wide impact regarding federal rights or interests, the lower courts are needed to enforce and apply it. Moreover, as Supreme court review becomes more selective, the lower courts have become the primary vindicators of federal rights.[81]

The lower federal courts, thus, must remain open to federal questions—including and especially constitutional ones—if the national judiciary is to retain its role in guaranteeing that federal law is supreme and uniformly applied throughout the country.

Perceptions of Unfairness

Finally, the door-closing developments reinforce perceptions of unfairness and discriminatory treatment. The burden of these developments has often been felt most heavily by those who have historically been the victims of discrimination: the poor, the disadvantaged, and members of minority groups. Closing the federal courts to them while leaving the doors open to other classes of litigants reconfirms a sense of powerlessness and alienation. As Justice Harlan observed, "When we automatically close the courthouse door . . . we implicitly express a value judgment on the comparative importance of classes of legally protected interests."[82] The value judgment expressed by the door-closing developments discussed in this book is clear—constitutional rights are not as deserving of protection as other federal rights.

That message is heard quite clearly by the victims of the door-closing doctrines. A number of years ago a bill was introduced in the U.S. Senate that would have relaxed the restrictive standing rules adopted in such cases as *Warth v. Seldin*.[83] A Senate subcommittee conducted hearings and invited victims of door-closing decisions to testify. Victor Vinkey, a plaintiff in the *Warth* case, testified that most people did not understand the standing doctrine and viewed the Court's decision as a way to avoid the serious issues raised by exclusionary zoning practices. He explained: "I would say that the predominant attitude was what is standing anyhow? People didn't understand. We also believe the court used the false issue of 'standing' to avoid facing the sensitive questions of race and class raised in the lawsuit—to avoid making a decision on the merits."[84]

Later in that same hearing Senator Howard Metzenbaum questioned former Solicitor General Erwin Griswold who was speaking on behalf of the American College of Trial Lawyers (ACTL). Griswold was opposed to any relaxation of the standing requirements and appeared to support the closing of the federal courts to constitutional litigants. Senator Metzenbaum sensed that Griswold's position was premised on the desire to keep the federal court dockets clear for cases brought by the private clients of the ACTL members. A heated exchange took place, and Senator Metzenbaum posed a series of rhetorical questions that in many ways summarize the concerns of this book. He asked: "Why is it more important that Burke Photo have a right of access to the Federal court in order to get a $14 million verdict against Kodak, whatever the facts are in the case, than it was for this group [from Penfield] to be concerned about the [exclusionary zoning] conditions in which they live?"[85] "The question is what cases are really more important? Which cases, really, as far as the body of politics of America, which ones ought to have access to the courts? To whom does the court system belong?"[86]

Over the past twenty years the Supreme Court has expressed its views on such questions and too often the answers have been the same: the federal courts do not belong to those alleging a deprivation of constitutional rights by state and local officials. Unfortunately, we pay a significant price for that answer. The authority of the federal judiciary—"possessed of neither the purse nor the sword—ultimately rests on sustained public confidence in its moral sanction."[87] That confidence is seriously eroded when the federal courthouse doors are selectively closed to those most needing access to the federal forum for protection of their rights.

A solution that shuts the courthouse door in the face of the litigant with a legitimate claim for relief, particularly a claim of deprivation of the constitutional right, seems to be not only the wrong tool but also a dangerous tool for solving the problem. The victims of the use of that tool are most often the litigants most in need of judicial protection of their rights—the poor, the underprivileged, the deprived minorities. The very life-blood of courts is popular confidence that they mete out even-handed justice and any discrimination that denies these groups access to the courts for resolution of their meritorious claims unnecessarily risks loss of that confidence.[88]

The door-closing developments undermine the popular confidence that the federal courts are available to mete out even-handed justice.

That confidence can be restored through a reaffirmation of the federal judiciary's essential character as guardian of federal constitutional rights. The reaffirmation might occur in either of two ways. The Supreme Court could reverse itself, as it did in the *Garcia* case, and conclude that it should not rely on federalism principles to resolve the kinds of issues discussed in this book.[89] Such a reversal is unlikely, at least in the forseeable future. The Rehnquist Court appears committed to the Burger Court's plan for closing the federal courts. Slogans about federalism continue to appear in the Court's opinions. Moreover, perceptions—some argue, misperceptions—about the litigation explosion in the federal courts provide additional pressure to keep the courthouse doors closed.[90]

Reaffirmation of the federal judiciary's role could also occur if Congress were willing to assert itself and exercise its constitutional power to determine the jurisdiction of the federal courts. Congress could repair much of the damage caused by the door-closing developments. Two such attempts were made within the past decade but neither was successful. The "Citizens' Right to Standing in Federal Courts Act" would have relaxed some of the restrictive standing rules.[91] Similarly, the appropriately named "Civil Rights Improvement Act"[92] would have eliminated some of the barriers created by the *Younger* line of cases.[93] The primary purpose of that latter bill was to reopen the federal courts and insure the continued vitality of Section 1983 that, in the words of one of the sponsors, "has been a principal tool in this Nation's efforts to fulfill its commitment to the protection of the civil rights and liberties of the American people."[94]

As we celebrate the 200th anniversary of the great First Judiciary Act it is especially appropriate for Congress to reassert itself in the dialogue about the proper role of the federal courts as guardians of constitutional rights. Ultimately, the issues in this book concern the character of the federal courts as an institution, and Congress has a significant role in shaping that character. Should federal courts be open to people like those who have been the focus of our story? Or, should the federal courthouse doors retain the sign: "Closed to individuals asserting constitutional rights against state and local officials?" These questions raise more than topics for debate among lawyers, judges, and law professors. They require, I believe, a reassessment of our national commitment to individual freedom and protection of federal constitutional rights.

Notes

1. For a compilation of recent articles, *see* Wells, *Is Disparity a Problem?*, 22 GA. L. REV. 283, 284 nn.3&4 (1988).

2. *See* Nowak, *Attacking the Judicial Protection of Minority Rights: The History Ploy*, 84 MICH. L. REV. 608 (1986).

3. *See* G. TARR & M. PORTER, STATE SUPREME COURTS IN STATE AND NATION (1988); Howard, *State Court and Constitutional Rights in the Day of the Burger Court*, 62 VA. L. REV. 873 (1976). *Developments in the Law—The Interpretation of State Constitutional Rights*, 95 HARV. L. REV. 1324 (1982).

4. Moore v. Sims, 442 U.S. 415, 430 (1979).

5. U.S. CONST. art. VI.

6. Stone v. Powell, 428 U.S. 465, 494 n.35 (1976).

7. *See, e.g.*, G. TARR & M. PORTER, *supra* note 3, at 13–14; Marvell, *The Rationales for Federal Question Jurisdiction: An Empirical Examination of Student Rights Litigation*, 1984 WIS. L. REV. 1315; Solimine & Walker, *Constitutional Litigation in Federal and State Courts: An Empirical Analysis of Judicial Parity*, 10 HASTINGS CONST. L. Q. 213 (1983).

8. Neuborne, *Myth of Parity* HARV. L. REV. 1105 (1977).

9. Neuborne, *Toward Procedural Parity in Constitutional Litigation*, 22 WM. & MARY L. REV. 725, 727 (1981).

10. Bator, *The State Courts and Federal Constitutional Litigation*, 22 WM. & MARY L. REV. 605 (1981).

11. Chemerinsky, *Parity Reconsidered: Defining a Role for the Federal Judiciary*, 36 UCLA L. REV. 233, 259 (1988).

12. Solimine & Walker, *supra* note 7, at 246. For criticism of the Solimine & Walker study, see Chemerinsky, *supra* note 11, at 261–69.

13. G. TARR & M. PORTER, *supra* note 3, at 13–14; Marvell, *supra* note 7. For criticism of the Marvell study, see Chemerinsky, *supra* note 11, at 269.

14. Bator, *supra* note 10, at 623.

15. *See generally* Neuborne, *supra* note 8.

16. *Id.* at 1127–28.

17. Sheran & Isaacman, *State Cases Belong in State Courts*, 12 CREIGHTON L. REV. 1, 41 n.217 (1978).

18. M. COMISKY & P. PATTERSON, THE JUDICIARY-SELECTION, COMPENSATION, ETHICS AND DISCIPLINE 9 (1987).

19. Sheran & Isaacman, *supra* note 17.

20. H. BALL, COURTS AND POLITICS (1987).

21. *Id.* at 177.

22. H. SCHWARTZ, PACKING THE COURTS (1988).

23. *Id.* at 131.

24. R. Neely, The Product Liability Mess 4 (1988).

25. R. Posner, The Federal Courts: Crisis and Reform 180 (1985).

26. *See* Maroney & Braveman, *"Averting the Flood": Henry J. Friendly, The Comity Doctrine and the Jurisdiction of the Federal Courts-Part II*, 31 Syracuse L. Rev. 469, 510 nn.284–286 (and articles cited therein).

27. Neuborne, *supra* note 8, at 1116 n.45.

28. H. Schwartz, *supra* note 22.

29. Neuborne, *supra* note 8 at 1124–27.

30. 449 U.S. 90 (1980).

31. Brennan, *Some Aspects of Federalism*, 39 N.Y.U.L. Rev. 945, 948 (1964) (quoting Texas v. White, 74 U.S. (7 Wall.) 700, 725 (1968)).

32. *See generally*, Neuborne, *supra* note 9.

33. Wells, *supra* note 1, at 325.

34. Fed. R. Civ. P. 23.

35. *See generally*, Braveman, *Class Certification in State Court Welfare Litigation: A Request for Procedural Justice*, 28 Buffalo L. Rev. 57 (1979).

36. Chayes, *The Role of the Judge in Public Law Litigation*, 89 Harv. L. Rev. 1281 (1976).

37. Braveman, *supra* note 35.

38. 415 U.S. 651 (1974). *See* ch. 5.

39. Braveman, *supra* note 35.

40. 38 N.Y.2d 785 (1975), *cert. denied*, 425 U.S. 985 (1976). The following discussion of the *Barton* case is based on my article cited in note 35, *supra*.

41. *See, e.g.*, United Farmworkers v. City of Delray Beach, 493 F.2d 799, 812 (5th Cir. 1974); Galvan v. Levine, 490 F.2d 1255, 1261 (2d Cir. 1973), *cert. denied*, 417 U.S. 936 (1974).

42. *See, e.g.*, Hurley v. Ward, 584 F.2d 609 (2d Cir. 1978).

43. *See* Maroney & Braveman, *supra* note 26, at 512 n.298.

44. Wells, *supra* note 1, at 319.

45. *Id.*

46. *See* H. Schwartz, *supra* note 22.

47. *Compare* Note, *All the President's Men: A Study of Ronald Reagan's Appointments to the U.S. Court of Appeals*, 87 Colum. L. Rev. 760 (1987) (Reagan's appointments are not significantly more conservative than their Republican colleagues) *with* H. Schwartz, *supra* note 22, at 154–55.

48. In some instances a defendant may remove a case from state to federal court. 28 U.S.C. §1441 (removal where a case could have been brought in federal court); 28 U.S.C. §1442 (removal by federal officers

sued or prosecuted in state court); 28 U.S.C. §1443 (removal by a person who cannot enforce in the state court a right guaranteed by a law providing for equal civil rights).

49. Chemerinsky, *supra* note 11, at 302.

50. *Id.* at 306.

51. *Id.* at 308.

52. Palmore v. United States, 411 U.S. 389, 401 (1973).

53. Cohens v. Virginia, 18 U.S. (6 Wheat.) 82 (1821). *See also* Wilcox v. Consolidated Gas Co., 212 U.S. 19, 40 (1909).

54. Mitchum v. Foster, 407 U.S. 225, 239 (1972).

55. *Id.* at 242.

56. *See generally*, Braveman, *Fair Assessment and Federal Jurisdiction in Civil Rights Cases*, 45 U. PITT. L. REV. 351, 370–76 (1984).

57. Younger v. Harris, 401 U.S. 37, 44 (1971) (emphasis added).

58. *See, e.g.*, Percy v. United States, 402 U.S. 146 (1971); Wickard v. Filburn, 317 U.S. 111 (1942); United States v. Darby, 312 U.S. 100 (1941).

59. 426 U.S. 833 (1976).

60. *Id.* at 857 (Brennan, J., dissenting).

61. *Id.* at 852.

62. 469 U.S. 528 (1985).

63. *Id.* at 550.

64. *Id.*

65. *Id.* at 550–51.

66. Wechsler, *The Political Safeguards of Federalism: The Role of the States in the Composition and Selection of the National Government*, 54 COLUM. L. REV. 543, 558 (1954).

67. 469 U.S. 528, 552 (1985).

68. *See* discussion in ch. 2.

69. *See* Monroe v. Pope, 365 U.S. 167 (1961).

70. *See generally* J. CHOPER, JUDICIAL REVIEW AND THE NATIONAL POLITICAL PROCESS 396 (1980); Redish, *Judicial Parity, Litigant Choice and Democratic Theory: A Comment on Federal Jurisdiction and Constitutional Rights*, 36 UCLA L. REV. 329 (1988).

71. The following discussion is derived from D. BRAVEMAN & W. BANKS, CONSTITUTIONAL LAW: STRUCTURE AND RIGHTS IN OUR FEDERAL SYSTEM 218–19 (1987).

72. Fried, *Federalism-Why Should We Care?*, 6 HARV. J. LAW & PUB. POL. 1, 2 (1982).

73. *See, e.g.*, Voting Rights Act, as amended, 42 U.S.C. §1973b; Title VII of the Civil Rights Act of 1964, as amended, 42 U.S.C. §2000e (equal employment opportunity law bars discrimination by state and local governmental employers).

74. *See,* POSNER, *supra* note 25, at 86.
75. New State Ice Co. v. Lieberman, 285 U.S. 262, 311 (1932) (dissenting).
76. *See,* G. TARR & M. PORTER, *supra* note 3, at 16–17.
77. Brennan, *supra* note 31, at 947.
78. *See Developments in the Law—The Interpretation of State Constitutional Rights, supra,* note 3.
79. Brennan, *State Constitutions and the Protection of Individual Rights,* 90 HARV. L. REV 489, 502—3 (1977).
80. Eisenberg, *Congressional Authority to Restrict Lower Federal Court Jurisdiction,* 83 YALE L.J. 498, 513 (1974).
81. *Id.* at 510–11.
82. Bivens v. Six Unknown Named Agents of Fed. Bureau of Narcotics, 403 U.S. 388, 411 (1971) (concurring).
83. See ch. 3.
84. Hearings on §3005 before the Subcommittee on Citizens and Shareholders Rights and Remedies of the Senate Comm. on the Judiciary and the Comm. on Governmental Affairs, 95th Cong., 2d Sess. 24 (Aug 16 & 23, 1978).
85. *Id.* at 55.
86. *Id.* at 57.
87. Baker v. Carr, 396 U.S. 186, 267 (1962) (Frankfurter, J., dissenting).
88. Brennan, *supra* note 79, at 498.
89. *See* discussion, *supra.*
90. *Compare* R. Posner, *supra* note 25 (federal courts are overburdened) *with* Eisenberg & Schwab, *The Reality of Constitutional Tort Litigation,* 72 CORN. L. REV. 1 (1987) (finding no litigation explosion in the area of Section 1983 cases); Galanter, *The Day After the Litigation Explosion,* 46 MD. L. REV. 3 (1986) (no exponential litigation explosion in the state or federal courts).
91. S. 3005, 95th Cong., 2d Sess., 124 Cong. Rec. S6497–6502 (daily ed. April 27, 1978).
92. S.35, 95th Cong., 1st Sess., 123 Cong. Rec. 557 (1977), reintroduced in 1979 as S.1983, 96th Cong., 1st Sess., 125 Cong. Rec. S15994 (daily ed. Nov. 6, 1979).
93. *See* ch. 4.
94. 123 Cong. Rec. 554 (1977) (remarks of Sen. Mathias, R-Md.).

Bibliography

Chapter 1

Althouse, A. "How To Build a Separate Sphere: Federal Courts and State Power." *Harvard Law Review* 100 (1987): 1485.

Blasi, V., ed. *The Burger Court: The Counter Revolution That Wasn't*, (New Haven, Conn.: Yale University Press, 1983).

Chemerinsky, E. "State Sovereignty and Federal Court Power: The Eleventh Amendment After Pennhurst v. Halderman." *Hastings Constitutional Law Quarterly* 12 (1985): 643.

Dwyer, J. "Pendent Jurisdiction and the Eleventh Amendment." *California Law Review* 75 (1987): 129.

Rudenstine, D. "Pennhurst and the Scope of Judicial Power To Reform Social Institution." *Cardozo Law Review* 6 (1984): 71.

Schwartz, H., ed. *The Burger Years: Rights and Wrongs in the Supreme Court, 1969–1986*, New York, N.Y.: Viking Press, 1987.

Shapiro, D. "Wrong Turns: The Eleventh Amendment and the Pennhurst Case." *Harvard Law Review* 98 (1985): 61.

Chapter 2

A Workable Government? The Constitution After 200 Years. (B. Marshall, ed.), New York, N.Y.: Norton Press, 1987.

Abramson and Gutmann, "New Federalism: State Constitutions and State Courts." In *A Workable Government? The Constitution After 200 Years* B. Marshall, ed. New York, N.Y.: Norton Press, 1987.

Barbash, F. *The Founding: A Dramatic Account of the Writing of the Constitution*, New York, N.Y.: Linden Press, Simon and Schuster, 1987.

Bell, D. "Brown v. Board of Education and the Interest-Convergence Dilemma." *Harvard Law Review* 93 (1980): 518.

Bickel, A. *The Least Dangerous Branch*, Indianapolis, Ind.: Bobbs-Merrill, 1962.

Blackmun, H. "Section 1983 and Federal Protection of Individual Rights—Will the Statute Remain Alive or Fade Away?," *New York University Law Review* 60 (1985): 1.

Braveman, D., and W. Banks. *Constitutional Law: Structure and Rights in Our Federal System*, New York, N.Y.: Matthew Bender, 1987.

Chaffee, Jr., Z. *How Human Rights Got Into the Constitution*, Boston, Mass.: Boston University Press, 1952.

Chayes, A. "The Role of the Judge in Public Law Litigation," *Harvard Law Review* 89 (1976): 1281.

Choper, J. *Judicial Review and the National Political Process*, Chicago, Ill.: University of Chicago Press, 1982.

Comment, Author Anonymous. "The Civil Rights Act: Emergence of an Adequate Federal Civil Remedy?" *Indiana Law Journal* 26 (1951): 361.

Ely, J. *Democracy and Distrust: A Theory of Judicial Review*, Cambridge, Mass.: Harvard University Press, 1980.

The Federalist Papers, (R. Fairfield, ed.) Baltimore, Md.: Johns Hopkins University Press, 1966.

Fallon, R. "A Constructivist Coherence Theory of Constitutional Interpretation." *Harvard Law Review* 100 (1987): 1189.

Farber, D., and Muench, J. "The Ideological Origins of the Fourteenth Amendment." *Constitutional Commentary* 1 (1984): 235.

Farrand, M., ed. *The Records of the Federal Convention of 1787*, Rev. Ed., New Haven, Conn.: Yale University Press, 1966.

Field, M. "The 11th Amendment and Other Sovereign Immunity Doctrines: Part One." *University of Pennsylvania Law Review* 126 (1978): 515.

Fiss, O. *The Civil Rights Injunction*, Bloomington, Ind.: Indiana University Press, 1978.

Fletcher, W. "A Historical Interpretation of the Eleventh Amendment: A Narrow Construction of an Affirmative Grant of Jurisdiction Rather Than a Prohibition Against Jurisdiction." *Stanford Law Review* 35, 1033.

Frankfurter, F. "Distribution of Judicial Power Between United States and State Courts." *Cornell Law Quarterly* 13 (1928): 499.

Gibbons, J. "Our Federalism." *Suffolk University Law Review* 12 (1978): 1087.

Gunther, G. *Constitutional Law* 11th ed. Mineola, N.Y.: Foundation Press, 1985.

Hand, L. *The Bill of Rights*, Cambridge, Mass.: Harvard University Press, 1958.

Hyman, H., and W. Wiecek. *Equal Justice Under Law*, New York, N.Y.: Harper and Row, 1982.

Jacobs, C. *The Eleventh Amendment and Sovereign Immunity*, Westport, Conn.: Greenwood Press, 1972.

Jensen, M. *The Making of the American Constitution*, Princeton, N.J.: Van Nostrand, 1964.

Johnson, E. *Justice and Reform: The Formative Years of the OEO Legal Services Program*, New York, N.Y.: Russell Sage Foundation, 1974.

Kammen, M. *A Machine That Would Go of Itself*, New York, N.Y.: Knopf, 1986.

Kelly, A., Harbison, W., and H. Belz. *The American Constitution: Its Origins and Development* New York, N.Y.: Norton Press, 6th ed. 1983.

Kluger, R. *Simple Justice*, New York, N.Y.: Knopf, 1976.

Kurland, P., and R. Lerner, eds. *The Founder's Constitution*, Chicago, Ill.: University of Chicago Press, 1987.

Marshall, B. A Workable Government, New York, N.Y.: Norton, 1987.

Nevins, A. *The American States During and After the Revolution, 1775–1789*, New York, N.Y.: Macmillan Co., 1924.

Orth, J. *The Judicial Power of the United States: The Eleventh Amendment in American History*, New York, N.Y.: Oxford University Press, 1987.

Palmer. "Liberties as Constitutional Provisions." In *Liberty and Community: Constitution and Rights in the Early American Republic* W. Nelson and R. Palmer eds., p. 55, New York, N.Y.: Oceana Publications, 1987.

Perry, R., and J. Cooper, eds. *Sources of Our Liberties*, Chicago, Ill.: American Bar Foundation, 1959.

Smith, R. *Justice and the Poor*, New York, N.Y.: The Carnegie Foundation for the Advancement of Teaching, 1919.

Story, J. *Commentaries on the Constitution*, 3rd. Ed., Boston, Mass.: Little Brown, 1858.

tenBroek, J. *Equal Under Law*, Rev. Ed., New York, N.Y.: Collier, 1965.

Tribe, L. "Intergovernmental Immunities in Litigation, Taxation, and Regulation: Separation of Powers Issues in Controversies About Federalism." *Harvard Law Review* 89 (1976): 682.

Van Alstyne, W. "A Critical Guide to Marbury v. Madison," *Duke Law Journal* 1.

Warren, C. "New Light on the History of the Federal Judiciary Act of 1789." *Harvard Law Review* 37 (1923): 49.

Warren, C. *The Supreme Court in United States History* 2d ed. Boston, Mass.: Little Brown and Co., 1970.

Wiecek, W. "The Reconstruction of Federal Judicial Power, 1863–1875," *American Journal of Legal History* 13 (1969): 333.

Williams, J. *Eyes on the Prize*, New York, N.Y.: Penguin, 1987.

Chapter 3

Bickel, A. *The Least Dangerous Branch*, Indianapolis, Ind.: Bobbs-Merrill, 1962.

Braveman, D. "The Standing Doctrine: A Dialogue Between the Court and Congress." *Cardozo Law Review* 31 (1980): 64.

Brilmayer, L. "The Jurisprudence of Article III: Perspective on the 'Case of Controversy' Requirement." *Harvard Law Review* 93 (1979): 297.

Ely, J. *Democracy and Distrust*, Cambridge, Mass.: Harvard University Press, 1980.

Frankfurter, F. "A Note on Advisory Opinions." *Harvard Law Review* 37 (1924): 1002.

Gunther, G. "The Subtle Vices of the "Passive Virtues"—A Comment on Principle and Expediency in Judicial Review." *Columbia Law Review* 64 (1964): 1.

Scott, K. "Standing in the Supreme Court—A Functional Analysis." *Harvard Law Review* 86 (1973): 645.

Tribe, L. *American Constitutional Law* Mineola, N.Y.: Foundation Press, 2d ed. 1988.

Tushnet, M. "...And Only Wealth Will Buy You Justice"—Some Notes on the Supreme Court 1972 Term." *Wisconsin Law Review* (1974): 177.

Yarbrough, T. "Litigant Access Doctrine and the Burger Court." *Vanderbilt Law Review* 31 (1978): 33.

Chapter 4

Bator, P. "The State Courts and Federal Constitutional Litigation." *William & Mary Law Review* 22 (1981): 605.

Brennan, W. "State Constitutions and Protections of Individual Rights." *Harvard Law Review* 90 (1977): 489.

Chayes, A. "The Role of the Judge in Public Law Litigation." *Harvard Law Review* 89 (1976): 1281.

Fiss, O. *The Civil Rights Injunction*, Bloomington, Ind.: Indiana University Press, 1978.

James, Jr., F. and G. Hazard, Jr. *Civil Procedure* 3d ed. Boston, Mass.: Little, Brown, 1985.

Gibbons, J. "Our Federalism." *Suffolk University Law Review* 12 (1978): 1087.

Maroney, T. and Braveman, D. " 'Averting the Flood': Henry J. Friendly, The Comity Doctrine, and the Jurisdiction of the Federal Court—Part II", *Syracuse Law Review* 31 (1980): 469.

Redish, M. *Federal Jurisdiction: Tensions in the Allocation of Judicial Power*, Indianapolis, Ind.: Michie Co., 1980.

Redish, M. "The Doctrine of Younger v. Harris: Deference in Search of a Rationale." *Cornell Law Review* 63 (1978): 463.

Wechsler, B. "Federal Court, State Criminal Law and the First Amendment." *New York University Law Review* 49 (1974): 740.

Zeigler, D. "A Reassessment of the Younger Doctrine in Light of the Legislative History of Reconstruction." *Duke Law Journal* (1983): 987.

Chapter 5

Amar, A. R. "Of Sovereignty and Federalism." *Yale Law Journal* 96 (1987): 1425.

Bandes, S. "Monell, Parratt, Daniels and Davidson: Distinguishing a Custom or Policy from Random Unauthorized Act." *Iowa Law Review* 72 (1986): 101.

Blackmun, H. A. "Section 1983 and Federal Protection of Individual Rights—Will the Statute Remain Alive or Fade Away?" *New York University Law Review* 60 (1985): 1.

Brown, G. D. "State Sovereignty Under the Burger Court—How the Eleventh Amendment Survived the Death of the Tenth: Some Broader Implications of Atascadero State Hospital v. Scanlon." *Georgetown Law Journal* 74 (1988): 363.

Brown, G. D. "Municipal Liability Under Section 1983 and the Ambiguities of Burger Court Federalism: A Comment on City of Oklahoma City v. tuttle and Pembaur v. City of Cincinnati—the 'Official Policy' Cases." *Boston College Law Review* 27 (1986): 833, 909.

Comment, "The Civil Rights Act: Emergence of Adequate Federal Civil Remedy?" *Indiana Law Journal* 26 (1951): 361.

Field, M. A. "The Eleventh Amendment and Other Sovereign Immunity Doctrines: Part One." *University of Pennsylvania Law Review* 126 (1978): 515.

Fletcher, W. "A Historical Interpretation of the Eleventh Amendment: A Narrow Construction of an Affirmative Grant of Jurisdiction

Rather than a Prohibition Against Jurisdiction." *Stanford Law Review* 35 (1983): 1033.

Low, P. and J. Jeffries. *Civil Rights Actions*, Mineola, N.Y.: Foundation Press, 1988.

Mead, S. M. "42 U.S.C. Section 1983; Municipality Liability: The Monell Sketch Becomes a Distorted Picture." *North Carolina Law Review* 65 (1987): 518.

Monaghan, H. P. "State Law Wrongs, State Law Remedies, and the Fourteenth Amendment." *Columbia Law Review* 86 (1986): 979.

Nowak, J. E. "The Scope of Congressional Power To Create Causes of Action Against State Governments and the History of the 11th and 14th Amendments." *Columbia Law Review* 75 (1975): 1413.

Orth, J. *The Judicial Power of the United States: The Eleventh Amendment in American History*, New York, N.Y.: Oxford University Press, 1987.

Schuck, P. *Suing Governments: Citizen Remedies for Official Wrongs*, New Haven, Conn.: Yale University Press, 1983.

Schwartz, M., and J. Kirklin. *Section 1983 Litigation: Claims Defenses and Fees*, New York, N.Y.: Wiley, 1986.

Shapiro, S. "Keeping Civil Rights Actions Against State Officials in Federal Court: Avoiding the Reach of Parratt v. Taylor and Hudson v. Palmer." *Journal of Law & Inequality* 3 (1985): 161.

Snyder, B. R. "The Final Authority Analysis: A Unified Approach to Municipal Liability Under Section 1983." *Wisconsin Law Review* 633, 1986.

Whitman, C. "Constitutional Torts." *Michigan Law Review* 79 (1980): 5.

Chapter 6

Braveman, D. and Goldsmith, R. "Rules of Preclusion and Challenges to Official Action: An Essay on Finality, Fairness, and Federalism All Gone Awry." *Syracuse Law Review* 39 (1988): 599.

James, Jr., F., and G. Hazard, Jr. *Civil Procedure* 3d ed. Boston, Mass.: Little, Brown, 1985.

Moore, J. 1B *Moore's Federal Practice*, Albany, N.Y.: Bender, 1984.

Newman, J. O. "Rethinking Fairness: Perspectives on the Litigation Process." *Yale Law Journal* 94 (1985): 1643.

Redish, M. *Federal Jurisdiction: Tensions in the Allocation of Judicial Power*, Indianapolis, Ind.: Michie Co., 1980.

Smith, R. "Full Faith & Credit and Section 1983: A Reappraisal." *North Carolina Law Review* 63 (1984): 59.

Smith, R. H. "Pennhurst v. Halderman: The Eleventh Amendment,

Erie and Pendent State Law Claims." *Buffalo Law Review* 34 (1985): 227.

Steinglass, S. *Section 1983 Litigation in State Courts*, New York, N.Y.: C. Boardman, 1988.

Chapter 7

Ball, H. *Courts and Politics*, Englewood Cliffs, N.J.: Prentice-Hall, 1987.

Bator, P. M. "The State Courts and Federal Constitutional Litigation." *William & Mary Law Review* 22 (1981): 605.

Braveman, D. "Fair Assessment and Federal Jurisdiction in Civil Rights Cases." *University of Pittsburgh Law Review* 45 (1984): 351.

———. "Class Certification in State Court Welfare Litigation: A Request for Procedural Justice." *Buffalo Law Review* 28 (1979): 57.

———. and W. Banks. *Constitutional Law: Structure and Rights in Our Federal System*, New York, N.Y.: Matthew Bender, 1987.

Brennan, W. J. "State Constitutions and the Protection of Individual Rights." *Harvard Law Review* 90 (1977): 489.

———. "Some Aspects of Federalism." *New York University Law Review* 39 (1964): 945.

Chayes, A. "The Role of the Judge in Public Law Litigation." *Harvard Law Review* 89 (1976): 1281.

Chemerinsky, E. "Parity Reconsidered: Defining a Role for the Federal Judiciary." *UCLA Law Review* 36 (1988): 233.

Choper, J. *Judicial Review and the National Political Process*, Chicago, Ill.: University of Chicago Press, 1980.

Comisky, M., and P. Patterson. *The Judiciary-Selection, Compensation, Ethics and Discipline*, Westport, Conn.: Quorom Books, 1987.

"Developments in the Law—The Interpretation of State Constitutional Rights." *Harvard Law Review* 95 (1982): 1324.

Eisenberg, T. "Congressional Authority To Restrict Lower Federal Court Jurisdiction." *Yale Law Journal* 83 (1974): 498.

———. and Schwab, S. "The Reality of Constitutional Tort Litigation." *Cornell Law Review* 72 (1987): 641.

Fried, C. "Federalism—Why Should We Care?" *Harvard Journal of Law and Public Policy* 6 (1982): 1.

Galanter, M. "The Day After the Litigation Explosion." *Maryland Law Review* 46 (1986): 3.

Howard, A.E.D. "State Court and Constitutional Rights in the Day of the Burger Court." *Virginia Law Review* 62 (1976): 873.

Maroney, T., and Braveman, D. " 'Averting the Flood': Henry J.

Friendly, The Comity Doctrine and the Jurisdiction of the Federal Courts—Part II." *Syracuse Law Review* 31 (1980): 469.

Marvell, T. B. "The Rationales for Federal Question Jurisdiction: An Empirical Examination of Student Rights Litigation," *Wisconsin Law Review* (1984): 1315.

Neely, R. *The Product Liability Mess* 4 New York, N.Y.: Free Press, 1988.

Neuborne, B. "Myth of Parity." *Harvard Law Review* 90 (1977): 1105.

———. "Toward Procedural Parity in Constitutional Litigation." *William & Mary Law Review* 22 (1981): 725.

Note, "All the President's Men: A Study of Ronald Reagan's Appointments to the U.S. Court of Appeals." *Columbia Law Review* 87 (1987): 760.

Nowak, J. E. "Attacking the Judicial Protection of Minority Rights: The History Ploy." *Michigan Law Review* 84 (1986): 608.

Posner, R. *The Federal Courts: Crisis and Reform*, Cambridge, Mass.: Harvard University Press, 1985.

Redish, M. "Judicial Parity, Litigant Choice and Democratic Theory: A Comment on Federal Jurisdiction and Constitutional Rights." *UCLA Law Review* 36 (1988): 329.

Schwartz, H. *Packing the Courts*, New York, N.Y.: Scribner's, 1988.

Sheran, R. J., and Isaacman, B. "State Cases Belong in State Courts." *Creighton Law Review* 12 (1978): 1.

Solimine, M. E., and Walker, J. L. "Constitutional Litigation in Federal and State Courts: An Empirical Analysis of Judicial Parity." *Hastings Constitutional Law Quarterly* 10 (1983): 213.

Tarr, G., and M. Porter. *State Supreme Courts in State and Nation*, New Haven, Conn.: Yale University Press, 1988.

Wechsler, H. "The Political Safeguards of Federalism: The Role of the States in the Composition and Selection of the National Government." *Columbia Law Review* 54 (1954): 543.

Wells, M. "Is Disparity a Problem?" *Georgia Law Review* 22 (1988): 283.

Index

Absolute immunity, public officials and, 116–18
Anti-Injunction Act, 87
Appellate jurisdiction, Supreme Court and, 15, 140
Article III: cases or controversies, 15; concerns of anti-federalists, 14; independent judiciary, 16; product of compromise, 14–15; Supreme Court appellate jurisdiction, 15; Supreme Court original jurisdiction, 15
Attorneys' fees, Section 1983 and, 127

Barron v. Mayor and City Council of Baltimore, 20–22
Barton v. Lavine, 171–72
Bell, Derrick, 45
Bickel, Alexander, 24
Bill of Rights: adoption of, 19–20; impact on state-federal relations, 20–22
Blackmun, Harry A., 37, 42, 124
Brennan, William J., 98, 183
Brown v. Board of Education, 43–46

Carey v. Piphus, 126–28
Cases of controversies, 15, 62
Chayes, Abram A., 83
Chisholm v. Georgia, 22–23, 108
Civil Rights Cases, 41
Civil War: civil rights acts, 34–37; concept of national citizenship, 32–33, 39; constitutional amendments, 33–34; impact on federal courts as protectors of constitutional rights, 37–42
Claim preclusion: effect of, 137, 145–52; federalism and, 144, 155–57; full faith and credit statute and, 142–44; need for flexible application of, 152–57; purpose of, 138–39; requirements of, 136–37
Cohens v. Virginia, 29–30
Colonial charters, protection of liberties and, 12
Colonial period, enforcement of rights durng, 13
Concurrent jurisdiction, 17, 174–75, 183–84
Confederation period, 12–13
Congress: control over federal court jurisdiction, 175–80; creation of federal courts, 15; po-

litical safeguards of federalism, 178–80

Constitution: Article III, 15; Bill of Rights, 19–22; creation of federal courts, 15; Fifteenth Amendment, 13; Fourteenth Amendment, 14; ratification, 17; supremacy clause, 15

Constitutional Convention: Article III, 15–17; creation of federal courts, 13–15; federalism concerns, 14–17; opponents of federal judiciary, 14; supporters of federal judiciary, 14; Virginia Plan, 14–15

Damages: absolute immunity from, 116–18; against local governmental units, 101–8; against public officials, 115–21; against states, 108–15; Eleventh Amendment, 110–15; federalism and, 107–30; kinds of, 125–30; policy or custom requirement and, 105–8; purposes of award of, 103; qualified immunity from, 119–20; Section 1983 and, 101–30

Due process: damages for denial of, 121–24; narrow definition of, 123–24; *Parratt v. Taylor* and, 121–24; state remedies and, 123

Duke Power Co. v. Carolina Environmental Study Group, Inc., 72

Edelman v. Jordan, 109–11

Eleventh amendment: damages and, 108–15; federalism, 108–15; injunctions, 80–82, 109; language of, 4; purpose of, 22, 109; relationship to Fourteenth Amendment and, 112–

13; Section 1983 and, 114; waiver of, 111–12, 113

England v. Louisiana State Board of Medical Examiners, 139–40

Ex parte Young, 42, 80–82, 109

Federal courts: Article III, 15–18; Civil War impact on, 32–37; congressional control of, 175–80; Judiciary Act of 1789, 18–19; Judiciary Act of 1801, 30–32; jurisdiction over constitutional cases after Civil War, 32–49; jurisdiction over constitutional cases before Civil War, 18–32; parity with state courts, 166–75; pending state proceedings, 88–96; procedures, 139, 170–73; Reconstruction, 33–37

Federal judiciary: appointment, 16, 168; independence, 16, 168–70; willingness and ability to protect constitutional rights, 166–75

Federalism: comity, 88, 93–98; Constitutional Convention and, 13–15; damages and, 107–30; definition of, 88; efficiency and, 182–83; Eleventh Amendment and, 108–15; Fourteenth Amendment, 112–13; full faith and credit statute and, 144, 155–57; individual liberty and, 181–82; injunctions and, 80–98; limit on jurisdiction of federal courts, 97–98; local control, 181; local experimentation and, 183; perceptions of unfairness and, 185–87; political safeguards of, 178–80; preclusion rules and,

144, 155–57; purposes of federal structure, 181–84
Federalist Papers: No. 78, 13, 16; No. 82, 17
Fourteenth Amendment: due process, 121–24; Eleventh Amendment, 112–13; history of, 34; language of, 34; privileges and immunities clause, 38–39
Frankfurter, Felix, 32
Full faith and credit statute: claim preclusion and, 142–44'deralism and, 144, 155–57; issue preclusion and, 143; language of, 142; Section 1983 and, 142–45

Garcia v. San Antonio Metropolitan Transit Authority, 178–80
Gargiul v. Tompkins, 145–52

Hamilton, Alexander, 13, 16, 17, 20
Home Telephone and Telegraph Co. v. Los Angeles, 42–43
Hudson v. Palmer, 122
Huffman v. Pursue, Ltd., 89

Immunity from damages: absolute, 116–18; local governments and, 101–8; public officials and, 115–21; qualified, 119–20; Section 1983 and, 101–30; states and, 108–15
Injunctions: civil rights cases and, 82–84; Eleventh Amendment and, 80–82, 109; federalism and, 80–98; historical use of, 79–80, 87; mandatory, 80; pending state civil cases and, 90–92, 95–96; pending state criminal cases and, 88–90, 95–

96; prohibitory, 80; public law litigation and, 82–84
Issue preclusion: effect of, 138; full faith and credit statute and, 143; need for flexible application of, 152–57; purposes of, 138; requirements of, 137–38

Judiciary Act of 1789: creation of inferior federal courts, 18–19; inferior courts and protection of constitutional rights, 19; jurisdiction over constitutional claims, 19; Supreme Court review of state courts, 18
Judiciary Act of 1801: history of, 30–31; jurisdiction over constitutional claims, 31; new federal courts created, 31; repeal, 31–32

Legal Services Program, 47
Local governmental units: damages against, 101–8; policy or custom requirement, 105–8; Section 1983 and, 101–8
Lombard v. Board of Education, 141–42

Madison, James, 14, 20
Marbury v. Madison, 23–25, 30, 63
Marshall, John, 23, 29
Martin v. Hunter's Lessee, 25–29, 30
Memphis Community School Dist. v. Stachura, 128–30
Migra v. Warren City School District, 143–45
Monell v. Department of Social Services, 104–5

Monroe v. Pape, 46–47, 101–4, 122–24

National League of Cities v. Usery, 177–78

Original jurisdiction, Supreme Court and, 15

Parratt v. Taylor, 121–24
Pennhurst State School and Hospital: conditions of, 1–2; litigation regarding, 2–4; settlement and, 4
Pennhurst State School and Hospital v. Halderman (1984), 4; impact of decision, 4–6
Pennzoil Co. v. Texaco, Inc., 90–92
Plessy v. Ferguson, 41
Policy or custom requirment: liability of local government units and, 105–8; Section 1983 and, 107–8
Preclusion rules: claim preclusion, 136–37; effect of, 137–38, 145–52; federalism and, 144, 155–57; full faith and credit statute and, 142–44; issue preclusion, 137–38; need for flexible application of, 152–57; purposes of, 138–39; Section 1983 and, 135–37
Public official immunity: absolute, 116–18; purpose of, 115–16; qualified, 119–20; Section 1983 and, 115–21

Qualified immunity, and public officials, 119–20

Reconstruction, and federal courts as protectors of constitutional rights, 33–37
Rizzo v. Goode, 92

Section 1983: attorney's fees and, 127; damages and, 101–30; Eleventh Amendment and, 80–82, 112–13; federalism and, 93–98; Fourteenth Amendment and, 112–13; historical background of, 35–36; injunctions and, 79–98; language of, 35; local governmental liability under, 101–8; official immunity, 115–21; person requirement, 103; policy or custom requirement, 104–8; state liability under, 108–15; under color of law requirement, 102; vehicle for protecting constitutional rights, 46
Slaughterhouse Cases, 37–40
Standing doctrine: effect of, 73–75; purposes of, 63–67; requirements of, 62; source of, 62
State civil proceedings, federal injunction of, 90–92, 95–96
State courts: concurrent jurisdiction, 17, 174–75, 183–84; parity with federal courts, 166–75; protection of federal constitutional rights, 165–87; review by U.S. Supreme Court, 25–30; Section 1983 and, 136; selection of judges, 168
State criminal proceedings, federal injunction of, 88–90, 95–96
Story, Joseph, 27, 30
Stump v. Sparkman, 116–18
Supremacy clause: history of, 15
Supreme Court (U.S.): appellate jurisdiction, 15, 140; caseload, 96; control of lower federal court jurisdiction, 175–80; fact-finding, 140; judicial re-

view, 23–25; legitimacy, 186–87; original jurisdiction, 15; review of state court decisions, 18, 25–30; usurping congressional power, 175–80

TenBroek, Jacobus, 33
Thirteenth Amendment, 33
Trainor v. Hernandez, 90

Under color of law, Section 1983 and, 102

United States v. SCRAP, 71
University of Tennessee v. Elliott, 144

Virginia Plan, 14–15

Warth v. Seldin, 57–61, 68–71
Wechsler, Herbert, 179

Younger v. Harris, 85–88

About the Author

DAAN BRAVEMAN is Professor of Law at Syracuse University College of Law, Syracuse, NY. After earning a law degree from the University of Pennsylvania, he was law clerk for Justice Samuel J. Roberts, Supreme Court of Pennsylvania, and staff attorney for the Greater Upstate Law Project, Rochester. He is coauthor of *Constitutional Law: Structure and Rights in Our Federal System* and author of many articles on costitutional law and federal courts.